THE INDIAN CHILD WELFARE ACT HANDBOOK

A Legal Guide to the Custody and Adoption of Native American Children

B. J. JONES

SECTION OF FAMILY LAW
AMERICAN BAR ASSOCIATION

Cover photograph: Eagle Feather, a Lakota woman, and her child, 1900, from *North American Indians: Photographic Prints* by F. A. Rinehart (Omaha: Rinehart-Marsden, 1900). Photo Courtesy of the Edward E. Ayer Collection, The Newberry Library, Chicago, Illinois.

Cover design by Catherine Zaccarine.

Printed in the United States of America.

Library of Congress Catalog Card Number 94-74277
ISBN 1-57073-136-5

99 98 97 96 95 5 4 3 2 1

CONTENTS

Foreword

In 1978, the U.S. Congress enacted the Indian Child Welfare Act to focus national attention on, and give priority to, the problems of Native American communities and their children. The act established procedures for notice to tribes and families in cases of adoption, foster placement, dependency and neglect proceedings against parents, and other situations where the parental rights of Native Americans were at risk. The "best interest" standard was defined in relation to Native American cultural standards. Burdens of proof were made stricter in proceedings involving Native American children.

Since the enactment of this law, courts have struggled with the intent and purpose of the act. This book will help the practitioner understand the breadth of the act, the specific notice requirements of the act and the standards of proof as these issues have been interpreted through different cases.

For family law practitioners working with any proceeding involving Native American children, this book offers an overview of the various requirements that must be met. There is no other book that offers this overview in such a manageable, accessible style. The list of tribal court and ICWA contacts, checklists, and forms are time savers for the busy lawyer.

For many attorneys dealing with the adoption of children, whether or not cultural heritage is at issue, this book will be important. Native Americans are residents of every state, and over the years, large numbers of Native Americans have moved to the major cities.

Native American issues can arise in any state, and attorneys should be prepared to raise the issue first rather than ignore it—or hope that no one will notice.

Many cases in the last few years, such as those involving Baby M, Baby Jessica, Baby Richard, and Gregory, have reached a certain level of national notoriety. The argument surfaces again and again over biological ties versus bonding and a new environment. The custodial fight between biological parents as opposed to psychological parents is a common thread woven through many of the ICWA cases involving adoption and foster placement. Thorough lawyers will want to read this book and look for parallel analysis of those issues to support their own arguments in their cases.

Many people have contributed to the completion of this book. B.J. Jones was a committed and dedicated author who met his deadlines, wrote well, and made working with him a pleasure. Others who have helped with comments, editing, and reading were Barbara Stark, Jean Cline, Hon. John Fitzgerald, Terry Pechota, and Donald Gecewicz.

Although the Indian Child Welfare Act is still evolving, this book will be an important volume in your library.

Mary McCusker

About the Author

B.J. Jones is the Litigation Director for Dakota Plains Legal Services, a nonprofit corporation set up under the aegis of the indigent residents of eight Sioux Indian reservations in South and North Dakota and adjoining counties. He is a 1984 graduate of the University of Virginia School of Law. He is admitted in the state courts of Virginia, South Dakota, and North Dakota and the United States Court of Appeals for the Eighth Circuit. His practice focuses on Indian law, domestic relations, and entitlements litigation. In that practice he has represented tribes, Indian children and Indian parents in hundreds of cases involving the application of the Indian Child Welfare Act. He has also served as a special tribal judge for the Turtle Mountain Band of Chippewa Indians, the Red Lake Band of Chippewa Indians, and the Cheyenne River Sioux Nation. He is a member of the Indian Law Committee of the South Dakota Bar Association, a Commissioner for the Sicangu Oyate Bar Commission, and the Chairman of the Rosebud CASA organization.

He lives in Mission, South Dakota with his wife, Dixie, and their son, Kipp.

Introduction

This book is designed to assist those persons, including lawyers, social workers, counselors, and others, whose professions and interests involve them with Native American children to understand the Indian Child Welfare Act of 1978. ICWA, as it is commonly referred to, was enacted by the U.S. Congress to ameliorate the problem of the massive removal of Native American children from their homes by both state welfare agencies and private agencies and to ensure that those children once removed would be placed in homes that reflect their Native American cultures and traditions. It is Congress's attempt to preserve distinct cultures by preventing future generations of Native American children from being alienated from those cultures.

Because ICWA is a federal law with a primary emphasis on the workings of the state social services agencies and court systems that process Native American children, it is in those venues that ICWA and its ramifications have been played out. Although it was passed less than twenty years ago, there are already several hundred state and federal court decisions discussing ICWA. Even the U.S. Supreme Court opted to pronounce upon ICWA in a 1989 decision that, although limited in its scope as far as its holding, broadly examines both the sociological and cultural antecedents of the law.

Native Americans, although a small minority in this country, live, work, and prosper in every state of the union. An examination of the court cases discussing ICWA reveals that cases involving Indian children do not simply arise in areas thought of as the last bastions of

Indian culture, reservations and their border towns, but instead may arise in large cities in the Northeast or in small hamlets in the southern United States. The need for a working understanding of ICWA among all persons engaged in promoting better lives for our children is therefore apparent.

It is hoped that through an examination of this book it will become apparent that the fate of Native American people as a discrete culture is inextricably intertwined with the future of Native American children. The traditions and practices that define Native American culture today and that preserve the understandings of the elders will be lost forever unless inculcated in future generations of Native Americans. This is the lesson understood by Congress when it enacted ICWA. I hope readers will appreciate this goal as they peruse the pages that follow.

CHAPTER • 1

The Indian Child Welfare Act and Its Foundations

> Let us put our minds together and see what kind of life we can build for our children.
>
> —Sitting Bull, Hunkpapa Sioux[1]

In 1978 the U.S. Congress heeded the call of the great Lakota leader Sitting Bull by passing the Indian Child Welfare Act of 1978, Public Law No. 95-608, 92 Stat. 3069 (Nov. 8, 1978), commonly known as ICWA. Codified at 25 U.S.C. Sections 1901–63, the law has had a substantial impact on the practices and procedures of state juvenile courts, state social services agencies, and private adoption agencies in this country.[2] The law has not been universally welcomed, with some deriding it as an illegitimate usurpation of the traditional powers of state courts and agencies.[3] An overwhelming majority of commentators, however, have praised it as requisite to eliminating the practices of state entities that had tended to remove an inordinately large number of Native American[4] children from their homes without a full appreciation of traditional Native American child-rearing practices.[5]

> ICWA, at 25 U.S.C. Section 1902, states as its purpose: The congress hereby declares that it is the policy of this Nation to protect the best interest of Indian children and to promote the stability and security of Indian tribes and families by the establishment of minimum federal standards for the removal of Indian children from their families and the placement of such children in foster or adoptive homes which will reflect the unique values of Indian culture, and by providing for assistance to Indian tribes in the operation of child and family programs.

Displacement of Indian Children

State Involvement

Before 1978, Congress noted, the wholesale removal of Native American children from their families and tribes by state social services agencies and courts was commonplace.[6] Surveys found that in states with large Native American populations an incredible 25 to 35 percent of all Native American children were removed from their homes and placed in foster or adoptive homes at one time in their lives.[7] In Minnesota, for example, one of every four Native American children under the age of one was adopted, usually by a non-Native American family.[8]

The disparity between the removal rates of Native American children and other children was just as austere. In South Dakota the number of Native American children in foster care was, per capita, sixteen times greater than the rate for other children.[9] In Washington the adoption rate for Native American children was nineteen times greater than the rate for other children.[10] What makes these statistics even more sobering is that in many of these states the overwhelming majority of Native Americans resided on reservations where ostensibly the state courts and welfare agencies had no authority to order the removal of Native American children.

Federal Involvement

The displacement of Indian children was even more of a national travesty because of the federal government's complicity in carrying out the destruction of Native American families. In 1971, 17 percent of Native American school-age children were removed from their homes to attend Bureau of Indian Affairs (BIA) boarding schools, where they were oftentimes isolated from their native families and instructed by teachers who had very little understanding and appreciation of the children's native languages and traditions.[11] In many of these boarding schools children were punished for speaking their native languages or practicing their religious beliefs. In others children were sent so far away from their birth communities that contact between them and their extended families was impractical.[12]

Grounds for Removal

Native American children were rarely removed because of physical abuse; instead, their families were routinely judged unfit by non-Native

American social workers and judges because of alleged neglect or emotional mistreatment.[13] A common ground for removal was that the natural parent had left the child with an extended relative for a prolonged period of time. To the non-Native American social worker ignorant of the traditional ways of child-rearing such behavior was unacceptable under Anglo-Saxon traditions.[14] To Native American families, however, such methods of raising children were commonplace because the notion of extended family included not only those in the nuclear family but also those related by marriage or by some other traditional bond. Another commonly cited ground for removal was the abuse of alcohol.

Although alcoholism was, and remains, a profound problem among Native American families, studies demonstrated that the number of Native American children removed from their homes because of this malady was disproportionate compared to other families afflicted by the disease.[15]

Removal without Due Process

Compounding the removal problem, in many states Native American children were taken from their families without a modicum of due process.[16] Many of the children were removed from families dependent on the federal and state governments for financial support. Congress documented instances of state welfare agencies pressuring Native American families into signing away custody of their children to the state under threat of the termination of welfare benefits.[17] State welfare departments often controlled the everyday lives of Native American people, and endearing oneself to non-Native American social workers was critical to financial survival.

The process provided in state courts was no more redeeming than the practices of state social services agencies.[18] In most states parents were provided with neither counsel nor interpreters, even if they spoke only their native tongues; instead, parents relied on the same social workers who were seeking to displace the children.[19] Non-Native American social workers, ignorant of the ways and traditions of the very people they worked with, were the "experts" who advised the courts that the abject poverty many Native American families survived in prevented the families from properly parenting their children. Courts rarely received the expert testimony of native people who could familiarize state judges with traditional child-rearing practices.[20] The result was oftentimes the judicial countenance of the abusive practices of state welfare agencies. As stated at 25 U.S.C. Section 1901(5), Congress specifically found that "the States, exercising their recognized jurisdiction over Indian child custody proceedings through administrative and judicial bodies, have often failed to recognize the essential tribal relations of Indian people and the cultural and social standards prevailing in Indian communities and families."

Placement of Indian Children Outside of Their Culture

In addition to the flawed process by which Native American children were dislodged from their homes, the fate of the children after removal gave Congress pause. In 1969 a survey of sixteen states revealed that approximately 85 percent of Native American children in foster homes were living in non-native homes.[21] Some 90 percent of nonrelative adoptions of native children involved non-Native Americans adopting native children.[22] If continued, this trend could conceivably have led to the alienation of Native American children from their unique cultural values and mores. Psychological and sociological studies have suggested that Native American children brought up in non-native homes suffer from a variety of adjustment disorders once they discover their unique racial ancestry.[23] These children have a foothold in the dominant society's world but eventually long to discover their indigenous roots. This longing often results in maladaptive behavior, contributing little to either the dominant society or the native traditions.[24]

Federal Policy behind ICWA

In 1978 the federal government was promoting Native American self-determination through a series of legislative enactments, including the Indian Child Welfare Act.[25] Preserving the unique nature of native traditions and values was more important to Congress than promoting the assimilation of native people into the dominant, predominately Anglo-Saxon, culture. Although this congressional objective has been subject to unpredictable shifts since the turn of the century,[26] an understanding of it as a motivation behind ICWA is key to understanding certain provisions of the act. Congress clearly felt that maintaining Native American children in homes that reflect the children's unique native cultures and values would be in their "best interest" and the best interest of Indian tribes.[27]

"Best Interest" of Indian Children

This policy objective may well clash with the commonly accepted theory of "best interest of the child" propagated by many in the non-native social work community and most popularly enunciated by Goldstein, Freud, and Solnit in their often-cited book *Beyond the Best Interest of the Child.* The theory emphasizes the importance of a child's psychological bonding with at least one adult who is perceived by that child as his or her psychological parent.[28] The book essentially speaks of the need for a psychological parent in universal terms—without acknowledging the cultural diversity of the American population and the essential tribal relations of Native American people. This theory, as applied to Native American children, has created consternation in certain state courts where the goals of ICWA have been perceived as counterproductive to promoting the best interest of the child.[29]

ICWA is a realization that Native Americans have unique practices and traditions regarding child-rearing that are not susceptible to judgment using a non-Indian barometer. Although generalizations are difficult because of the diversity of native people who flourished in North America before the arrival of Europeans, there seems to be certain characteristics shared by most North American tribes.

First and foremost, Native Americans were tribal people whose existence as individuals depended on the survival of the "whole" to which they belonged.[30] This type of holistic thinking was impressed upon Indian children at an early stage, both through the social structure[31] and through the oral storytelling tradition, which focused on the role the land and animals played in a tribe's existence.[32] Indian children were raised by their families within the context of a larger clan, oftentimes related either by blood or marriage, whose responsibilities extended to all children in the clan and not just lineal descendants. Although many children were raised outside of the nuclear family, it was the ultimate loss for a child to be cast out of the collective group.[33]

Second, within the collective group, children were taught unwritten rules regarding their relations with almost everyone in the group. These rules were not enforced through corporal punishment but instead through storytelling typically involving animals and the earth.[34] To Native Americans both the animals and the earth were larger models of their own existence and the habits of animals were often used as models for human behavior.

This knowledge of the role people played in the social order was passed along to future generations primarily through the oral storytelling tradition and not through any formal educational process. Thus, the removal of a child from the tribe or clan severely curtailed that child's ability to foster an understanding of his or her role in life.

It is apparent, therefore, that fundamental differences exist between the primarily Judeo-Christian values imparted to non-Indian children, which tend to stress the superiority of man and individual responsibility, and those values ingrained in Native American children. It is perhaps this clash of values that explains the difficulties Indian children have in meshing with the non-Indian world. These differences have also engendered a misunderstanding in the non-Indian community of Indian child-rearing practices. It is not uncommon for a grandparent[35] to raise an Indian child even when the natural parents are quite fit to do so. Such a practice is not an indication of parental neglect but, rather, a fulfillment of the grandparent's obligation to the extended family, which, if defied, may result in a rift in the extended family.

Congress did not adopt the standard espoused in *Beyond the Best Interest of the Child* when it enacted ICWA. Instead, as the legislative history professes, Congress concluded that proper implementation of the act itself would serve the best interest of the Native American child.[36] In this way, Congress believed, the act would eliminate the many subjective standards regarding the best interest of the Native American child that had led to the perilous situation that existed before 1978.

Indian Law as a Foundation for ICWA

Under what authority, however, did Congress intervene in this area of law traditionally left to the states? An examination of the answer requires some historical background on the area of Indian law.

Indian tribes are sovereign entities whose existences predate the ratification of the U.S. Constitution.[37] The Supreme Court long ago recognized tribes as "domestic dependent nations" with a unique relationship to the federal government.[38] The sovereignty of Indian tribes is subject to the paramount authority of the federal government over the affairs of tribes.[39] However, the federal government can exercise that paramount, or plenary, authority only if the exercise of that authority is consistent with certain obligations the government has toward Indian tribes.[40]

Those obligations, characterized by the Supreme Court as the obligations a guardian has toward a ward, have often been referred to as a trust responsibility.[41] That responsibility has been described as the duty of one nation toward "a nation claiming and receiving the protection of one more powerful, not that of individuals abandoning their national character and submitting as subjects to the laws of a master."[42] The obligations of the United States toward Indian tribes are primarily borne out of treaties entered into by the parties as well as federal laws enacted for the benefit of Indian tribes.[43]

This relationship between Indian tribes and the federal government is a "political" relationship between two nations, not a relationship based on the racial classification of Native Americans. The Supreme Court has recognized that Congress can treat Native Americans differently from other racially distinct groups and not run afoul of traditional equal protection notions because of the unique relationship between the tribes and the government.[44]

Congress has the exclusive authority to regulate the affairs of Indian tribes through the provision in the U.S. Constitution granting the federal government the exclusive authority to regulate "commerce with Indian tribes."[45] This grant of authority is broad and expansive and is limited only by the constraints of the Bill of Rights. One product of this broad grant of authority to Congress is that, as a general principle, states are preempted from exercising any authority over Indian tribes if that exercise of authority clashes with federal authority.[46]

Indian nations have long been recognized as retaining the inherent authority to regulate domestic relations among their members.[47] Even before the enactment of ICWA, the courts had acknowledged that Indian tribes, and not the states, could regulate marriage among tribal members;[48] adoption of Native American children;[49] divorce and property distribution among Native Americans;[50] and the rights and privileges of children.[51] In many ways, therefore, ICWA is simply a realization and codification of the legal landscape that existed before its passage. ICWA reaffirms the continuing authority of Indian tribes over their members who reside within reservation boundaries.

In other ways, however, ICWA represents an extension of Congress's authority to enact remedial legislation for Native American people. Before ICWA, it was a generally recognized tenet of the law that once a Native American ventured off a reservation and into state territory his or her actions would be governed by state law.[52] This was especially true in the area of domestic relations, an area traditionally governed by the well-recognized police powers of the state.[53] The idea that the federal government could dictate to state courts and social services agencies in an area traditionally relegated to them did not sit well with many commentators, and the resistance to that intrusion perhaps explains many of the judicially created exceptions to ICWA, discussed hereinafter, that have been carved out by many state courts.

Constitutional Challenges to ICWA

Predictably, there have been constitutional challenges to ICWA by parties claiming that the act countenances disparate treatment of parties in state courts based on the parties' race. The act has been upheld in the face of every challenge, including in Maine,[54] South Dakota,[55] Arizona,[56] Michigan,[57] Oklahoma,[58] and Oregon.[59] In those cases the courts have held that, as long as a rational basis existed for Congress to legislate as it did, the authority of Congress extended to the legislative purpose achieved by ICWA. In upholding the constitutionality of ICWA, the courts have referred to the commerce clause of the U.S. Constitution as a justification for congressional action in the arena of the welfare of Native American children.

This chapter has reviewed the legislative purpose behind the enactment of ICWA. The chapters that follow will discuss the act with a degree of specificity. The reader, however, should always keep the objective of Congress in mind while reviewing specific provisions of the act, with an eye toward how the specific provision achieves Congress's stated objective of furthering the best interest of Native American children and protecting the integrity and future of Indian tribes.

Notes

1. Sitting Bull apparently made this statement upon his return from exile in Canada, when it was becoming apparent that the nomadic lifestyle of his Hunkpapa people was being proscribed by the white settlers. *See* ROBERT M. UTLEY, THE LANCE AND THE SHIELD: THE LIFE AND TIMES OF SITTING BULL (Henry Holt and Company, 1993).

2. The need for a working knowledge of ICWA is perhaps best exemplified by a recent Alaska decision, Doe v. Hughes, 838 P.2d 804 (Alaska 1992), wherein the Alaska Supreme Court held that a law firm had committed malpractice by not obtaining the consent of the natural mother of an Indian child conceived by artificial insemination in a private adoption in violation of ICWA.

3. *See* Atwood, *Fighting Over Indian Children: The Uses and Abuses of Jurisdictional Ambiguity*, 36 UCLA L. REV. 1051 (1989); Barsh, *The Indian Child Welfare*

Act of 1978: A Critical Analysis, 31 HASTINGS L.J. 1287 (1980); Bennett, *Native American Children: Caught in the Web of the Indian Child Welfare Act,* 16 HAMLINE L. REV. 953 (1993).

4. In this book the terms "Native American" and "Indian" will be used interchangeably.

5. *See, e.g.,* Goldsmith, *Individual v. Collective Rights: The Indian Child Welfare Act,* 13 HARV. WOMEN'S L.J. 1 (1990); Strickland, *Indian Law and the Miner's Canary: The Signs of Poison Gas,* 39 CLEV. ST. L. REV. 483 (1991).

6. There are three separate documents evidencing the legislative history behind ICWA. The House Report, H.R. REP. NO. 1386, 95th Cong., 2nd Sess. (1978), *reprinted in* 1978 U.S. CODE CONG. & AD. NEWS 7530 (hereinafter House Report); the Senate Report, S. Rep. No. 597, 95th Cong., 1st Sess. (1977); and the Senate Hearings, *Hearing before the U.S. Senate Select Committee on Indian Affairs, 95th Cong., 1st Sess., on S.1214. To Establish Standards for the Placement of Indian Children in Foster or Adoptive Homes, to Prevent the Breakup of Indian Families, and for other Purposes* (Aug. 4, 1974).

7. *See* House Report at 9

8. House Report at 9.

9. *Id.*

10. *Id.*

11. *Id.*

12. *Id.*

13. House Report at 10.

14. *Id.*

15. *Id.* An increasingly prevalent condition among some Native American families is the high incidence of fetal alcohol syndrome or fetal alcohol effects present in young children of alcoholic mothers. Such a condition potentially may lead to growth deficiencies, mental retardation, and learning and behavioral problems. *See* M. DORRIS, THE BROKEN CORD (1989); A. Streissgurth, A MANUAL ON ADOLESCENTS AND ADULTS WITH FETAL ALCOHOL SYNDROME WITH SPECIAL REFERENCE TO AMERICAN INDIANS (Washington, D.C., Indian Health Services, 1988). This problem was recently the subject of a television movie, *The Broken Cord,* based on the book of the same title.

16. House Report at 11.

17. The House cited to a South Dakota entrapment case where parents signed away custody of their children under duress and that relinquishment was later used as evidence of abandonment. House Report at 11.

18. ICWA is not an indictment against state courts and institutions for intentional racism directed against Native Americans; rather, it is a realization of the lack of ethnic diversity in many state courts and social services agencies in this country. *See* Melton, *2020 Vision: A Plan for the Future of California's Courts: Children, Families and the Courts in the Twenty-First Century,* 66 S.CAL. L. REV. 1993 (1993); *Symposium on Racial Bias in the Judicial System,* III, *Juvenile and Family Law,* 16 HAMLINE L. REV. 624 (1993).

19. House Report at 11.

20. *Id.*

21. House Report at 9.

22. The 90 percent figure was derived from statistics out of the state of Minnesota, which Congress noted was one of the few states to keep detailed statistics.

Congress believed, however, that Minnesota's statistics were representative of other states. House Report at 9.

23. R. McCartney, *The American Indian Child Welfare Crisis: Cultural Genocide or First Amendment Preservation,* 7 Columbia Hum. Rts. L. Rev. 529 (1975); I.N. Berlin, Anglo Adoptions of Native Americans: Repercussions in Adolescence 387–88 (American Academy of Child Psychiatry, 1978); J. Westermeyer, *The Apple Syndrome in Minnesota: A Complication of Racial-Ethnic Discontinuity,* Journal of Operational Psychiatry, 10(2), 134–40 (1979).

24. There has been surprisingly little empirical data addressing the impact of the removal of Indian children from their culture and their placement in the non-Indian, predominately Anglo-Saxon culture, especially in light of the fact that Congress believed the problem was so serious that it threatened the existence of an entire culture. Much of what Congress relied on was anecdotal and statistical information and the inferences drawn from that. The studies that do exist generally pertain to transracial adoptions and the effect on minority children, which are clearly apposite to the plight of Indian children. *See* Forde-Mazrui, *Black Identity and Child Placement: The Best Interests of Black and Biracial Children,* 92 Mich. L. Rev. 925 (1994); Glynn, *The Role of Race in Adoption Proceedings: A Constitutional Critique of the Minnesota Preference Statute,* 77 Minn. L. Rev. 925 (1993); Eubanks, *Transracial Adoption in Texas: Should the Best Interests Standard Be Color-Blind?,* 24 St. Mary's L.J. 1225 (1993); Bartholet, *Where Do Black Children Belong? The Politics of Race Matching in Adoption,* 139 U. Pa. L. Rev. 1163 (1991). The studies that do exist suggest that the problems confronting Indian children who grow up in the non-Indian world are serious. *See* note 23, I.N. Berlin, *Suicide Among Native American Adolescents: An Overview, Suicide and Life Threatening Behavior,* 17(3), 218–32 (1987); D. McShane, *An Analysis of Mental Health Research with American Indian Youth,* special issue, Journal of Adolescence, 11(2), 87–116.

25. *See, e.g.,* Indian Self-Determination Act, 25 U.S.C. § 450 et seq.

26. *See* Felix S. Cohen, Handbook of Federal Indian Law 127–206 (1982 ed., Michie Bobbs-Merrill). Federal policy has shifted from a desire to assimilate Indians into the mainstream American society, as exemplified by the era of allotment from 1871 to 1928 and termination from 1943 to 1961, to a desire to maintain tribal independence and sovereignty, as exemplified by the enactment of the Indian Reorganization Act, 25 U.S.C. § 461 *et seq.,* in 1934 and the period of self-determination of which the enactment of ICWA is an extension.

27. *See In re* Adoption of M.T.S., 489 N.W.2d 285 (Minn. App. 1992) (court holds that it is presumptively in the best interest of an Indian child to be placed with Indian grandmother rather than with non-Indian foster parents for adoption because of child's need to be raised in his culture).

28. Joseph Goldstein, Anna Freud and Albert J. Solnit, Beyond the Best Interest of the Child (New York Free Press, 1973), at 53.

29. An example of this is a case from Montana, Matter of T.S., 801 P.2d 77 (Mont. 1990), where a guardian ad litem for an Indian child questioned whether ICWA does further the best interests of Indian children. *See also In re* Baby Girl A., 230 Cal. App. 3d 1611, 282 Cal. Rptr. 105 (Cal. App. 4 Dist. 1991) (tribe allowed to intervene in voluntary adoption proceeding by Indian mother raised by non-Indian adoptive parents, but court strongly suggests that the rights of the mother to keep child out of Indian home more important than cultural attachment to child's native family).

30. *See generally* JOHN F. BRYDE, MODERN INDIAN PSYCHOLOGY (Institute of Indian Studies, University of South Dakota, 1971).

31. An excellent discussion of traditional Lakota (Sioux) child-rearing practices can be gleaned through reading the novel *Waterlilly,* by Ella Cara Deloria, published by the University of Nebraska Press. The novel, set in the mid-1800s when the Lakota culture was flourishing, details a Lakota woman's life from birth to old age.

32. *See* MICHAEL J. CADUTO AND JOSEPH BRUCHAC, KEEPERS OF THE ANIMALS: NATIVE AMERICAN STORIES AND WILDLIFE ACTIVITIES FOR CHILDREN (Fulcrum Publishing, 1991).

33. *See* Deloria at 20.

34. One of the greatest Lakota storytellers was Fools Crow, who had the ability to enthrall young children with his stories about animals and traditional values. *See* THOMAS MAILS, FOOLS CROW: WISDOM AND POWER (Council Oak Books, 1991).

35. A "grandparent" is not necessarily a lineal ancestor of an Indian child, but in many Indian societies great-aunts and uncles as well as cousins are considered grandparents. *See* Gray v. Pann, 513 N.W.2d 154 (Mich. App. 1994) (grandmother of Indian child brings action to obtain custody of child against father).

36. *See* House Report at 19, where the House stated that compliance with ICWA is "in the best interest of an Indian child."

37. *See* Cherokee Nation v. Georgia, 30 U.S. (5 Pet.) 1 (1831).

38. *Id.* at 17.

39. United States v. Wheeler, 435 U.S. 313 (1978).

40. For example the United States cannot exercise its plenary power in a manner that results in a taking of property without just compensation, *see* United States v. Sioux Nation, 100 S. Ct. 2716 (1980), or in a manner that is violative of the due process clause in the Fifth Amendment. Delaware Tribal Business Committee v. Weeks, 430 U.S. 73 (1977).

41. *See* Cherokee Nation, *supra,* at 15; United States v. Mitchell, 463 U.S. 206 (1980).

42. Worcester v. Georgia, 31 U.S. (6 Pet.) 515, 555 (1832).

43. *See, e.g.,* Seminole Nation v. United States, 316 U.S. 286 (1942).

44. *See* Morton v. Mancari, 417 U.S. 535 (1974).

45. U.S. Const., art. I, sec. 8, cl. 3.

46. *See* Williams v. Lee, 358 U.S. 217 (1959).

47. *See, e.g.,* Fisher v. District Court, 424 U.S. 382 (1976) (exclusive authority to grant on-reservation adoption); No Fire v. United States, 164 U.S. 657 (1897) (authority to grant marriage license); Conroy v. Conroy, 575 F.2d 175 (8th Cir. 1978) (authority to divide marital property).

48. Carney v. Chapman, 247 U.S. 102 (1918).

49. Fisher, note 47.

50. Conroy, note 47.

51. *See, e.g.,* Heart v. Ellenbecker, 689 F.Supp. 989 (D.S.D. 1988).

52. *See, e.g.,* Mescalero Apache Tribe v. Jones, 411 U.S. 145 (1973).

53. Popovici v. Agler, 280 U.S. 379 (1930).

54. *In re* Marcus S., 638 A.2d 1158 (Me. 1994).

55. *In re* D.L.L. and C.L.L., 291 N.W.2d 278 (S.D. 1980).

56. *In re* Appeal of Pima County Juvenile Action, S-903, 635 P.2d 187 (Ariz Ct.

Appeals 1981), *cert. denied,* 455 U.S. 1007 (1982).

57. Matter of Miller, 182 Mich. App. 70, 451 N.W.2d 576 (Mich. App. 1990) (non-Indian parent's challenge to ICWA on ground that it gave Indian parents preferential treatment denied).

58. Matter of Two Babies (Okla. Dist. Ct. #JF 79-1121, 1980).

59. State *ex rel.* CSD v. Graves, 848 P.2d 133 (Or. App. 1993); *see also* Angus v. Joseph, 60 Or. App. 546 (Ore. Ct. App. 1982).

CHAPTER • II

Applicability of ICWA

The beginning point for any analysis of the Indian Child Welfare Act is an understanding of what type of proceeding the act is intended to cover. The act applies only to child custody proceedings in state courts.

At 25 U.S.C. Section 1903(1), a "child custody proceeding" is defined as any of four separate proceedings.

- i "foster care placement" which shall mean any action removing an Indian child from its [sic] parent or Indian custodian for temporary placement in a foster home or institution or the home of a guardian or conservator where the parent or Indian custodian cannot have the child returned upon demand, but where parental rights have not been terminated;
- ii "termination of parental rights" which shall mean any action resulting in the termination of the parent-child relationship;
- iii "preadoptive placement" which shall mean the temporary placement of an Indian child in a foster home or institution after the termination of parental rights, but prior to or in lieu of adoptive placement; and
- iv "adoptive placement" which shall mean the permanent placement of an Indian child for adoption, including any action resulting in a final decree of adoption.

Proceedings Not Covered

Divorce Proceedings

ICWA does not apply to a child custody dispute between the natural parents of a child, even if the child is Native American, that arises in the course of a divorce action.[1] The legislative language of ICWA makes that distinction clear. Nor, as some courts have held, does ICWA apply to a custody dispute between the unwed parents of a Native American child.[2] This is true even if the child's parents are both Native American, if neither one is Native American, or if one is native and the other is not. ICWA clearly did not intend to supplant parents' rights to custody of their children in divorce or similar proceedings.

Intrafamily Disputes

If a nonparent of a Native American child were awarded custody in a divorce or similar proceeding, the provisions of the act might be triggered, but thus far there is insufficient case law to discuss this possibility. The act is triggered, however, if a nonparent applies to a court for the guardianship of a minor Indian child against the wishes of a parent.[3] The act also clearly applies if a parent awarded custody in a divorce or similar proceeding attempts to terminate the parental rights of the noncustodial parent for purposes of commencing a stepparent adoption.[4]

Delinquency Proceedings

As stated at 25 U.S.C. Section 1903(1), ICWA does not apply to a placement outside of the home if it is a result of an "act which, if committed by an adult would be deemed a crime. . . ."[5] There are several exceptions to this general rule, many of which are discussed in the guidelines enacted by the Department of Interior to guide state courts in the implementation of ICWA.[6]

25 U.S.C. Section 1952 orders the secretary of interior to promulgate final regulations to implement ICWA. The secretary has failed to follow this mandate; instead, the secretary has published "guidelines" for state courts to follow in administering ICWA. These guidelines, as many courts have noted, do not have the weight of administrative regulations.[7] Notwithstanding the secretary's clear instructions in the guidelines that they were not published as regulations, many courts have devoutly followed them.[8] They are included in this book in the appendix at A.

The guidelines give several instances where delinquency proceedings would be covered by ICWA. If, for example, a state court were to attempt to terminate the parental rights of a parent over a Native American child because of delinquent acts committed by that child, ICWA would govern the termination proceeding, though not the adjudication of delinquency.[9] Similarly, if the gravamen of the delinquency petition were acts of truancy[10] instead of criminal behavior, ICWA would govern the adjudication of delinquency as well as disposition.[11] In the majority of cases, however, when a Native American child commits a delinquent act neither his or her placement nor the proceedings whereby he or she is adjudicated delinquent are governed by ICWA.

Voluntary Placements

The definition of "foster care placement" excludes placements where the parent can regain custody of the child upon demand.[12] This encompasses most educational and religious placements, which continue to be common occurrences among Native American families.[13]

The reader should not confuse this with a voluntary placement for purposes of an adoption, which is clearly governed by ICWA.[14]

Judicially Created Exceptions

Along with the clearly expressed exceptions to the coverage of ICWA stated in the legislation and the legislative history, some courts have adopted exceptions to the coverage of ICWA based on these courts' interpretation of the act's intent. These courts have held that the provisions of ICWA are inapposite in a "child custody proceeding" in which a Native American child is not being removed from a Native American family or a Native American cultural setting. These cases routinely involve non-Native American parents attempting to terminate the parental rights of Native American parents where the Native American parents and the family have had little or no contact with the child. Relying on the legislative history behind the enactment of ICWA, these courts, which have embraced the "existing Indian family" exception, have held that the act should not apply unless the child is being removed from an existing Native American family or from a family where the child was exposed to Native American culture.

The earliest decision to sanction this exception was in *Baby Boy L.*,[15] wherein the Kansas Supreme Court refused to follow the dictates of ICWA when a non-Native American mother petitioned to terminate the parental rights of an incarcerated Native American father. The court held that its application of ICWA to that factual situation would not serve the purposes articulated by Congress in enacting the law. Many state courts quickly followed suit, including courts of South Dakota,[16] Indiana,[17] Missouri,[18] Oklahoma,[19] and Mississippi.[20]

The U.S. Supreme Court granted certiorari in the Mississippi case, albeit for a different issue, and apparently laid the existing Indian family exception to rest in *Mississippi Band of Choctaw Indians v. Holyfield,*[21] the Court's only incursion into the realm of ICWA. In that decision the Court examined a situation where a reservation-domiciled Native American couple placed their twins with a non-Native American family residing off the reservation for adoption. The adoption was permitted by the state court despite the Indian tribe's contention that the state court lacked jurisdiction under the provision of ICWA vesting Indian tribal courts with exclusive jurisdiction over child custody proceedings involving reservation-domiciled Native American children. The Mississippi Supreme Court affirmed the adoption, holding that ICWA did not apply because the children had never resided with a Native American family and were not domiciled on the reservation.

The Supreme Court rejected the Mississippi Supreme Court's conclusion that the children were not domiciled on the reservation and reversed the state adoption order, sending the case back to the tribal court. In so doing, the Court strongly suggested that the exception adopted by the Mississippi Supreme Court and others to the application of ICWA was doctrinally flawed. The Court stated that the fact the parents gave up the children did not defeat the application of ICWA, especially since the Choctaw Tribe had rights under ICWA that could not be frustrated by the parents' actions.

After *Holyfield* the South Dakota Supreme Court specifically held that the existing Indian family exception had been dealt its death knell in reversing its previous holding that the exception defeated the application of ICWA.[22] However, notwithstanding the clear language in *Holyfield* repudiating the exception, numerous state courts have resurrected it in a further attempt to defeat the application of ICWA. Recent state court decisions in Washington,[23] Oklahoma,[24] and Alabama[25] have held that the exception is alive and well in those states.[26] A Louisiana appellate court has even altered the science of genetics in an attempt to show that a Native American child is not a Native American.[27]

The majority of courts, however, have applied the clear language of the statute and held that ICWA applies to any child custody proceeding in which the child involved is Native American. This includes courts in Alaska,[28] Arizona,[29] Illinois,[30] Colorado,[31] Iowa,[32] Minnesota,[33] Montana,[34] New Jersey,[35] Idaho,[36] California,[37] and New York.[38] It is apparent that this area of the law is in a state of flux, and readers are cautioned to review their state court decisions to determine whether ICWA applies to a particular fact situation.[39]

Proceedings Covered by ICWA

Definition of Indian Child

The beginning point for any determination of whether ICWA applies to a particular proceeding is an inquiry into whether the child involved is an "Indian child" as that term is defined at 25 U.S.C. Section 1903(4). The definition requires that the child be a member of or eligible for membership in an Indian tribe and be the biological child of a member of an Indian tribe. The secretary of interior annually publishes a list of Indian tribes eligible for federal services and programs. A recent list is included in Appendix B.[40] It should be noted that ICWA applies to those children who are members of or eligible for membership only in federally recognized tribes and Alaska native villages and corporations.[41] Certain tribes are recognized by the states in which they are located but are not eligible for federal services.[42] Other tribes were federally recognized at one time but had their status as federally recognized tribes terminated in the 1950s when Congress terminated several tribes during a period of assimilation.[43] Many of the tribes were terminated under legislation that specifically stipulated that federal law applicable to Native Americans would no longer apply to those tribes.[44] Many of these tribes are seeking to have their status restored; therefore it is important to make proper inquiry with the Department of Interior to determine whether a particular tribe is eligible for federal services. A last group not encompassed in the definition of Indian tribe is Canadian tribes,[45] even if those tribes can show a historical and genealogical relationship to tribes of the United States.[46]

The situation confronting Alaska tribes is a unique one. ICWA applies to "any Alaska Native Village defined in section 1602(c) of Title 43." The reference in ICWA is to the Alaska Native Claims

Settlement Act, codified at 43 U.S.C. Sections 1601–28. That act was an attempt by Congress to settle the land rights of Alaska natives and to set up regional corporations that would then select for their use some of the lands set aside by Congress for the use of the native corporations. The reference to the Claims Settlement Act in ICWA, however, is not meant to exclude native village Alaskans from the coverage of ICWA, an Oregon court has held.[47] Instead, under ICWA all Alaska natives, including those from native villages as well as resident and nonresident members of the regional corporations set up by the Claims Settlement Act, are protected by the provisions of ICWA. A list of native villages eligible for federal services is periodically listed, along with other federally recognized tribes, in the *Federal Register.* A recent list is included in Appendix B.

The inclusion of native villages under the coverage of ICWA has created some consternation in the courts because many of the covered villages are so small that the state and federal courts applying ICWA have expressed concern about the ability of native village judicial entities to administer the exclusive jurisdiction given them by Section 1911(a) of the act. This concern has led both the Alaska Supreme Court[48] and the U.S. Court of Appeals for the Ninth Circuit[49] to rule that villages in Alaska cannot exercise the jurisdiction vested in them by ICWA absent a retrocession of jurisdiction to them under the provisions of Section 1918 of ICWA. Congress enacted that section, discussed in more detail *infra* at 44–45, to allow tribes in states that the federal government had vested with jurisdiction over Indian country,[50] or in states that had opted to exercise jurisdiction over Indian country, to petition the federal government to reassume jurisdiction over child custody proceedings to permit them to exercise the jurisdiction vested them under ICWA. This is especially important for tribes that previously had no need for a tribal court system because the state in which the tribe was located exercised judicial jurisdiction over child custody proceedings arising even on the reservation.

The best way to obviate the need to establish that a child is an Indian child for the purpose of coverage under ICWA is to have the relevant tribe declare that the child is either a member or eligible for membership in the tribe. Such a determination is entitled to deference by the state court because of a long line of federal decisions recognizing that Indian tribes have the inherent authority to determine their own memberships and that such determinations are binding on the federal and state governments.[51] Such a conclusion is also entitled to full faith and credit under Section 1911(d) of ICWA. The guidelines for state courts also state that a tribal determination of membership is conclusive.[52] State courts cannot look beyond a tribe's determination of membership even if it appears that the member child does not possess the necessary blood quantum for membership under the tribe's own organic laws.[53] This has created inequities in cases where tribes mistakenly assert that a child is a member and then, on further inquiry, determine that the original determination was erroneous. In one case a state court held that it was bound by a tribal determination that, although erroneous, deprived another tribe of the right to assert that a child was eligible for membership.[54]

ICWA requires that a child be a member or eligible for membership in an Indian tribe and be the biological child of a member of an Indian tribe. This would seem to preclude coverage in a case where a non-Indian child has been adopted by a Native American family, although if the particular tribe allows that child to become a member, ICWA would apply. Membership in a tribe should not necessarily be equated with enrollment with the tribe. Enrollment with a tribe is the most common method for tribes to compile a list of tribal members, but it certainly is not the exclusive manner.[55] Each tribe may have its own method of determining its membership, and therefore that tribe needs to be consulted in any case where it appears that a child may have some affiliation with the tribe. A determination by the Department of Interior that a child is not a member or eligible for membership with a tribe, although probative, certainly is no substitute for a tribal determination. The guidelines for state courts provide that if a tribe fails to make a determination of membership or eligibility thereof, the Department of Interior can make the determination and that decision is conclusive upon a state court.[56] Absent a determination by the tribe as to a child's membership or eligibility for membership, the burden falls on the state court to make an independent determination with the evidence it has before it. This determination, at least one court has held, must be made even if the tribe in question does not unambiguously assert that the child is eligible for membership.[57] Such a review may require the acquisition of the tribe's organic documents, including the tribal constitution and ordinances governing membership.

In certain cases it will not become apparent that a child custody proceeding involves an Indian child until the proceeding is fairly advanced. In that case the courts that have dealt with the issue have held that the late discovery will not vitiate the proceedings up to that point but that ICWA would have to be adhered to in future proceedings.[58] However, if the court or any officer of the court, including guardians ad litem and lawyers in the case, were aware of certain circumstances, more adequately set out in the guidelines, that would put the court on notice that an Indian child is involved, the proceedings may be invalidated if certain mandates of ICWA were not followed, including the notice requirements discussed *infra* at 51–54.[59]

Foster Care Placements

The provisions of ICWA apply to both voluntary and involuntary "foster care placements."[60] The relevant procedural and substantive provisions of the act applicable to each type are discussed *infra* at 71–73 (voluntary) and at 57–63 (involuntary). As previously stated, any placement of an Indian child, whether voluntary or involuntary, is governed by ICWA if the natural parent or Indian custodian cannot regain custody of the child upon demand.[61] The act therefore applies to an Indian parent who places his or her child with a state social services agency or private agency on a temporary basis, even though Section 1913(c) seems to mandate that the parent could regain custody of the child upon demand. Certainly the agency should not be allowed to claim that ICWA does not govern the placement because Section 1913(c) allows the parent or Indian custodian to regain custody upon demand as such a contention would clearly frustrate the intent of Congress to abate some social workers' common practice of encouraging Indian parents to place their children with social services agencies at a time of crisis in their lives and then using that placement as a sign of parental unfitness.[62]

On its face, the definition of foster care placement does not seem to encompass involuntary proceedings wherein physical custody of the Indian child remains with the natural parent or Indian custodian pending dependency and neglect proceedings because such does not involve a removal of the child from the home. Such a proceeding would, however, fall under the definition of a "termination of parental rights" proceeding if termination were a possible aftermath of the proceedings.[63]

A proceeding resulting in the return of an Indian child to his or her natural parents would not trigger the various provisions of ICWA even in a situation where the child is being involuntarily removed from an "Indian custodian" and returned to the natural parents.[64]

A finding that a proceeding is a foster care placement activates both the procedural requirements, including notice requirements, discussed *infra* at 51–54, and the substantive provisions relating to foster care placements, discussed *infra* at 84–91.

Termination of Parental Rights Proceedings

ICWA applies to any proceeding "resulting in the termination of the parent-child relationship."[65] Although that language seems to imply that ICWA only applies to those proceedings that actually result in the termination of parental rights, it is clear from legislative history and case law that the act governs any proceeding in which the termination of parental rights is a potential disposition.[66] This includes stepparent adoptions, although it is in this area that many state courts have concocted the "existing Indian family" exception, discussed *supra* at 15–17, to hold that the provisions of ICWA do not apply to the termination of parental rights of an Indian parent who has had little or no contact with the Indian child.

In those states that permit adoptions without the consent of a natural parent, because of an abandonment or other commission or omission by the natural parent, the ICWA provisions relating to termination of parental rights, especially Section 1912(f), supersede state law and govern those state court proceedings.[67] The adoption of an Indian child must necessarily be preceded by a lawful termination, either voluntary or involuntary, of the parental rights of the parents in compliance with the provisions of ICWA.

ICWA has provisions applicable to both voluntary and involuntary termination of parental rights that differ notably from many state court procedures. The ICWA provisions relating to the involuntary termination of parental rights, discussed *infra* at 63–65, were designed to ensure that the parental rights of Indian parents are terminated only after all possible remedial and rehabilitative services have made available to the parents and only upon the testimony of those persons qualified to opine upon the capacity of the parents to provide for their children. The burden of proof needed to sustain a termination also differs from termination proceedings in non-ICWA cases, although some states have amended their codes to harmonize the standard for termination in non-ICWA cases with ICWA.[68]

ICWA does not prohibit the practice of allowing Indian parents to voluntarily terminate their parental rights, but it does place stringent requirements on the procedures for termination.[69] ICWA also allows a parent to withdraw a consent to voluntary termination if that is done before an entry of a decree terminating parental rights or a decree of adoption.[70]

Preadoptive Placements

The third kind of proceeding covered by ICWA is a "temporary placement. . . in a foster home or institution after the termination of parental rights, but prior to or in lieu of adoptive placement."[71] It is oftentimes difficult to determine when a child custody proceeding ceases to be a termination proceeding and becomes a preadoptive placement. As discussed *infra* at 35–36, the distinction is important for jurisdictional purposes because ICWA does not literally permit an Indian tribe to transfer a preadoptive placement proceeding to the tribal court, whereas a termination proceeding is subject to a transfer to tribal court.[72] No court has apparently drawn this distinction in a transfer matter, but with the number of cases increasing, it will probably be the subject of some contention in the future.

Preadoptive placements include any long-term foster care placement, provided the parental rights of one or both of the natural parents are terminated.

Most of the ICWA provisions germane to preadoptive placements pertain to where Indian children should be placed and not to any particular procedural formalities a state court must satisfy to effect a preadoptive placement. Those placement preference provisions are discussed *infra* 84–91.[73]

Adoptive Placements

The last type of proceeding regulated by ICWA is "the permanent placement of an Indian child for adoption, including any action resulting in a final decree of adoption."[74] This section covers adoptions arranged by state social services agencies as well as private adoption agencies. It also encompasses stepparent adoptions, although it is difficult to reconcile the adoptive placement preference provisions with the stepparent adoption scenario, especially when the custodial parent is non-Indian.[75]

The last part of the definition of adoptive placement strongly suggests that the provisions of ICWA continue to apply up to the point of a final adoption decree being rendered by a state court and not only up to the point where an adoptive placement is effected.[76]

This may be important in certain cases when an Indian tribe or relatives of an Indian family become aware of an Indian child being placed for adoption after the placement is accomplished.[77] ICWA clearly permits these parties to advance the goals of the law even though the placement has already been effected.

Indeed, ICWA even applies to certain matters that arise after a final decree of adoption has taken place, as one provision allows certain parties collaterally to attack a final decree of adoption[78] and yet another provision allows a parent to petition for the return of an adopted Indian child if the adoption is vacated.[79]

This chapter has explored the type of proceeding to which ICWA applies and the determination of when an Indian child is involved. The chapters that follow discuss in more detail the jurisdictional, procedural, and substantive provisions of the act.

Notes

1. *See* 25 U.S.C. § 1903 (1); *In re* Marriage of Baisley, 749 P.2d 446 (Colo. App. 1987); Malatarre v. Malatarre, 293 N.W.2d 139 (N.D. 1980).

2. *See* Application of Defender, 435 N.W.2d 717 (S.D. 1989); *In re* Custody of Sengstock, 165 Wis. 2d 86, 477 N.W.2d 310 (Wis. App. 1991) (both of these cases hold that ICWA does not apply to a custody dispute between the unwed parents of an Indian child).

3. Two recent cases have held that the provisions of ICWA do apply to proceedings wherein a nonparent is seeking placement of the child with her or him. In Matter of Ashley Elizabeth R., 863 P.2d 451 (N.M. App. 1993), the New Mexico Court of Appeals held that the placement of an Indian child with a non-Indian paternal great-aunt was a foster care placement covered by ICWA. In Custody of A.K.H., 502 N.W.2d 790 (Minn. App. 1993), the Minnesota Court of Appeals held that the lower court had erred in disallowing intervention by an Indian tribe in a custody dispute between a grandparent and a parent as ICWA applied. *See also In re* Guardianship of Q.G.M., 808 P.2d 684 (Okla. 1991); A.B.M. v. M.H. and A.H., 651 P.2d 1170 (Alaska 1982); *In re* Custody of S.B.R., 719 P.2d 154 (Wash. App. 1986). Dissenting from this point of view is the Montana Supreme Court's decision in *In re* Bertelson, 617 P.2d 121 (Mont. 1980).

4. *See, e.g.,* Matter of Application of Baade, 462 N.W.2d 485 (S.D. 1990). It is in the area of stepparent adoptions, however, that many courts have recognized an exception to the application of ICWA, discussed *infra,* at 15–17.

5. *See, e.g.,* State in Interest of T.D.C., 748 P.2d 201 (Utah App. 1988) (court rejects application of ICWA to placement of an Indian child for the commission of criminal conduct even though conduct was not serious under 42 U.S.C. § 5603(14)).

6. Department of Interior, Bureau of Indian Affairs Guidelines for State Courts; Indian Child Custody Proceedings, 44 Fed. Reg. No. 228, 67584 (Nov. 26, 1979). The BIA Guidelines are set out in Appendix A of this book.

7. *See* Matter of Adoption of F.H., 851 P.2d 1361, 1364 (Alaska 1993).

8. Matter of Ashley Elizabeth R., 863 P.2d 451, 454 (N.M. App. 1993). In a recent Minnesota decision the Supreme Court of Minnesota held that the guidelines would be strictly adhered to in determining whether a non-Indian couple had demonstrated good cause to deviate from the placement preference provisions of ICWA, discussed *infra,* at 91–92. Matter of Custody of S.E.G., 521 N.W.2d 357 (Minn. 1994).

9. BIA Guidelines, Rule B.3 Commentary at 67587–88.

10. ICWA also applies to proceedings in which the state claims that a child is in need of assistance or supervision because of no fault of the parents or guardians. *See* In Interest of B.B., 500 N.W.2d 9 (Iowa 1993) (ICWA applies to a proceeding in which a mentally retarded Indian child is declared a minor in need of assistance).

11. *See* note 9.

12. 25 U.S.C. § 1903 (1).

13. One reason there has been a high incidence of "voluntary" placements of Indian children for education purposes has been the failure of the Bureau of Indian Affairs to construct schools that are in close proximity to many Indian population bases. In the 1984 Oversight Hearings on the Indian Child Welfare Act, the Association on American Indian Affairs cited BIA statistics showing that almost one out of every two Indian students in the BIA education system had to be placed at a boarding school because of the absence of local day schools. This, as Congress noted at Title IV of ICWA, 25 U.S.C. § 1961(a), contributed to the displacement problems that ICWA was enacted to address. This problem has been somewhat alleviated by new standards for BIA schools; *see* 25 U.S.C. § 2001e, which stresses the need for local day schools.

14. *See* 25 U.S.C. § 1913(a). The Department of Interior has promulgated recent amendments to 25 C.F.R. § 23.1 *et seq.,* in which the department defines "child custody proceeding" to also include "other tribal placements made in accordance with the placement preferences of the Act, including the temporary or permanent placement of an Indian child in accordance with tribal children's codes and local tribal customs or traditions." 59 Fed. Reg. No. 9, 2257 (January 13, 1994). The import of this amendment is unclear.

15. 643 P.2d 168 (Kan. 1982).

16. Claymore v. Serr, 405 N.W.2d 650 (S.D. 1987).

17. *In re* Adoption of T.R.M., 525 N.E.2d 298 (Ind. 1988). *T.R.M.* was criticized but not reversed in *In re* D.S., 577 N.E.2d 572 (Ind. 1991).

18. *In re* S.A.M., 703 S.W.2d 603 (Mo. Ct. App. 1986).

19. *In re* Baby Boy D., 742 P.2d 1059 (Okla. 1985).

20. Matter of B.B., 511 So. 2d 918 (Miss. 1987), *rev'd sub nom.* Mississippi Band of Choctaw Indians v. Holyfield, 490 U.S. 30 (1989).

21. 490 U.S. 30 (1989).

22. Matter of Adoption of Baade, 462 N.W.2d 485 (S.D. 1990).

23. *In re* Crews, 825 P.2d 305 (Wash. 1992). In a decision that a Washington appeals court rendered subsequent to *Crews,* the appellate court seemed to distance itself from the ruling in *Crews* by applying ICWA to a child custody proceeding involving a child who had lived primarily in a non-Indian home and whose parents petitioned to voluntarily terminate their parental rights. Matter of Adoption of M., 832 P.2d 518 (Wash. App. 1992). The court seemed to suggest that *Crews* was an aberration because of the strange facts there.

24. *In re* S.C., 833 P.2d 1249 (Okla. 1992) (court holds that ICWA does not apply to the foster care placement of an Indian child removed from a non-Indian mother). *S.C.* seems inconsistent with a previous ruling from the same court, which held that ICWA did apply to a dispute between the non-Indian grandparents and Indian mother over custody of a child. *See In re* Q.G.M., 808 P.2d 684 (Okla. 1991).

25. S.A. v. E.J.P., 571 So. 2d 1187 (Ala. Civ. App. 1990) (child who had been raised by non-Indian mother and non-Indian aunt and uncle and where Indian father had never supported the minor child was not an Indian child for purposes of ICWA).

26. A Missouri appeals court has also suggested in rather strong dicta that the existing family exception is doctrinally correct, although the court there went on to apply the act. *See* C.E.H. v. L.M.W., 837 S.W.2d 947 (Mo. App. W.D. 1992).

27. Barbry v. Dauzat, 576 So. 2d 1013 (La. App. 1991). There a Louisiana appellate court relied on a state statute that declared that an illegitimate child assumed the race of the mother in holding that ICWA did not apply to a child custody proceeding.

28. *In re* Adoption of T.N.F., 781 P.2d 973 (Alaska 1989).

29. *In re* Coconino County, 737 P.2d 829 (Ariz. App. 1989).

30. *In re* Adoption of S.S., 622 N.E.2d 832 (Ill. App. 1993). This decision contains a very thoughtful analysis of the existing Indian family exception and the cases that have adopted it. 835–38.

31. *In re* C.A.J., 709 P.2d 604 (Colo. App. 1985).

32. *In re* J.R.H., 358 N.W.2d 311 (Iowa 1984).

33. *In re* T.J.J., 366 N.W.2d 651 (Minn. App. 1985).

34. *In re* M.E.M., 679 P.2d 1241 (Mont. 1984).

35. *In re* Adoption of a Baby Child of Indian Heritage, 543 A.2d 925 (N.J. 1988).

36. Matter of Baby Boy Doe, 849 P.2d 925 (Idaho 1993).

37. *In re* Adoption of Lindsay C., 280 Cal. Rptr. 194 (1991).

38. *In re* Oscar C., 559 N.Y.S.2d 431 (Fam. Ct. 1990).

39. For a thorough discussion of the existing Indian family exception to ICWA, *see* Hahn Davis, *The Existing Indian Family Exception to the Indian Child Welfare Act,* 69 N.D. L. Rev. 465 (1993).

40. If an Indian tribe does not appear in the list of tribes eligible for services from the Bureau of Indian Affairs, that does not necessarily preclude the application of ICWA to proceedings involving that tribe's children. *See, e.g.,* In Interest of C.H., 510 N.W.2d 119 (S.D. 1993) (on remand from South Dakota Supreme Court, trial court holds that the Mowa Band of Choctaw Indians is a federally recognized tribe although not on the list in the *Federal Register*). A tribe should still be able to offer proof of its eligibility for federal services.

41. *See, e.g., In re* M.C.P., 153 Vt. 275 , 571 A.2d 627 (Vt. 1989) (membership of children in Micmac Tribe of Indians not sufficient to invoke ICWA because that tribe is not entitled to federal services. Case remanded, however, for proper notice of Mohawks who were eligible); *In re* John V., 5 Cal. App. 4th 1201, 7 Cal. Rptr. 2d 629 (Cal. App. 6 Dist. 1992) (Creoles not Indians for purpose of application of ICWA).

42. *See* Cohen, Handbook of Federal Indian Law 3–19.

43. Some examples of terminated tribes include the Klamath Tribe of Oregon, the Ponca Tribe of Nebraska, the Menominee Tribe of Wisconsin, and the Catawbas of South Carolina. The Catawbas have recently regained their federal

recognition under express federal legislation. *See* Cohen at 170–75. The Nebraska Poncas have also been re-recognized. Before their re-recognition, however, the Nebraska Supreme Court held that ICWA did not apply to children whose father was Ponca because that tribe had been terminated. *In re* Interest of J.L.M., 451 N.W.2d 377 (Neb. 1990).

44. *See, e.g.,* Pub. L. 87-629, codified at 25 U.S.C. §§ 971–80 (Ponca Termination Act).

45. *See, e.g., In re* Wanomi P., 264 Cal. Rptr. 623 (Ct. App. 2 Dist. 1989); In the Matter of T.I.S., 586 N.E.2d 690 (Ill. App. 1 Dist. 1991); *In re* Stairwalt, 190 Ill. App. 3d 547, 546 N.E.2d 44 (Ill. App. 2 Dist. 1989). 25 C.F.R. 83.1(f) defines an Indian tribe as a group within the continental United States and who are indigenous to the continental United States. There are many Indian tribes, such as the Micmacs of Maine, that have indigenous ties to the continental United States but who are recognized only by the Canadian government. *See In re* M.C.P., 571 A.2d 627 (Vt. 1989). These tribes do not have a political relationship with the U.S. government and it is perhaps for this reason that they were excluded under ICWA.

46. One tribe that does have a connection to Canadian bands of Indians is the Standing Rock Sioux Tribe, home of the Hunkpapa Sioux, Sitting Bull's band. During Sitting Bull's exile in Canada, many members of the band went over the border and remained there even after his return. Robert M. Utley, *The Lance and the Shield: The Life and Times of Sitting Bull* (1993).

47. State *ex rel.* Juvenile Dep't v. Tucker, 710 P.2d 793 (Or. App. 1985).

48. Native Village of Nenana v. State, 722 P.2d 219 (Alaska 1986), *cert. denied,* 479 U.S. 1008 (1986); Matter of K.E., 744 P.2d 1173 (Alaska 1987).

49. Native Village of Venetie I.R.A. Council v. State of Alaska, 944 F.2d 548 (9th Cir. 1991).

50. *See* Pub. L. 280, 67 Stat. 588, codified in part at 18 U.S.C. § 1162.

51. *See* Santa Clara Pueblo v. Martinez, 436 U.S. 49 (1978).

52. BIA Guidelines, B.1(b)(i) at 67586.

53. In a South Dakota case, Matter of Dependency and Neglect of A.L., 442 N.W.2d 233 (S.D. 1989), the court held that a tribe's enrollment of a Caucasian child required the lower court to apply ICWA to the proceedings.

54. *See* People in Interest of J.J., 454 N.W.2d 317 (S.D. 1990).

55. United States v. Broncheau, 597 F.2d 1260, 1263 (9th Cir. 1979); Nelson v. Hunter, 132 Or. App. 361, 888 P.2d 124, (1995) (court, after concluding that person can be member of a tribe without being enrolled, determines that mother of Indian children was not Indian under ICWA because she could not prove "membership"); BIA Guidelines, B.1 Commentary, at 67586. (*See* Appendix A.)

56. BIA Guidelines, B.1(b)(ii) at 67586.

57. *See* Matter of Baby Boy Doe, 849 P.2d 925, 930–31 (Idaho 1993), holding that a state court must make a determination of whether a child is an Indian even if the tribe and BIA are unable to make that determination. Other courts are in apparent disagreement with this requirement and have held that if the parents fail to come forward with evidence that ICWA applies, it is not error to ignore the mandates of ICWA. *See* Matter of Johanson, 402 N.W.2d 13 (Mich. App. 1986) (failure of mother to come forward with proof of membership in tribe dooms argument that ICWA applies); People in Interest of A.E., 749 P.2d 450 (Colo. App. 1987); Matter of

Shawboose, 438 N.W.2d 272 (Mich. App. 1989) (failure of mother to show she was enrolled with tribe and failure of tribes to intervene sufficient cause not to apply ICWA); Matter of Adoption of Baby Boy W., 831 P.2d 643 (Okla. 1992) (father's claims that school records show that he is Indian not sufficient to invoke ICWA.)

58. *See, e.g.,* People in Interest of A.E., 749 P.2d 450 (Colo. App. 1987); Matter of Adoption of Child of Indian Heritage, 543 A.2d 925 (N.J. 1988); Matter of Welfare of B.W., 454 N.W.2d 437 (Minn. App. 1990); Matter of Adoption of Crews, 825 P.2d 305 (Wash. 1992).

59. *In re* Kahlen W., 285 Cal. Rptr., 507 (Cal. App. 5 Dist. 1991); *see also In re* Interest of J.L.M., 451 N.W.2d 377 (Neb. 1990).

60. *See* 25 U.S.C. § 1913(a) (voluntary placements) and § 1912(e) (involuntary placements).

61. *See* 25 U.S.C. § 1903(1)(i) defining foster care placement.

62. Though ICWA allows a parent to regain custody of a child upon demand by revoking a voluntary placement, one court has held that a parent is not entitled to regain custody of the child from the other parent by revoking a consent to adoption. *See* Harvick v. Harvick, 828 P.2d 769 (Alaska 1992).

63. *See* State *ex rel.* Juvenile Dep't v. Cooke, 744 P.2d 596 (Or. App. 1987) (ICWA applies even if the result of the dependency petition is not the removal of the child from the parents' home).

64. *See* 25 U.S.C. § 1916(b). This section of ICWA can be read two different ways. First, because of its placement in the law, after the placement provisions of ICWA, it could be construed to mean that only the placement preference provisions of ICWA are inapplicable in a proceeding where a child is returned to his or her parents. In the alternative, it may mean that all the provisions of ICWA are inapplicable to a proceeding wherein a parent seeks the return of his or her child. This interpretation appears to conflict with those cases holding that ICWA applies to a custody dispute between a parent and a nonparent. *See* note 3.

65. 25 U.S.C. § 1903(1)(ii).

66. *See* note 63.

67. *See, e.g.,* Matter of Adoption of Baade, 462 N.W.2d 485 (S.D. 1990).

68. *See* State *ex rel.* CSD v. Greaves, 848 P.2d 133 (Or. App. 1993) (denying a constitutional claim of a non-Indian parent that the higher burden of proof in ICWA cases violated the privileges and immunities clause of the Oregon Constitution); *In re* Marcus S., 638 A.2d 1158 (Me. 1994).

69. *See* 25 U.S.C. § 1913(a).

70. *See* 25 U.S.C. § 1913(c). *See* Matter of Kiogma, 472 N.W.2d 13 (Mich. App. 1991) (mother cannot regain custody of child by withdrawing consent to termination of parental rights after order terminating rights has been entered).

71. *See* 25 U.S.C. § 1903(1)(iii).

72. *See* 25 U.S.C. § 1911(b).

73. *See* 25 U.S.C. § 1915.

74. 25 U.S.C. § 1903(1)(iv).

75. The adoption placement preference provisions address the placement of an Indian child when neither parent is able to care for the child. They do not conform well to the stepparent adoption scenario where the minor child remains with one of the parents after adoption. However, at least one court has held that a state

court is still bound to apply the placement preferences even in a stepparent adoption. *In re* Adoption of Lindsay C., 229 Cal. App. 3d 404, 280 Cal. Rptr. 194 (Cal. App. 1 Dist. 1991).

76. *See* E.A. v. Alaska, 623 P.2d 1210 (Alaska 1981); *but see* People in Interest of A.E.V., 782 P.2d 858 (Colo. App. 1989).

77. *See, e.g.,* In Matter of J.R.S., 690 P.2d 10 (Alaska 1984).

78. 25 U.S.C. § 1913(d).

79. 25 U.S.C. § 1916(a).

CHAPTER • III

Jurisdictional Provisions of ICWA

The Supreme Court noted in *Mississippi Band of Choctaw Indians v. Holyfield*[1] that the jurisdictional provisions of the Indian Child Welfare Act are at the very heart of the law.[2] Those provisions are designed to maximize the opportunity for tribal court judges, who in most cases are more knowledgeable than state court judges about Indian child-rearing traditions and customs, to determine the fate of Indian children. As a result, ICWA vests tribal courts with exclusive jurisdiction over child custody proceedings "when an Indian child resides or is domiciled within the jurisdiction of such tribe. . . ."[3]

When a child custody proceeding arises outside of the jurisdiction of a tribe (i.e., in a state court's jurisdiction), the act provides that the proceeding shall be transferred to the tribal court absent declination by the tribal court, objection by a parent, or upon a showing of good cause to the contrary.[4] This transfer jurisdiction of a tribal court was referred to by the Supreme Court as the tribal court's "presumptive" jurisdiction.[5] ICWA also allows states and tribes to enter into agreements allocating jurisdiction, which has engendered much positive development in the area of cooperative agreements between tribes and states.[6]

Exclusive Jurisdiction

ICWA prescribes that a tribal court exercise exclusive jurisdiction over any child custody proceeding involving an Indian child domiciled within the reservation, except when jurisdiction is otherwise vested in the state.[7] The tribal court retains exclusive jurisdiction over any Indian child who remains a "ward" of the tribal court, notwithstanding the child's domicile.[8]

The exclusive jurisdictional provisions of ICWA apply to all Indian children residing within a tribal court's jurisdiction, regardless of whether a child who is the subject of a custody proceeding is a member of the tribe that is exercising jurisdiction, provided the exercise of jurisdiction is consistent with the particular tribe's organic laws.[9] Recently, certain states have insisted that Indian tribes only possess the inherent authority to regulate the affairs of their own members residing on a reservation. This argument is a progeny of a Supreme Court decision holding that an Indian tribe does not possess the inherent right to prosecute nonmember Indians for criminal violations committed within Indian country.[10] This argument is inapposite in the ICWA context, however, because in the act itself Congress has expressly vested Indian tribes with exclusive jurisdiction over all Indian children, much the same way Congress vested tribal courts with criminal jurisdiction over all Indians after the Supreme Court decision mentioned above.

There has been confusion, however, about whether ICWA vests tribal courts in certain states, called Public Law 280 states, which were granted jurisdiction over Indian tribes within their borders or opted to exercise jurisdiction under federal statutes authorizing them to opt, with exclusive jurisdiction over child custody proceedings, concurrent jurisdiction with state courts, or no jurisdiction at all.[11] Public Law 280 was enacted by Congress in the early 1950s to allow states to fill what Congress felt was a vacuum in the enforcement of misdemeanor criminal laws on Indian reservations. The law vested five states with mandatory civil and criminal jurisdiction over reservations in those states and permitted other states to exercise an option to extend their jurisdiction over reservations within their borders.

Although not clear from the language of Public Law 280, most courts have ruled that in Public Law 280 states tribal courts retained concurrent jurisdiction over the civil and criminal matters that state courts assumed jurisdiction over as the result of the law.[12] Nevertheless, many tribes in Public Law 280 states, believing that their jurisdiction had been preempted by state authority, disbanded their court systems; so when ICWA was enacted, many of these tribes did not have tribal courts to exercise the jurisdiction granted them by ICWA. This appears to be the congressional focus behind Section 1918 of ICWA, which allows those tribes in Public Law 280 states to reassume jurisdiction over child custody proceedings by petitioning the secretary of interior. Such a procedure, put in place by Congress, intimates that those tribes lost their jurisdiction when it was vested in the states.

This confusion has led to a diversity of viewpoints on the effect of the exclusive jurisdiction provisions of ICWA, as well as the transfer of jurisdiction provisions, on tribes in Public Law 280 states. Courts in Alaska have held that Alaska native villages cannot exercise any jurisdiction over child custody proceedings absent the exercise of the procedure to reassume jurisdiction detailed at Section 1918 of ICWA.[13] Others have concluded that under ICWA the tribes can exercise concurrent jurisdiction over reservation-domiciled children within Public Law 280 states.[14] Still other courts have suggested that Public Law 280 did not vest state courts with the authority to entertain in state court a "child custody proceeding" involving a reservation-domiciled child because that type of proceeding is a public action rather than a private action.[15]

Obviously, some confusion reigns in this area. Readers should acquaint themselves with the law of the state in which they work if that state is a Public Law 280 state. In a Public Law 280 state a tribe that is resurrecting its tribal court system in an attempt to exercise the jurisdiction vested in it by ICWA may want to use the procedure outlined at Section 1918 to reassume jurisdiction even in a state where the tribal courts retained concurrent jurisdiction after the enactment of Public Law 280. In that way the tribe can supplant state court jurisdiction and exercise its exclusive jurisdiction under the parameters of Section 1911(a).

Domicile on Reservation

If an Indian child is domiciled on or resides on an Indian reservation, the tribal court, with a few exceptions, has exclusive jurisdiction over a child custody proceeding involving that child.[16] The only exceptions to this rule are Public Law 280, discussed *supra* at 30, and a section in ICWA that gives state officials and courts the authority to remove an Indian child temporarily and place him or her in an emergency foster home in a situation where the child is temporarily off the reservation.[17] In that circumstance, the state must immediately notify tribal officials so that they may take appropriate action. The definition of "reservation" under ICWA is a broad one. The definition refers to a criminal statute, the Major Crimes Act, that broadly defines "Indian country" as: (a) any territory located within the exterior boundaries of an Indian reservation, including fee-owned land; (b) any dependent Indian community; and (c) any Indian allotment and the rights of way running through them.[18] There are hundreds of law review articles, treatises, and cases discussing what constitutes "Indian country" under the Major Crimes Act. This book cannot possibly detail every nuance and interpretation of this definition. In brief, there are certain reservations in this country that have been disestablished.[19] This means that these reservations have lost part of their land base, because of certain congressional enactments in which Congress purchased surplus lands for non-Indians to homestead out of the original land set aside for tribes by treaty or congressional enactment. Some may not even have exterior boundaries defining their reservation.[20]

Certain Indian communities located on land held in trust for the tribe or individual Indians are still located in those areas that were taken from the tribes by congressional enactment. These communities are called dependent Indian communities because they retain much similarity to the communities located within the exterior boundaries of the reservation. Other lands, called allotments, were parceled out to individual Indians by Congress out of the original tribally owned land base in an effort to break up reservations and assimilate Indians into the dominant white society. Many of these allotments are located outside of the exterior boundaries of reservations but are nonetheless considered part of Indian country for jurisdictional purposes.[21] The best way to determine whether a particular area is Indian country is to confer with the Department of Interior or individual tribes about the status of the land ownership in the area. If the land is still administered by the United States and is populated predominately by Indians, it most likely remains "Indian country."

Other reservations retain their land base as set out in the individual treaty or congressional enactment setting up that reservation. For those reservations, any land that lies within the exterior boundaries of the reservation is Indian country, even if the land is held by non-Indians in fee simple.[22]

In *Holyfield* the U.S. Supreme Court dealt with the definition of "domicile" contained in the exclusive jurisdiction provisions of ICWA. In that case the Mississippi Supreme Court held that Indian twins born outside of the reservation borders to an Indian mother domiciled on the reservation were not "domiciled" on the reservation for purposes of the exclusive jurisdiction provisions of ICWA.[23] The U.S.

Supreme Court reversed this determination. *Holyfield* held that a state court, in determining the domicile of an Indian child, should look to generally accepted federal and common-law concepts of domicile. The Court distinguished between residence and domicile in concluding that a person's domicile need not necessarily be his or her residence, especially with respect to minor children who usually assume the domicile of their natural parents.[24]

Importantly, the *Holyfield* Court noted that state courts should not interpret "domicile" in a manner that frustrates the congressional intent behind the enactment of ICWA. Therefore, because ICWA expresses an intent to allow tribal courts to exercise exclusive jurisdiction over Indian children domiciled on the reservation, it would be violative of that intent to allow natural parents to circumvent a tribe's rights to exercise its jurisdiction by placing children off the reservation shortly after birth.[25] The Supreme Court therefore adopted a broad definition of domicile, one that maximizes a tribal court's opportunity to exercise its authority in ICWA cases.

Holyfield teaches that a tribal court's jurisdiction is not preempted by a natural parent arranging to have a child off the reservation or by placing that child for adoption off reservation shortly after birth. Although some may criticize this principle as violative of the natural parents' rights to determine the destiny of their child, Congress clearly weighed the tribe's interests in preserving tribal culture and values against the rights of natural parents in finding that the rights of the tribe are paramount in a situation where the natural parents desire to terminate their rights.[26] This balancing of tribal interests versus parental rights is evident throughout ICWA and is discussed more thoroughly in the area of transfer of jurisdiction issues, *infra* at 34–44, and placement issues, *infra* at 88.

Holyfield did resolve a simmering dispute among state courts on the issue of domicile in cases where the natural parent made a concerted effort to avoid tribal court jurisdiction. However, certain state courts have apparently continued to interpret ICWA in a result-oriented manner, even after *Holyfield*.[27] Thus one should familiarize oneself with the particular domicile rules in her or his state of practice before drawing any conclusions on jurisdictional questions. A good rule of thumb, however, is that any child custody proceeding, including an adoption, should be commenced in the tribal court if the mother of the child resided on the reservation immediately preceding the birth.[28]

Tribal Court Wardship

A second basis for exclusive tribal court jurisdiction is when the Indian child is a ward of the tribal court.[29] "Ward" is not defined under ICWA and there is very little guidance in the legislative history or BIA guidelines as to its import. In *Holyfield* the Supreme Court, without defining the term, stated that it means that tribal courts exercise exclusive jurisdiction over "wards. . . regardless of domicile."[30] The most commonly accepted understanding of wardship is that when a tribal court has exercised legitimate jurisdiction over an Indian child in a child custody proceeding and continues to exercise that jurisdiction, a state court's exercise of jurisdiction is precluded, except, of course, on an emergency basis.[31]

One court has held that a child is not a ward of a tribal court for ICWA purposes simply because a tribal court exercised jurisdiction over a custody dispute between parents.[32] The cases that create friction are those in which the Indian child is located off the reservation but the tribal court nonetheless exercises some authority over the child in a child custody proceeding. The language in *Holyfield* stresses that a child need not be domiciled on a reservation for a tribal court to continue to exercise its exclusive jurisdiction, contrary to a finding from at least one court.[33] Is a finding that a child is a ward of a tribal court, however, entitled to the same deference as a finding that the child is a member or eligible for membership in the tribe? Clearly, the latter finding is entitled to full faith and credit by the state court under Section 1911(d). Full faith and credit is not synonymous with blind allegiance, however, and, as with the federal and constitutional full faith and credit provisions, it appears that a state can make proper inquiry into whether the tribal court's exercise of jurisdiction is consistent with federal law and its own internal governing documents before deferring its otherwise proper jurisdiction to the tribal court.[34]

The wardship provision covers the situation in which a tribal court is exercising its proper jurisdiction over an Indian child when that child is placed off the reservation or moves off with his or her parents or other relatives. In that situation, the tribal court clearly has the exclusive authority to continue its jurisdiction over that child.[35]

Transfer Jurisdiction

If an Indian child is the subject of a foster care placement or termination of parental rights proceeding in state court, the state court shall transfer the proceeding to the tribal court, absent objection by either parent, upon a petition by either the parents, Indian custodian, or tribe.[36] Transfer shall not take place if the state court finds good cause not to transfer or the tribal court declines to accept jurisdiction.

This provision has perhaps resulted in the most litigation in the ICWA arena, primarily because Congress permitted denials of transfer because of "good cause" and many state and tribal officials vehemently disagree on what that term means. Although a very fractious issue, it is apparent, at least from the Supreme Court's discussion of transfer in *Holyfield*, that Congress believed that transfer should be the rule and not the exception.[37] If one recalls the discussion of the legislative impetus behind the enactment of ICWA, one of Congress's concerns was that state courts and social services personnel, because of the cultural gap between predominately non-Indian judges and social workers and Indian families, were perhaps incapable of passing judgment on the fitness of Indian child-rearing practices. The transfer provision was inserted into ICWA to further the best interest of Indian children by permitting a tribal judge, who optimally would have more knowledge of traditional native child-rearing practices, to assess a family's capability to provide for a child.

It is important to note that under ICWA "transfer" refers to a transfer of jurisdiction and not necessarily to a physical transfer of a child back to a reservation. This confusion often permeates discussion of transfer and leads to state courts and officials misunderstanding the plight of an Indian child after a transfer is granted, which in turn may color a judge's decision in determining a transfer issue.[38] Many tribes, after a transfer of jurisdiction, may choose to leave a child at his or her placement immediately preceding a transfer request and may even request that state officials monitor the placement. Some states and tribes have entered into cooperative agreements addressing this issue as well as others that are subject to resolution by agreement under the provisions of ICWA.

Proceedings Covered by the Transfer Provisions

The transfer provisions of ICWA only apply to two types of child custody proceedings—foster care placements and termination of parental rights proceedings.[39] ICWA does not explain why transfer is not permissible in preadoptive and adoptive placements, nor is there much discussion of this apparent discrepancy in the case law. Conceivably, Congress could have felt that allowing transfer after the termination of parental rights had occurred was too late and would interfere with a state's attempts to find an adoptive home for an Indian child. Notwithstanding the lack of statutory authority to transfer, many states do transfer preadoptive and adoptive placement proceedings to tribal courts, primarily because tribes may be in a better position to find an adoptive placement in compliance with the placement preference provisions discussed *infra* at 91–92.

Standing to Request Transfer and to Object

Under ICWA four separate parties may request a transfer of jurisdiction to tribal court. Either parent, the Indian child's tribe, or an "Indian custodian" may request a transfer. All four of these parties are defined by ICWA in important ways. Only a natural parent can absolutely veto a transfer of jurisdiction by interjecting an objection.[40]

Definition of "Parent"

"Parent" is defined under ICWA as any biological parent of an Indian child or any Indian person who has lawfully adopted an Indian child.[41] The term excludes fathers whose paternity has not been acknowledged or established.

A few things are apparent from this definition. ICWA does not give an Indian parent more rights than a non-Indian parent, except for non-Indian adoptive parents. A natural parent of an Indian child, either Indian or non-Indian, can prevent a transfer of a child custody proceeding to tribal court by objecting to a transfer. Only an Indian adoptive parent has standing, however, to object to a transfer.

The right of a parent to veto absolutely a transfer of jurisdiction to tribal court is one area where Congress recognized that the rights of natural parents are paramount to the rights of a tribe. Regardless of how fit a natural parent is, or the severity of charges of abuse or neglect, that parent retains the right to overrule a transfer request. Some have commented that the right to veto a transfer request even survives the termination of parental rights because the definition of parent under ICWA refers to biological, not legal, parent, though such a right may cease to exist under prevailing state law.[42]

ICWA excludes the unwed father of an illegitimate child from its definition of parent unless the father has either acknowledged the child or has had his paternity judicially established. Therefore, if a putative father has not been adjudicated the father of an Indian child or has not acknowledged the child, either in writing or orally, he has no rights to veto a transfer of jurisdiction to a tribal court.[43]

This should not be confused with the right of a putative father to notice of proceedings that may lead to the termination of his inchoate rights. As the Supreme Court recognized in *Stanley v. Illinois,*[44] a putative father may still be entitled to notice of any proceedings implicating his rights. At least one court in New Jersey has apparently concluded that ICWA's definition of parent does not require notice to a putative father who only orally acknowledged a child before the child's placement with an adoptive home, although that same court did conclude that the child there was Indian for purposes of application of ICWA.[45]

Definition of "Indian Custodian"

Another party to a child custody proceeding who may request a transfer to tribal court, but who has no standing to veto a transfer request, is an Indian custodian. "Indian custodian" is defined under ICWA as any Indian person who has legal custody of an Indian child under tribal or state law or who has been granted custody by the natural parent.[46]

The inclusion of an Indian custodian as a person vested with certain rights under ICWA is an acknowledgment by Congress of the role the extended Indian family plays in the rearing of Indian children. In many instances, for example, the right to request a transfer and to notice of proceedings, ICWA treats an Indian custodian the same as a natural parent. The only proceeding in which the Indian custodian is not granted the privileges and procedural protections of ICWA is when the child is removed from the Indian custodian and returned to the natural parent. In that situation, the Indian custodian can neither request a transfer of the proceeding to tribal court nor demand compliance with the standard of proof necessary to effect a foster care placement.[47] However, if the Indian custodian of the child had custody immediately before the foster care placement, ICWA is not implicated when the child is returned to the Indian custodian. Non-Indian custodians of Indian children do not qualify as Indian custodians under ICWA even if the person is a blood relation to one of the natural parents. That person, however, does qualify for a relative placement, discussed *infra* at 86.

An Indian custodian in most circumstances is a relative of the Indian child, but a blood relationship is not a prerequisite to finding a person an Indian custodian. The first type of Indian custodian is one who has been granted "legal" custody under either state or tribal law, including the customs and traditions of the particular tribe. At least two courts have held that an Indian relative foster care placement is not an Indian custodian under ICWA because the state, in that circumstance, retains the legal custody of the child.[48] Legal custody is not synonymous with the existence of a court order granting custody, however, because the legislative history makes it clear that Congress appreciated that a person could have custody under the traditions and practices of a tribe without having followed the formalities of obtaining a custody order from the tribal court. If a person claims legal custody of a child under the traditions of a particular tribe, consultation with that tribe may be necessary to verify those traditions.

The second type of Indian custodian is one who has received the custody of the child voluntarily from a natural parent, a not uncommon occurrence among Indian people. In that situation, ICWA does not seem to require the formalization of the placement arrangement. However, the courts that have addressed this issue have concluded that Indian relatives with physical custody of children but nothing to prove that a natural parent acquiesced in the placement were not Indian custodians.[49] A consent to custody or some type of temporary guardianship executed by a natural parent would perhaps eliminate any confusion over the status of an Indian custodian.

Definition of "Indian Child's Tribe"

Lastly, an Indian child's tribe can request a transfer to tribal court. The tribe can also prevent a transfer to the tribal court by declining to exercise jurisdiction over the case on a transfer basis.[50]

In many cases, determining which tribe is the "Indian child's tribe" is not difficult because the child and his or her family only claim affiliation with one tribe. However, in a case where the child is a member of more than one tribe, which is rare, or eligible for membership in more than one tribe, the BIA guidelines set out some factors for a court to consider in determining which tribe is the Indian child's tribe.[51] Only one tribe can be declared the Indian child's tribe, even if substantial contacts between the child and more than one tribe exist.[52] Every tribe that the child claims some affiliation with must be notified of the proceedings, however, to allow each of the tribes some input in the state court decision-making process.[53]

If a child is a member of only one tribe, that tribe is the Indian child's tribe and only that tribe can request a transfer of jurisdiction.[54] If the child is eligible for membership in or an actual member of more than one tribe, the guidelines require the state court, after notice has been provided to all tribes with a potential interest as required under Section 1912(a), to consider a variety of factors—all of which concern the affinity of the child and the child's parents to a particular tribe—before deciding which tribe qualifies as the Indian child's tribe.[55] After the court makes a decision, it is required to reduce that decision to writing and notify all parties, including the tribes that are the unsuccessful suitors.[56]

Obviously, the state court needs to make the Indian child's tribe determination before addressing transfer issues. The only circumstance justifying a state court reconsidering its determination of an Indian child's tribe is when the child becomes a member of a different tribe during the pendency of the action, at which time the state court is to consider the tribe where the Indian child is a member as the child's tribe from that point on.[57] Any proceedings that took place before that occurrence will not be vitiated.

Only those tribes that are federally recognized are eligible to be declared an "Indian child's tribe" under ICWA. For a discussion of the meaning of federally recognized, see the "Definition of Indian Child" section, *supra* at 17–20.

Grounds for Denying Transfer Request

In the absence of good cause to the contrary or a declination by the tribal court, a state court is to transfer a child custody proceeding to the tribal court upon an appropriate request by a natural parent, an Indian custodian, or the Indian child's tribe. The request need not be a conventional petition but can be made orally. In Appendix G, Form 4, is a copy of a form motion as well as a form order from the tribal court accepting jurisdiction. Protocol would perhaps call for a motion to the tribal court to accept jurisdiction before moving the state court to transfer, but an affirmative acceptance of jurisdiction by the tribal court is not a prerequisite to the state court transferring jurisdiction.

The legislative history of ICWA, in discussing good cause for a state court to deny a transfer request, declares that a state court should apply a "modified doctrine of *forum non conveniens,* in appropriate cases, to ensure that the rights of the child as an Indian, the Indian parents or custodian, and the rights of the Tribe are fully protected."[58]

The burden of proving good cause to deny a transfer of jurisdiction to tribal court is upon the party opposing transfer to establish, by clear and convincing evidence, that good cause exists not to transfer a case.[59] There are numerous reported state court decisions discussing transfer issues. Most of the courts that have denied transfer have relied on the good cause grounds enumerated in the BIA guidelines. Several courts have adopted a "contrary to the best interest of the child" standard in denying transfer requests, whereas many others have fervently criticized the use of this criterion.[60]

"Best Interest of the Child" Standard

The only reference in ICWA to use of the "best interest of the child" standard, commonly used in non-Indian child custody proceedings, is the section allowing an Indian parent to petition a state court for the return of her or his child if an adoption of that child is set aside.[61] The phrase is conspicuously absent from the section of the law discussing transfer of jurisdiction issues. Nonetheless, numerous courts have used the congressional declaration of policy at Section 1902, which does refer to the best interest of Indian children, to hold that it is legitimate for a state court to consider whether a transfer to tribal court would be in the best interest of an Indian child.[62] This seems to be inconsistent with legislative intent, which clearly expresses that it would be in the best interest of an Indian child for a tribal judge to decide the child's fate, except in the rare situation.

Thus far Arizona, Nebraska, Montana, South Carolina, Indiana, California, and South Dakota have employed the "best interest of the child" standard to deny a transfer of jurisdiction request.[63] A close examination of these cases reveals that many of them involve Indian children who have been in foster homes and bonded with the foster parents. Resultantly, the state's or guardian ad litem's argument against transfer revolves around the issue of separation from the foster parents and the psychological impact such a separation would have on the child.[64]

A similar argument was made by the adoptive parents of the Indian twins in *Holyfield* in opposition to the tribe's *exclusive* jurisdiction there and in similar cases.[65] The argument was soundly rebuffed by the Supreme Court, which held that the only issue before it was who should make the decision about the placement of an Indian child, not what that decision should be.

This distinction also exists in the transfer of jurisdiction arena. The concrete issue in a transfer proceeding is whether the tribal court is in a position to hear all the evidence and make a decision without causing a hardship on the parties and witnesses, not whether the tribal court will make the right decision.[66] Congress found that tribal courts were better equipped than state courts to make decisions regarding the future of Indian children.

It is often difficult, however, to appreciate this distinction, especially when a tribe seems eager to remove children from homes where the children have resided for a prolonged period of time. Many courts have noted the distinction and criticized those courts that have adopted the "best interest of the child" standard to deny transfer requests. Among those criticized have been courts in Illinois and Minnesota as well as a recent Colorado appeals court decision.[67]

No Tribal Court

The BIA guidelines give several definitions of good cause to deny a transfer request. An obvious one is when the tribe lacks a tribal court to adjudicate the matter.[68] This may be common in those states that were vested with jurisdiction over Indian country and have been exercising that jurisdiction to the exclusion of tribal jurisdiction (see *supra* at 30–31). The definition of "tribal court" under ICWA is an expansive one, however, and would include informal, traditional dispute resolution bodies such as a council of elders or tribal leaders. A conventional judicial entity is not mandated in order to receive a transfer of jurisdiction. The definition of tribal court includes any administrative body vested with authority over child custody proceedings.[69]

Proceeding at Advanced Stage When Transfer Request Is Made

If the state court proceedings are at an advanced stage when the request is made *and* it appears that the requesting party did not act promptly to request a transfer after receiving notice of the proceedings, the state court may find good cause to deny a transfer request.[70] In this way a party is prevented from engaging in forum shopping when it appears that the case is not proceeding in his or her favor in state court. Giving the state court the prerogative to deny a transfer request for untimeliness also prevents potential disruption of the state court proceedings, which may prolong the child's stay in foster homes.[71]

There are two elements to this good cause denial: untimeliness of the request and advanced stage of the proceedings. If any party to a case who is entitled to notice of the proceedings does not receive adequate and timely notice, this ground should not be used to defeat that party's transfer request,[72] although at least one court has disagreed with that proposition.[73] If a party makes an untimely request for transfer but the proceedings are still in the early stages (e.g., preadjudication), this would not appear to be a ground to deny a transfer as it would not serve either of the objectives cited by the drafters of the BIA regulations.

Many tribes feel that their court systems are ill-equipped to deal with expensive and time-consuming adjudication trials and, resultantly, they routinely delay their transfer requests until the child is adjudicated a dependent or neglected child by the state court. In most cases this tactic does not hinder a transfer request, although it could if the child is in a foster home and the foster parents attach to that child and begin inquiring about a potential adoption, as many state courts routinely transfer already adjudicated cases to tribal courts for disposition. Every case is unique, however, and the conscious decision to delay a transfer request could foreordain a denial of the request.[74]

Child over Twelve Objects to Transfer

The BIA guidelines state that a good cause ground to deny a transfer request is when the Indian child is over the age of twelve and objects to the transfer.[75] This ground was included in the guidelines despite Congress's express rejection of its inclusion in the statutory language of the act itself.[76]

It is interesting to observe how Congress treated the rights of the Indian child in ICWA. The child has no standing to request a transfer of jurisdiction to the tribal court nor does the child have an absolute right to veto that transfer.[77] Nor is there any voice given to the child in the selection of his or her placement, either on a temporary or permanent basis, as compared to the law of most states, which grant to most children over a certain age the right to assert some input into placement decisions. The BIA, in promulgating the guidelines, obviously felt that children over a certain age should be able to assert some control over their own destiny in a transfer of jurisdiction dispute.

An objection by a child over twelve, or, more likely, the guardian ad litem appointed for the child, does not portend failure of the transfer request, but it should be considered. The presence in the guidelines of this ground for denying a transfer request could be construed as a limitation on the right of a guardian ad litem to object to a transfer of jurisdiction if the child in question is under the age of twelve. However, the guidelines seem to permit any party to the case—including the guardian ad litem—to purport that good cause exists not to transfer to tribal court.[78] The guardian ad litem would, therefore, appear to have standing to object to a transfer even if the parents, state, and tribe are in agreement that transfer would be appropriate.[79]

Child Has Little Contact with Tribe and Members

In certain cases the natural parents of an Indian child may be unavailable or have had their parental rights terminated and therefore are not in a position to decide whether transfer to tribal court would be appropriate. In that case *and* when the child has had little or no contact with the tribe and its members, the guidelines permit a state court to deny a transfer request for good cause if the child is over five years old.[80] Younger children would better be able to adapt to the different cultural milieu present on an Indian reservation.

Inconvenient Forum

The most commonly cited ground for denying a transfer request is when the evidence necessary to decide the case could not be adequately presented in the tribal court without undue hardship to the parties or witnesses.[81] This appears to be the original impetus behind granting state courts the authority to deny transfer requests as it is referred to in the legislative history. There does not appear to be any clearly delineated benchmark in the case law for deciding when transfer would cause undue hardship, as some courts have held that transferring a case hundreds of miles away from the location of the state court would not cause hardship,[82] whereas another court has ruled that transferring a case to a tribal court some thirty miles away from the state court would.[83]

Tribal courts, in an attempt to foreclose the use of this ground for denying transfer, may wish to convene hearings at a more convenient location to the parties and witnesses. The guidelines contemplate this as a possibility, so state courts should not automatically deny a transfer request from a tribe or other party when it appears that travel to the tribal court would be burdensome without examining the possibility of the tribal court adjusting venue or even conducting telephonic proceedings.[84] None of the cases discussing this ground for denying transfer discuss this possibility, quite likely because none of the parties to the case brought it to the attention of the trial courts. When a state court does refuse to transfer a case or opts to transfer a case, the standard for reviewing that decision is under an abuse of discretion standard.[85]

Finally, a ground that clearly cannot be used by the state court to deny a transfer request is a showing that the relevant socioeconomic conditions on the reservation are not conducive to the child leading a healthy lifestyle or that the tribal court system is incapable of handling the case.[86] This prohibition was placed in the guidelines to forbid parties from parading out before a state court judge a variety of statistics regarding life expectancy, unemployment, poverty, alcoholism, and other maladies on certain reservations in an effort to convince the judge that no child should suffer the fate of a reservation Indian child. These problems do plague certain reservations in this country, but Congress clearly concluded that Indian families remain the focal point for the conservation of traditional values and cultures that are inimical to many of the problems facing reservation Indians and, indeed, may be the solution to those problems.[87]

Reassumption of Jurisdiction

For those tribes in states that assumed jurisdiction over Indian country under federal law, discussed *supra* at 30–31, a procedure is laid out in ICWA for the reassumption of jurisdiction over child custody proceedings governed by ICWA.[88] This procedure should not be confused with the recognition procedure whereby a tribe is petitioning the federal government to be recognized, or re-recognized in the case of terminated tribes, for the purpose of entitlement to certain federal benefits. A certain tribe may be federally recognized but not have a fully functioning court system because the state courts have been exercising authority over tribal members even on the reservation.

A certain amount of confusion exists over the need of tribes in those certain states to petition for reassumption of jurisdiction because specific cases have held that those tribes never lost concurrent jurisdiction over civil and criminal cases arising on reservations.[89] Other cases have held that state courts never gained the authority to adjudicate a case involving primarily regulatory authority, as opposed to purely private litigation.[90]

Nonetheless, Congress obviously believed that for tribes in certain states to guarantee the exercise of their exclusive jurisdictional rights, as well as their rights to request transfers to their court systems, they would have to use the procedure set out in Section 1918. That procedure requires the tribe to demonstrate that its plan to reassume jurisdiction would be feasible in light of the racial makeup of the area it would be reassuming jurisdiction over as well as the tribe's capability to administer cases that it would have jurisdiction over. If a total reassumption is denied, the federal government is nonetheless permitted to allow a partial reassumption so the tribe can exercise exclusive jurisdiction over certain communities or transfer jurisdiction.[91] Some tribes have reassumed jurisdiction and have court systems that essentially hear only ICWA cases. In those cases when a tribe has reassumed jurisdiction under ICWA, the state in which the tribe is located must be notified by the secretary of interior of that department's approval of the petition.

Notes

1. 490 U.S. 30, 109 S.Ct. 1597, 104 L.Ed 2d 29 (1989).
2. *Id.* at 36.
3. 25 U.S.C. § 1911(a).
4. 25 U.S.C. § 1911(b).
5. *Holyfield* at 36.
6. 25 U.S.C. § 1919.
7. In *Holyfield* the Supreme Court noted that the language in § 1911(a) excepting its coverage from cases where jurisdiction is otherwise vested in federal or state courts applies to tribes in Pub. L. 280 states where jurisdiction was vested in the state courts. *Id.* at 42 n.16.
8. *See, e.g.,* In Matter of J.M., 718 P.2d 150 (Alaska 1986); Matter of Guardianship of D.L.L., 291 N.W.2d 278 (S.D. 1980).
9. It should be noted that ICWA does not govern child custody proceedings in tribal courts. Those proceedings are governed by the individual tribe's code and constitution as well as the provisions of the Indian Civil Rights Act, 25 U.S.C. § 1301 *et seq.* Therefore, it is possible that under a tribe's code it cannot exercise jurisdiction over a member child from another tribe. *See, e.g.,* Twin City Construction v. Turtle Mountain Band of Chippewa Indians, 857 F.2d 1177 (8th Cir. 1988), *vacated,* 911 F.2d 137 (8th Cir. 1990).
10. *See* Duro v. Reina, 110 S.Ct. 2053 (1990). Duro was later legislatively repealed by Congress, restoring tribal jurisdiction over tribal members from other reservations. *See* Pub. L. 101-511, § 8077.
11. Under Pub. L. 280 certain states, called mandatory states, were vested with jurisdiction irrespective of their wishes. Those states include Alaska, California, Minnesota, with the exception of the Red Lake Reservation, Nebraska, Wisconsin, and Oregon, with the exception of the Warm Springs Reservation. 18 U.S.C. § 1162. All other states, called option states, were permitted to exercise jurisdiction by the performance of certain acts. *See* Washington v. Confederated Bands of the Yakima Indian Nation, 439 U.S. 463 (1979). Pub L. 280 has been amended to require tribal approval before the assumption of further jurisdiction by state courts. 25 U.S.C. § 1322.

12. *See* Native Village of Venetie I.R.A. Council v. Alaska, 944 F.2d 548 (9th Cir. 1991).

13. Native Village of Nenana v. State, 722 P.2d 219 (Alaska 1986).

14. *See* note 12.

15. *See* Bryan v. Itasca County, 426 U.S. 373 (1976); *contra* County of Inyo v. Jeff, 227 Cal. App. 3d 487, 277 Cal. Rptr. 841 (Cal. App. 4 Dist. 1991); Becker County Welfare Dep't v. Bellcourt, 453 N.W.2d 543 (Minn. App. 1990) (states have jurisdiction in Pub. L. 280 states to pursue absent parents for welfare reimbursement and ICWA does not apply).

16. *See, e.g., In re* Adoption of S.S., 622 N.E.2d 832 (Ill. Ct. App. 2nd 1993) (domicile of Indian child shifted to that of natural parent after father, who had legal custody of child, died).

17. 25 U.S.C. § 1922; *see* State *ex rel.* Juvenile Dep't of Clackamas County v. Charles, 106 Or. App. 637, 810 P.2d 393 (Or. App. 1991) (court holds that notice need not be given to tribe when state takes emergency custody until such time as the state decides to file a dependency petition).

18. 18 U.S.C. § 1151.

19. *See* Hagen v. Utah, U.S. Sup. Ct. #92-6281, 62 U.S.L.W. 4118; Solem v. Bartlett, 465 U.S. 463 (1980).

20. This is the case with the Lake Traverse Band of Indians in South Dakota, who had their land base diminished by the Supreme Court's decision in DeCoteau v. District Court, 420 U.S. 425 (1975).

21. *See* Rosebud Sioux Tribe v. Kneip, 430 U.S. 584, 615 n. 48 (1977).

22. 18 U.S.C. § 1151.

23. Matter of B.B., 511 So.2d 918 (Miss. 1987).

24. *Holyfield* at 49.

25. *Holyfield* at 51 n.26; *but see* Matter of W.L., 260 Mont. 325, 859 P.2d 1019 (Mont. 1993) (state court does not lose the jurisdiction it originally lawfully exercised by the actions of the mother in moving back to the reservation).

26. *See, e.g.,* Matter of Baby Girl Doe, 865 P.2d 1090 (Mont. 1993), holding that the tribe's rights are paramount in a situation where the natural mother desires to terminate her parental rights.

27. For instance, the Mississippi Supreme Court in *Holyfield* actually held that the ICWA did not apply to the adoption proceeding there because the children had not lived in an Indian home. The *Holyfield* Court gave little credence to such an argument in concluding that ICWA applied to defeat the state court's jurisdiction. Despite this apparent renunciation of the existing Indian family exception to ICWA, several state courts have continued to adhere to it. *Supra,* at 15–17.

28. *See also* Matter of Adoption of Halloway, 732 P.2d 962 (Utah 1986).

29. 25 U.S.C. § 1911(a).

30. *Holyfield* at 36.

31. *See* Matter of Parental Placement of M.R.D.B., 787 P.2d 1219 (Mont. 1990) (tribal court has exclusive jurisdiction over adoption proceeding after mother withdrew consent to adoption and the tribal court had declared the child a ward of the tribal court).

32. *See* Application of Defender, 435 N.W.2d 717 (S.D. 1989).

33. Matter of Adoption of T.R.M., 525 N.E.2d 298 (Ind. 1988).

34. *See, e.g.,* Matter of Welfare of R.I., 402 N.W.2d 173 (Minn. App. 1987) (state court not obliged to give full faith and credit to tribal court finding of wardship if it appeared that child was not domiciled on reservation at the time the tribal court entered its order and the state court was properly exercising jurisdiction); DeMent v. Oglala Sioux Tribal Court, 874 F.2d 510 (8th Cir. 1989).

35. Matter of Guardianship of D.L.L., 291 N.W.2d 278 (S.D. 1980) (tribal court has exclusive jurisdiction over guardianship petition filed by parties in state court involving Indian child residing off the reservation).

36. 25 U.S.C. § 1911(b).

37. Indeed, the Supreme Court called the tribe's jurisdiction over children living outside the reservation boundaries its presumptive jurisdiction. *Holyfield* at 36.

38. An example of this appears to be the South Dakota Supreme Court's insinuation in People in Interest of J.J., 454 N.W.2d 317, 328 (S.D. 1990), that an Indian tribe was being used as a pawn by a grandmother seeking the return of her grandchildren.

39. 25 U.S.C. § 1911(b).

40. 25 U.S.C. § 1911(b). A parent is absolutely entitled to veto a transfer of jurisdiction by objecting. One court has held that a parent who does not concur in a transfer of jurisdiction nonetheless has acquiesced in transfer by taking the child back to the reservation and placing the child with relatives. Matter of Welfare of R.I., 402 N.W.2d 173 (Minn. App. 1987).

41. 25 U.S.C. § 1903(9).

42. Under Santosky v. Kramer, 455 U.S. 745 (1982), the Court seems to suggest that once the parental rights of a parent are severed that parent loses any rights with respect to the child. This holding would seem to preclude a parent whose rights have been terminated from objecting to a transfer to tribal court. There is an unreported decision from a district court in North Dakota allowing a parent to object even after termination. Matter of J.W.M., Cass County Dist. Ct., June 1989.

43. *But see* the discussion in Matter of Adoption of Child of Indian Heritage, 543 A.2d 925 (N.J. 1988), regarding how a child who is allegedly the natural child of an Indian father whose rights have not been determined is to be treated for purposes of the application of ICWA.

44. 405 U.S. 645 (1972).

45. *See* note 43.

46. 25 U.S.C. § 1903(6).

47. *See* 25 U.S.C. § 1916(b).

48. *See* People in Interest of J.J., 454 N.W.2d 317 (S.D. 1990); State *ex rel.* Juvenile Dep't v. England, 640 P.2d 608 (Or. 1982).

49. *See* note 48.

50. 25 U.S.C. § 1911(b).

51. BIA Guidelines, B.2, at 67586–87.

52. *Id.*

53. *Id.,* Commentary at 67587. If the state court fails to notify all tribes that may have an interest in the child such failure constitutes error, which requires a remand back to the trial court for service of notice, although it may not justify reversal if, on remand, it is determined that the newly notified tribe is not the "Indian child's tribe." *See* People *ex rel.* South Dakota Dep't of Social Services in Interest of

C.H., 510 N.W.2d 119 (S.D. 1993); *In re* M.C.P., 153 Vt. 275, 571 A.2d 627 (Vt. 1989); *In re* Junious M., 144 Cal. App. 3d 786, 193 Cal. Rptr. 40 (Cal. App. 1 Dist. 1983).

54. *Id.*

55. Those factors stress the contacts the child has had with each tribe's members, the activities of the tribe, and the language. BIA Guidelines at 67587.

56. *Id.*

57. *Id.*

58. House Report at 21.

59. *In re* M.E.M., 625 P.2d 1313 (Mont. 1981); People in Interest of J.J., 454 N.W.2d 317 (S.D. 1990). BIA Guidelines, C.3(d), at 67591.

60. An Illinois appellate court has strongly condemned the practice of denying transfers based on a "contrary to the best interest of the child" standard as being violative of the intent of Congress. *In re* Interest of Armell, 550 N.E.2d 1060 (Ill. App. 1990).

61. *See* 25 U.S.C. § 1916(a).

62. *See In re* Interest of C.W., 479 N.W.2d 105 (Neb. 1992); Matter of Maricopa County Juvenile Action, 828 P.2d 1245 (Ariz. App. 1991); Matter of T.S., 801 P.2d 77 (Mont. 1990); Dep't of Social Services v. Coleman, 399 S.E.2d 773 (S.C. 1990); People In Interest of J.J., 454 N.W.2d 317 (S.D. 1990); *In re* Robert T., 200 Cal. App. 2d (Cal. 1988); Matter of N.L., 754 P.2d 863 (Okla. 1988); Matter of Adoption of T.R.M., 525 N.E.2d 298 (Ind. 1988); People In Interest of M.E.M., 635 P.2d 1313 (Mont. 1991).

63. *See* note 62.

64. *See, e.g.,* Matter of Adoption of Halloway, 732 P.2d 962 (Utah 1986) (psychological bonding between foster parents and Indian child not a sufficient reason to ignore the mandates of ICWA).

65. A good example of why perhaps the bonding argument is an inappropriate consideration in a transfer of jurisdiction issue is the fate of the twins in *Holyfield.* After remand of that case from the Supreme Court the case was transferred to the Choctaw Tribal Court, where the tribal court held a hearing and determined that the twins should remain with the non-Indian family that was attempting to adopt through state court as that disposition was in the twins' best interests. This tends to demonstrate that those courts that deny transfers to tribal court because such would be contrary to the best interest of the child fail to appreciate that the tribal court will always attempt to act in the best interest of the child.

66. *Cf.* Matter of Welfare of B.W., 454 N.W.2d 437 (Minn. App. 1990).

67. In Interest of Armell, 550 N.E.2d 1060 (Ill. App. 1990); Matter of Welfare of B.W., 454 N.W.2d 437 (Minn. App. 1990); *see also* Colorado in Interest of J.L.P., 870 P.2d 1252 (Col. App. 1994); Matter of Appeal in Pima County, 635 P.2d 187 (Ariz. App. 1981); BIA Guidelines, C.3 Commentary, at 67591.

68. BIA Guidelines, C.3(a), at 67591.

69. 25 U.S.C. § 1903(12).

70. *See, e.g.,* Matter of Dependency and Neglect of A.L., 442 N.W.2d 233 (S.D. 1989); Matter of Wayne R.N., 757 P.2d 1333 (N.M. App. 1988); Matter of Maricopa County Juvenile Action, 828 P.2d 1245 (Ariz. App. 1991); *In re* Robert T., 246 Cal. Rptr. 168 (1988); Matter of Laurie R., 760 P.2d 1295 (N.M. App. 1988); *In re* Interest of C.W., 479 N.W.2d 105 (Neb. 1991).

71. BIA Guidelines, C.1 Commentary, at 67590.

72. *See* Matter of D.S., 577 N.E.2d 572 (Ind. 1991).

73. People in Interest of J.J., 454 N.W.2d 317 (S.D. 1990).

74. *See* Matter of Dependency and Neglect of A.L., 442 N.W.2d 233 (S.D. 1989) (Supreme court criticizes the lack of involvement from tribe in an ICWA case).

75. BIA Guidelines, C.3(ii), at 67591.

76. The BIA recommended to Congress that this ground be included in the statute as grounds for denial of transfer. Congress declined the invitation; thus, the BIA included the ground in its guidelines. House Report at 32.

77. *But see* note 62.

78. *See* Matter of T.S., 801 P.2d 77 (Mont. 1990) (GAL permitted to argue against the application of ICWA on the purported ground that ICWA is not in the best interest of an Indian child).

79. *See* BIA Guidelines, C.2(b), at 67590; People in Interest of M.C., 504 N.W.2d 598 (S.D. 1993).

80. BIA Guidelines, C.3(iv), at 67591; *see also* Matter of G.L.O.C., 668 P.2d 235 (Mont. 1983); People in Interest of J.J., 454 N.W.2d 317 (S.D. 1990).

81. In Interest of J.R.H., 358 N.W.2d 311 (Iowa 1984); *In re* Interest of Bird Head, 331 N.W.2d 787 (Neb. 1983); Chester County Dep't of Social Services v. Coleman, 399 S.E.2d 773 (S.C. 1990); *In re* Adoption of K.L.R.F., 515 A.2d 33 (Pa. Super. 1986); In Interest of C.W., 479 N.W.2d 105 (Neb. 1992); Matter of Wayne R.N., 757 P.2d 1333(N.M. App. 1988).

82. *See* In Interest of Armell, 550 N.E.2d 1060 (Ill. App. 1990).

83. *See In re* Interest of Bird Head, 331 N.W.2d 787 (Neb. 1983).

84. BIA Guidelines, C.3 Commentary, at 67591.

85. People in Interests of M.C., 504 N.W.2d 598 (S.D. 1993); *In re* Interest of C.W., 239 Neb. 817, 479 N.W.2d 105 (Neb. 1992).

86. BIA Guidelines, C.3(c), at 67591.

87. *See* Pommersheim, *The Reservation as Place: A South Dakota Essay,* 34 S.D. L. Rev. 246 (1989).

88. 25 U.S.C. § 1918.

89. *See* note 12.

90. *See* note 15.

91. 25 U.S.C. § 1918(b)(2).

CHAPTER • IV

Procedural Requirements of ICWA

Once a state court has determined that a proceeding is governed by the Indian Child Welfare Act, there are numerous procedural requirements that a court must follow in both voluntary and involuntary proceedings to comport with ICWA. These procedures were enacted to ensure maximum involvement from the Indian child's tribe as well as to secure the sanctity of the Indian family by ensuring that the removal of an Indian child from his or her family would be done pursuant to stringent requirements. Many courts have concluded that these procedural requirements are jurisdictional in nature; thus failure to adhere to them may invalidate state court proceedings.[1]

The reader will note that many of the requirements mandated by ICWA are similar to procedures states must follow pursuant to the Adoption Assistance and Child Welfare Act.[2] In certain areas, however, ICWA expands upon the procedural protections afforded parents to require more from a state to remove an Indian child from her or his family, on either a temporary or permanent basis. In a situation, however, where applicable federal or state law provides a higher standard of protection to Indian parents or custodians than ICWA, that higher standard must be applied.[3] To implement ICWA, many states have adopted state laws and guidelines that are more stringent than the federal law.[4] In those cases the state law or regulation would apply. Other states, in an apparent response to ICWA, have amended their dependency and neglect laws to conform to ICWA, resulting in a higher standard of process and proof required in non-Indian cases as well.[5]

All provisions of Title IV-E of the Social Security Act apply to ICWA cases, even though ICWA itself does not incorporate these provisions. These include the requirement of "reasonable efforts" to prevent the removal of children as well as various criteria related to a periodic review of each foster child's case.[6] ICWA should be read in *pari materia* with the provisions of Title IV-E and not as an alternative scheme for Indian children only. The procedural protections that are discussed below, however, relate specifically to ICWA.

Notice Requirements

One of the fundamental underpinnings of ICWA is the notion that a child's Indian tribe has a discrete interest, separate from a parent's or Indian custodian's, in any proceeding involving the child that must be protected throughout.[7] To protect that interest, ICWA grants the tribe an unqualified right to intervene in the proceedings[8] as well as the right to request a transfer to tribal court.[9] The exercise of that right is, of course, contingent upon the tribe receiving timely and adequate notice of the proceedings.[10]

Under ICWA, in any involuntary proceeding where the party initiating the proceeding knows or has reason to know that an Indian child is involved, that party must notify the parent, custodian, and tribe by registered mail, with return receipt requested, of the commencement of the proceedings.[11] The failure to serve proper notice is a jurisdictional defect that spoils the proceedings.[12]

When Notice Is Required

A finding by a state court that a child custody proceeding involves an Indian child is not a prerequisite to the giving of notice to an Indian custodian or tribe under ICWA.[13] Notice must be given even if doubts remain whether the child is an Indian child. This is so because often only with the input of an Indian tribe will a state court be able to determine whether a child is Indian under the act. Thus, an Indian tribe plays a critical role in the initial determination of the applicability of ICWA and notice to it is imperative any time the court or any of the parties have reason to suspect that an Indian child is involved.[14] Some of the factors sufficient to trigger notice to the tribe are set out in the BIA guidelines.[15] Failure to give notice cannot be justified by a later determination that the child in question is not Indian, as some have attempted to argue.[16]

If a child is a member of only one tribe, only that tribe is entitled to notice of the proceedings.[17] However, in many cases the only way to determine where a child is a member is to give notice to every tribe to which the child claims some affiliation. Failure to do so may interfere with the state court's ability to establish where the child is a member or eligible for membership. If tribal affiliation is undetectable, ICWA permits the state court to notify the Department of Interior, which is then charged with the responsibility to make a determination of the child's affiliation.[18] Addresses for the various BIA area offices where notice can be sent are set out in 25 CFR Section 23.12. Once a tribe proclaims that a particular child is a member of that tribe, one court has declared, that decision is binding on the state court even if proper and legal notice was not effected upon another tribe claiming an interest.[19] A partial list of tribal contacts in ICWA cases is included in Appendix E.

The ICWA provision relating to notice unfortunately uses a term that is not defined under the law. The section provides that "in any involuntary proceeding" notice must be provided to the tribe. One court has declared that an adoptive placement is not an involuntary proceeding under the act, although that court went on to find that notice was required under state law.[20] Certainly, an adoptive placement that is effected after an involuntary termination of parental rights is an involuntary proceeding and notice would be mandated to the termination as well as the adoption proceedings.

When a proceeding is commenced as a voluntary one, however, ICWA does not seem to mandate notice to the tribe. Most courts that have addressed this issue have held as much.[21] This creates some problems, especially when the child's domicile is not clear.

There are several inconsistencies in ICWA that have not yet been remedied by congressional amendments to the law. One of these deals with the interplay between ICWA's notice provisions and the provisions related to the right of a tribe to intervene in a foster care placement or termination of parental rights proceeding, voluntary or involuntary, discussed *infra* at 54–55. A tribe is entitled to intervene in any foster care placement or termination of parental rights proceeding[22] yet is apparently entitled to notice only in involuntary proceedings.[23] This, of course, begs the question of how a tribe is to know of a proceeding in which it can intervene if it receives no notice of the proceeding.

This appears to be another instance in which Congress balanced the rights of Indian parents against the interest of the tribe and concluded that Indian parents should be able to effect a voluntary foster care placement or voluntary termination of parental rights without their tribe becoming cognizant of their actions.[24] The failure of a state court to notify a tribe in a voluntary proceeding, however, may lead to more adoptions, like the one struck down by the Supreme Court in *Holyfield,* where an Indian parent attempts to defeat the tribal court's exclusive jurisdiction by placing the children off the reservation for adoption immediately after birth. If the tribe in *Holyfield* had never found out about the adoption, it appears unlikely that any party would have challenged the state court's jurisdiction there and an illegal adoption would have taken place. Such an adoption, because it is capable of being upset at any time[25], does not lend stability to the lives of the adopted children and should be avoided.

A good rule of thumb would thus be that if a parent seeks to use the state court to terminate her or his parental rights voluntarily or to consent to an adoption and there is a question of that parent's domicile on a reservation, the tribe or its court should be notified to avoid inevitable problems arising later. However, if the parent and child are clearly domiciled off the reservation and the parent seeks to place the child voluntarily, there may be no requirement of notice unless, of course, some requirement is present under state law. The state court and agency are, nonetheless, still required to comply with the placement provisions discussed *supra* at 84–92. The tribe would also be entitled to notice, under Section 1915(e), of the placement of the child even if the parent requests anonymity.[26]

Type of Notice Required

ICWA requires service of notice by registered mail, return receipt requested, to the parents, Indian custodian, and tribe, or if the tribe cannot be identified, to the Department of Interior.[27] The department can usually be served by serving the area office of the BIA. A list of these offices is included in Appendix D. The BIA guidelines allow personal service in lieu of registered mail.[28] One should also look to state law for proper service of process because many states mandate personal service upon the natural parents when a dependency and neglect action is commenced. A child custody proceeding cannot advance until at least ten days after notice has been effected.[29]

The notice shall include the following:

1. The name of the child;
2. The child's tribal affiliation, if known;
3. A copy of the petition or other document which initiates the action;
4. The name of the petitioner and his attorney;
5. A statement informing the parents, Indian custodian, and Tribe of their respective rights to intervene;
6. A statement that if the parents or Indian custodian are unable to afford counsel one will be appointed for them;
7. A statement that the parents, Indian custodian, or Tribe can have up to twenty days to prepare for the proceedings;
8. The location, mailing address, and telephone number of the Court;
9. A statement informing the parents, Indian custodian, or Tribe of the right to request a transfer to Tribal Court;
10. The potential legal consequences on the rights of the Parties if the child is adjudicated dependent;
11. A statement that child custody proceedings should be kept confidential.[30]

A typical notice is included in Appendix G, Form 1. Failure to follow this format for notice is not a jurisdictional defect, but the failure to give notice is.[31] If a new child is born to the parents during the pendency of a child custody proceeding, that child can be added to the proceeding without the necessity of serving a new and discrete notice.[32]

If the state court discovers during the pendency of an action that an Indian child is involved, notice shall be required, but the proceedings up to that point will not be rendered null and void.[33]

Right to Intervene

ICWA grants to the parents, Indian custodian, and tribe the unqualified right to intervene at any stage of a foster care placement or termination of parental rights proceeding, even when the case is on appeal.[34] The right to intervene is not limited to involuntary cases, as is the entitlement to notice. Once again, as with the right to request a transfer of jurisdiction, the right to intervene does not extend to preadoptive and adoptive placements even though the tribe may have important information regarding the availability of appropriate relative or Indian adoptive homes. Some courts, however, have ruled that the right of an Indian custodian, tribe, or even family member to intervene may derive from the general principles regarding rights of intervention and not necessarily from ICWA itself.[35] That type of intervention seems to be permissive in nature, whereas ICWA clearly grants to certain parties the right to mandatory intervention. Intervention in preadoptive and adoptive placement proceedings would therefore be governed by the permissive intervention rules of the particular state court.

Only the Indian child's tribe is entitled to intervene as a matter of right. However, the BIA guidelines contemplate a state court allowing another tribe that has some connection with the child to intervene in the proceeding and suggests that such may be beneficial when attempting to find a relative or Indian placement for the child.[36] Several courts have permitted more than one tribe to participate in ICWA proceedings.[37]

Unlike a request to transfer, there is no timeliness requirement for intervention in a proceeding. Also, there is no requirement that the intervention be sought by a licensed attorney representing the tribe. Many tribes do not have the resources to hire private counsel in every state in which an ICWA case may arise. Resultantly, many times they send social services representatives or even tribal judges to advocate the tribe's interests. Although not discussed in the statute or in the BIA guidelines, there appears to be no reason a tribe cannot appear *in propria persona,* which is essentially what it does when it sends a representative instead of being represented by counsel.[38] The request to intervene may also be rudimentary, but because of the absolute nature of that right under ICWA even oral requests should be routinely granted.

Once a tribe intervenes, it becomes a party to the case and is entitled to receive service of all motions and pleadings from that point forward. It is also entitled, along with the parents or Indian custodian, to examine all relevant documents filed with the court on which a decision in the case may be based.[39]

Right to Counsel

ICWA mandates that the state court appoint counsel for an indigent parent or Indian custodian in a "removal, placement, or termination proceeding."[40] If there is no state law mandating appointment of counsel, the state court can apply to the Department of Interior for reimbursement of court-appointed lawyer's fees in an ICWA case.[41] ICWA also allows a state court to appoint a lawyer for the Indian child but does not make that appointment mandatory.[42]

The right to counsel attaches in both proceedings initiated by the state and those initiated by private parties, such as in stepparent adoption proceedings and intrafamily disputes.[43] The right to counsel also seems to extend to preadoptive and adoptive placement proceedings and not simply to foster care placement and termination proceedings. As the result of *Santosky v. Kramer*[44] many states already provide for the appointment of counsel in foster care and termination proceedings, but few mandate the appointment of counsel in purely private disputes, such as adoption proceedings where the state is not involved or in a guardianship matter where a private individual is seeking guardianship over an Indian child. ICWA guarantees counsel in those types of proceedings, although it is unclear whether parents and custodians are being adequately apprised of that right. It is equally unclear how many states have attempted to seek reimbursement from the Department of Interior for fees paid to court-appointed lawyers in ICWA cases.[45]

25 CFR Section 23.13 sets out the procedure for a state court to follow in obtaining reimbursement from the Department of Interior for court-appointed lawyer's fees in ICWA cases, and Section 23.12 lists the addresses of the BIA area offices to which the requests can be sent. It should be noted that one of the criteria for denying reimbursement, listed in Section 23.13, is that no money is available for payment of the expenses. Historically, very little money has been appropriated by Congress for funding tribal ICWA programs or for implementation of ICWA by the Department of Interior.[46] The Department of Interior's solicitor's office has opined that even if no funding for state court lawyer reimbursement exists at the area office level, the monies should be paid out of a reserve account held at the national level.[47]

The appointment of counsel for the Indian child is purely discretionary with the state court judge, although state law may mandate the appointment of counsel. The BIA reimbursement regulations seem to imply that a state may apply to the BIA for reimbursement of lawyer's fees paid to a guardian ad litem, provided that state law does not mandate an appointment.[48] This appears to be somewhat inconsistent with the use of discretionary, rather than precatory, language in the ICWA section discussing the appointment of counsel.

Standards of Proof

A party, be it a state social services entity or a private party, attempting to effect a foster care placement of an Indian child or a termination of the parental rights or the custodial rights of an Indian custodian must satisfy the standards of proof established by ICWA. These standards of proof are unique to child custody proceedings involving Indian children, although in some instances they share similarities to the requirements set out in Title IV-E of the Social Security Act.[49] Once again, the reader should remember that the requirements in ICWA are not mutually exclusive of requirements set out by state or federal law and applicable to child custody proceedings but instead are inclusive of those other requirements.[50]

Foster Care Placements

A party seeking to accomplish a foster care placement of an Indian child must establish (1) that active efforts have been made to provide remedial and rehabilitative services designed to prevent the breakup of the Indian family but which have been unsuccessful[51] and (2) clear and convincing evidence, supported by the testimony of qualified expert witnesses, that the continued custody of the child by the parent or Indian custodian is likely to result in serious emotional or physical damage to the child.[52]

Indian custodians are treated the same as parents in involuntary child custody proceedings under ICWA, with the exception that they lack the right to veto a transfer of jurisdiction to tribal court. Therefore, if a person is determined to be an Indian custodian, under ICWA a proceeding that involves the involuntary removal of the Indian child from the Indian custodian requires the same proof as the removal of the child from a natural parent, except when the removal is for the purpose of returning the child to a natural parent. This is proof again of Congress's cognizance of the important role extended family members play in the rearing of Indian children.

Remedial Services and Rehabilitative Programs

There is nothing unique about requiring a state foster care placement agency to provide services to families whose children have been removed because of neglect or abuse in the home.[53] Title IV-E of the Social Security Act requires efforts to reunite a family by the provision of services to the family. ICWA, however, requires that "active" services be provided "before" the removal of the Indian child in an attempt to avoid the necessity of removal. The legislative history of ICWA evinces a clear congressional bent for energetic efforts to be made by state agencies in Indian communities for the development of culturally relevant programs designed to address the problems that lead to the removal of Indian children. Some examples cited by the Senate include home counseling, homemaker care, residential treatment facilities, day care, and group homes.[54] Of course, there is a universal need for these types of services, not only in Indian communities but in all communities. Congress mandated a showing that such services were offered to an Indian family before a foster care placement, as opposed to a showing that such services were offered as part of a case service plan entered into by the parent after placement.

There is no need for the state to demonstrate compliance with Section 1912(d) before removal of the Indian child, only as part of the foster care or termination proceedings.[55] Otherwise, the state court would be required to convene a full-blown adversarial hearing before removal, which might be impossible if an emergency situation existed. The courts have also held that Section 1912(d) does not apply in voluntary placement or termination proceedings.[56] Section 1912(d) does not cite to a standard of proof, as do Subsections (e) and (f), which has led most courts to rule that the same standard applicable to the particular proceeding, that is, clear and convincing evidence for foster care placements and beyond a reasonable doubt for termination of parental rights proceedings,[57] applies to the showing that Subsection (d) has been complied with. There are, however, at least two courts dissenting from that point of view.[58]

The BIA guidelines describe in very general terms the types of remedial and rehabilitative services a state should attempt to provide to avoid the need for the breakup of an Indian family.[59] The guidelines stress that the state should attempt to use the resources of the tribe, tribal social services, and "individual Indian caregivers," defined in the commentary as medicine men or other traditional tribal leaders, such as elders, whose skills can be used to keep the family together.[60] Of course, if the custody proceeding arises in a venue distant from where such resources can be tapped, using them may be exacting. In many cities, however, urban Indian cultural centers exist that may have the human resources available to assist and advise state social services agencies in the implementation of ICWA. There are also numerous urban ICWA programs funded by the Department of Interior under Title II of ICWA that could be of assistance in finding culturally relevant services. The Department of Interior has a list of the programs funded.

There are a variety of opinions that discuss the requirement of remedial and rehabilitative services that must be made available to Indian families before displacement of the child or termination of parental rights.[61] Most do not seem to differentiate between the ICWA standard for the provision of remedial services and the mandate imposed on states by the Adoption Assistance Act.

Qualified Expert Testimony

Before a court can order the foster care placement of an Indian child, the court must be persuaded by clear and convincing evidence that continued custody by the parent or Indian custodian will result in serious emotional or physical damage to the child.[62] That finding must be supported by the testimony of "qualified expert witnesses." Although this term is not defined in the statute, the legislative history proclaims that the term is designed to require more from a witness than the "normal social worker qualifications."[63] Ideally, the term was meant to encompass those persons who are, because of their knowledge of Indian culture and traditions, capable of opining on the question of whether an Indian child is suffering some form of emotional or physical harm because of the commissions or omissions of the family.[64]

The BIA guidelines further flesh out the Department of Interior's understanding of the qualifications of an expert witness for ICWA cases.

a. Persons with the following characteristics are likely to meet the requirements for a qualified expert witness for purposes of Indian child custody proceedings;

i A member of the Indian child's Tribe who is recognized by the Tribal community as knowledgeable in tribal customs as they pertain to family organization and childrearing practices.

ii A lay expert witness having substantial experience in the delivery of child and family services to Indians, and extensive knowledge of prevailing social and cultural standards and childrearing practices within the Indian child's tribe.

iii A professional person having substantial education and experience in the area of his or her specialty.[65]

Some states have enacted laws that require even more of a showing of expertise in Indian child-rearing practices before a person is qualified as an expert witness.[66]

The purpose of the qualified expert testimony requirement is "to provide the Court with knowledge of the social and cultural aspects of Indian life to diminish the risk of any cultural bias."[67] This ICWA provision does not mean that an otherwise qualified expert who has very little academic or personal experience working with Indian families cannot testify in an ICWA proceeding, but only that a foster care placement or termination of parental rights must be founded on the testimony of qualified experts. The BIA guidelines aim at steering state courts toward permitting the testimony in ICWA proceedings of certain individuals with concrete knowledge of cultural and societal standards not necessarily gained from academic achievements, although they may not be expert witnesses under state law.[68] Once again, this provision was an attempt to eliminate what Congress perceived to be a cultural bias, borne of ignorance, in state courts toward Indian families.

A literal reading of ICWA would permit only those qualified expert witnesses who testify in favor of a foster care placement or termination of parental rights to introduce testimony at trial. Many Indian parents and tribes, however, have used the broad definition of qualified expert testimony to offer evidence to counter a contention that an Indian child should be removed from his or her home.[69] In those cases it appears that the state court is not entitled to give greater weight to a witness merely because of academic achievement but must give equal or more weight to lay witnesses with a particularized knowledge of Indian customs and traditions.[70]

A few courts have carved out an exception to the requirement for qualified expert testimony in holding that such testimony is only necessary in cases involving the potential for "cultural bias" and is not necessary otherwise.[71] One of those courts held that because the child involved lived in an Indian home that had little or no contact with a reservation there was no chance of cultural bias and therefore expert testimony was not necessary.[72] This appears to be the same type of reasoning that has led some courts to rule that ICWA does not apply to certain cases involving Indian children who have never resided in an Indian culture or home. It is perhaps a misperception, however, for a court to find that an Indian family that lacks ties to a reservation is not in touch with its cultural values and tradition since many urban Native Americans are more cognizant of their cultural and traditional antecedents than reservation Indians.

Most courts that have addressed the requirement of qualified expert testimony have concluded that social workers with some experience working with Indian children qualify as experts under ICWA, notwithstanding their lack of formal training or education in the field.[73] The practical effect of the requirement of qualified expert testimony has been to expand the potential pool of witnesses in ICWA cases to include those Indian persons who otherwise would not qualify as experts under state law rather than proscribing the role of social workers who routinely testify in child custody proceedings.[74] Two courts have held that the failure of a parent to object at trial to the state's failure to call qualified expert witnesses bars appeal of that issue.[75]

Serious Emotional or Physical Damage

To accomplish a foster care placement of an Indian child, the petitioning party must demonstrate by clear and convincing evidence that the continued custody by the parent or custodian would likely result in serious emotional or physical damage to the child.[76] In many states this standard is an immense modification of the state standards for the removal of children, many of which focus on the best interest of the child and the abilities of the parents to conform their behavior to what is expected of an adequate parent. The focus in ICWA cases, on the other hand, is on whether the actions of the parents or Indian custodian have or will likely result in serious emotional or physical harm to the child.

The BIA guidelines discuss in some detail Congress's motivation for heightening the standard for the removal of Indian children from their homes.[77] The guidelines state at Section D.3, Commentary, that

> A child may not be removed simply because there is someone else willing to raise the child who is likely to do a better job or that it would be "in the best interest of the child" for him or her to live with someone else. Neither can a placement or termination of parental rights be ordered simply based on a determination that the parents or Indian custodians are "unfit parents." It must be shown that it is dangerous for the child to remain with his or her present custodians. . . .
>
> The legislative history makes it pervasively clear that Congress attributes many unwarranted removals to cultural bias on the part of the courts and social workers making the decisions. In many cases children were removed merely because the family did not conform to the decision maker's stereotype of what a proper family should be—without any testing that a family that conforms to that stereotype could successfully raise children.[78]

Some courts have apparently adopted the clear and convincing standard from Section 1912(e) but have applied it to the state criteria for a determination of whether a child is abused or neglected. If the state criteria place more of an onus on the petitioning party than proving serious emotional or physical damage to the child, ICWA demands that the higher standard be the basis for a foster care placement.[79] However, if the state standard requires less than such proof, ICWA precludes its use under *Holyfield* because of the Supreme Court's admonition there against the use of state standards that conflict with the policy behind the enactment of ICWA.

Readers should examine their state laws defining abused or neglected children and determine whether proof of any of the state criteria for defining an abused or neglected child necessarily satisfies the ICWA standard. For example, most states define an abused or neglected child as one who has been abandoned by his or her parent. This is one of the criteria that was perhaps cited most often by non-Indian social workers in support of the removal of Indian children who had been placed with extended family members, such as grandparents, to be raised.[80] Clearly, the mere fact that a parent has placed a child with another person, be it a relative or not, and the other person has the primary responsibility to raise that child does not satisfy the ICWA criteria for a foster care placement. Otherwise, ICWA's granting of a protected status to the Indian custodian would be rendered superfluous.

Other states require foster care placement when a child has been sexually abused in the home of the parent or other relative. Proof of sexual abuse would probably satisfy the ICWA criteria, provided, of course, that qualified expert testimony supported the proposition that the sexual abuse has resulted in physical or emotional abuse to the child. It is in areas where non-Indian social workers and judges tend to be culturally naive that state courts should tread carefully. These areas include allegations of deprivation of medical care, when the child is perhaps being treated by a medicine man, or when the child is being taught at home in a traditional manner. A judge or social worker, unsophisticated in the traditions and cultures of Indian people, may unabashedly conclude that a child who is being deprived of Anglo-Saxon medicine or a conventional education is being subjected to the threat of physical or emotional harm. The requirement of qualified expert testimony in those types of cases becomes a *sine qua non* if a judge wishes to comply with ICWA.[81]

The ICWA standard for a foster care placement applies even in those cases where the parent has not had custody of the child.[82] Many ICWA cases have arisen in situations where children have been removed from non-Indian mothers of children whose fathers are Indian but have had little or no contact with the children. In that scenario, it seems maladroit to apply the ICWA standard that requires the court to address whether "continued custody" by the parent would result in serious emotional or physical harm to the child.[83] A court must do so, however, by determining whether placing the custody of the child with the absent parent would lead to serious emotional or physical harm to the child.[84] However, some courts have chosen to apply state law making it irrelevant whether the absent parent was an active participant in the abuse inflicted on a child in holding that the custodial parent's neglect or abuse alone is a sufficient predicate to a foster care placement.[85]

Finally, it is important to observe that any parent, Indian or non-Indian, of an Indian child can claim the protections of ICWA, including the higher standard of proof for placement of an Indian child in foster care. The exception to that rule, of course, is the existing Indian family exception to ICWA, discussed *supra* at 15–17, where certain courts have held that ICWA should not apply unless the Indian child is being removed from an Indian family or Indian cultural setting. In most of those cases it is a non-Indian parent that is arguing that ICWA does not apply in that context. Ironically, those very decisions may be depriving the non-Indian parent of the protections of ICWA should the state ever see fit to remove the Indian child from her or him.

Termination of Parental Rights

The most drastic remedy a court can order for the neglect and abuse of a child is the termination of the parents' rights. As the Supreme Court noted in *Santoksy v. Kramer,* "parents retain a vital interest in preventing the irretrievable destruction of their family life."[86] That interest requires, at a minimum, that the state require clear and convincing evidence to support a finding that the parental rights should be terminated.[87] The Supreme Court, however, rejected the parents' arguments in *Santosky* that the termination of parental rights was such a drastic remedy that a "beyond a reasonable doubt" standard should be mandated by the Fourteenth Amendment's due process clause.[88] In so doing, the Court implicitly criticized Congress's application of that standard to the termination of the parental rights of Indian children by concluding that the type of medical and psychiatric testimony commonly used in termination proceedings was not susceptible to proof beyond a reasonable doubt.[89]

Numerous state courts obviously disagree with the Supreme Court's observations regarding the obstacles to applying a beyond a reasonable doubt standard to termination of parental rights proceedings because the overwhelming majority of state courts that have addressed the issue have concluded that sufficient evidence existed to justify the termination of parental rights over Indian children. The factual predicates for the various cases in which the courts have concluded that sufficient evidence existed to terminate parental rights vary greatly. In some of the cases the courts applied state grounds to find that termination was justified,[90] while in others courts applied the serious emotional or physical harm standard to sustain a termination order.[91] Yet in other cases the courts have held that both the state and federal standards for termination have to be met.[92]

ICWA requires that to support a termination of parental rights a petitioning party must establish, by evidence beyond a reasonable doubt, that the continued custody of the parents or Indian custodian would result in serious emotional or physical harm to the child.[93] In addition, as with a foster care placement, the burden rests with the petitioning party to demonstrate that remedial services and rehabilitative programs have been provided to prevent the breakup of the Indian family. Some courts have held that this must be established beyond a reasonable doubt in a termination proceeding.[94] Another has held that a mere preponderance of the evidence is sufficient.[95] Lastly, the finding that the continued custody of the child by the parent or custodian would result in serious emotional or physical harm must be supported by the testimony of qualified expert testimony. Again, the reader should refer to state law to determine what other showings a petitioning party must demonstrate to support a termination of parental rights (e.g., least restrictive alternative, all rehabilitative services after placement have been exhausted, and best interest of the child) because these factors would also have to be demonstrated to support termination if required by state law.[96] These required findings would be in addition to the ultimate finding under ICWA that serious emotional or physical damage would befall the Indian child.

The BIA guidelines are virtually silent as to family circumstances that would constitute serious emotional or physical harm to a child. The guidelines do cite several conditions that would not justify such a finding.[97]

> Evidence that only shows the existence of community or family poverty, crowded or inadequate housing, alcohol abuse, or nonconforming

> social behavior does not constitute clear and convincing evidence that continued custody is likely to result in serious emotional or physical damage to the child.[98]

Clearly, if such findings would not warrant a foster care placement they would not call for termination of parental rights. Yet these are among the factors that several courts have pointed to in terminating the parental rights of Indian parents and Indian custodians under ICWA. Certain courts appear to be ill at ease with the provisions in ICWA and to be more comfortable applying state law to termination proceedings, ostensibly because state law gives the court certain parameters to evaluate whether termination is appropriate and because of an obvious judicial disdain for long-term foster placements, which appear to increase the instability in the lives of children.

Alcoholism is a commonly used ground for termination,[99] as are a nomadic lifestyle,[100] mental illness,[101] sexual abuse,[102] abandonment,[103] failure to comply with a case plan,[104] failure to visit,[105] need for stability of the child,[106] trauma associated with removing the child from long-term foster parents,[107] trauma associated with placing the child in an Indian home,[108] and leaving the child with a relative.[109] A review of these cases will not reveal any pattern for the type of evidence presented, although one could argue that the overriding consideration seems to be the need for stability in the child's lifestyle, a concept closely resembling the psychological parent theory espoused by the authors of *Beyond the Best Interest of the Child,* discussed *supra* at 5–6. Although the courts diverge on what evidence is needed to support a termination order, most are in agreement that the evidence must demonstrate the ground beyond a reasonable doubt, although some do not concede this point.[110] With respect to the required showings under state law to support a termination of parental rights most courts appear to apply the state burden of proof rather than the standard under ICWA.[111]

Voluntary Proceedings

ICWA was enacted not only to censure the unwarranted involuntarily removal of Indian children from their families but also to make the common practice of voluntary displacement more difficult. Congress pointed to instances of Indian parents voluntarily signing away custody of their children under threats by state and federal social services agencies to terminate their cash welfare payments.[112]

To prevent similar abuses, in ICWA Congress made it more difficult for a parent or custodian to execute a voluntary termination of parental rights by requiring some semblance of formality to the act and by permitting the Indian parent or custodian to regain custody of the child under certain circumstances. In this way the pernicious removal of Indian children from their families under the guise of a "voluntary" act would, one hopes, be curtailed.

ICWA applies to voluntary placements with both public and private agencies.[113] Although the discussion in the legislative history deals primarily with the biases of public welfare officials who sought to place Indian children, it is clear that the intent of ICWA to provide a home for Indian children that adequately reflects their cultural values and traditions would not be realized if private agencies were to arrange adoptions based on the ability of the adoptive parents to pay the fee to the agency.[114]

Voluntary Foster Care Placements

25 U.S.C. Section 1913 governs the procedures for a voluntary foster care placement. It is important to remember that not all voluntary placements are governed by the provisions of ICWA. As discussed *supra* at 20, the definition of foster care placement contained in ICWA explicitly excludes placements in which the parent can regain custody of the child upon demand.[115] This would include most placements done pursuant to a power of attorney appointment or guardianship appointment, such as educational placements or religious placements, which continue to be common among some Indian families. This exclusion was apparently included in the act to not burden state and tribal courts with the requirement of conducting some formal proceeding every time a parent is desirous of temporarily placing a child and to exempt such placements from the foster care placement preference procedures discussed *infra* at 84–87.

Certain placements that may not initially be governed by ICWA may be converted into such by the actions of the party with whom custody was vested. For example, if an Indian mother temporarily places her child with a social services agency because of some family emergency and after the emergency desists the agency refuses to return the child, the provisions of ICWA govern even though the original intent of the parties may have been to permit return upon demand. Custody would then have to be returned to the mother under the provisions of Section 1913(b), although the placement was not a foster care placement under the act when initially done.[116] On the other hand, if an involuntary proceeding is commenced and the parent or Indian custodian admits to the petition alleging that the child is abused or neglected, the parent or custodian would not be entitled to revoke his or her admission or consent and demand the return of custody of the child under Section 1913(b).[117] Such a proceeding would clearly be governed by the involuntary procedures set out in Section 1912.

If, however, as part of an involuntary proceeding the parent consents to the termination of parental rights as a disposition, at least one court has held that the parent retains the right to withdraw that consent, provided that it is done before an order terminating parental rights is entered, even if the consent has become irrevocable under state law.[118]

Necessity of Consent

Once again, for purposes of the execution of a voluntary consent to foster care placement the Indian custodian is treated in much the same way as the parent, with ICWA requiring the valid consent of either for a legal placement.[119] The legislative history is unclear on whether each would have to consent to a foster care placement in a case where the Indian custodian has the custody of the child, but the use of the disjunctive "or" in the language of Section 1913(a) indicates that consent need be given only by the party with the custody of the child for a lawful foster care placement.[120]

For a valid consent to be given the consent must be (1) given in writing; (2) recorded before a judge of a court of competent jurisdiction; (3) certified to by the presiding judge that the consequences of the consent were fully explained; (4) certified to by the court that the parent or custodian understood the explanation in English or had the explanation translated into a language understood by the person; and (5) executed after the child is ten days old.[121] The legislative history suggests that the consent be executed in open court unless the parent requests confidentiality.[122] A model consent form is contained in Appendix G, Form 5.

It is unclear what the ramifications of a failure to follow the voluntary consent procedure would be. This is because there appears to be an irreconcilable conflict between the definition of foster care placement, excluding a placement where the parent can regain custody upon demand,[123] and the various provisions of ICWA, including

Sections 1913(b) and 1920, requiring that an Indian child be returned to the parent or custodian upon revocation of consent or a showing that consent was obtained improperly. If the definition of foster care placement were construed literally, there would be no such thing as a voluntary foster care placement under ICWA because the parent can always regain custody of the child upon demand. At least one court has discussed this inherent conflict in holding that Section 1913(b) permits a parent to withdraw a consent to a foster care placement at any time before termination of parental rights, provided that the placement was consensual, regardless of compliance with Section 1913(a).[124]

A party who obtains the custody of an Indian child without following the mandates of Section 1913(a) should not be permitted to contend that ICWA does not apply to the proceeding, because the placement is not a foster care placement under the definition section, thereby defeating the provisions of ICWA demanding the return of the child to the parent or custodian. One court, however, has suggested that a voluntary placement that, under its own terms, permits the parent to withdraw consent and regain custody of the child is not governed by ICWA even if the parent later seeks to regain custody of the child and is rebuffed.[125] This seems to render Section 1913(a) superfluous and could potentially perpetuate the practice of agencies obtaining voluntary placements of Indian children without any modicum of due process. To avoid challenge, any agency seeking a placement of an Indian child should follow the procedures set out in Section 1913(a).

COURT OF COMPETENT JURISDICTION In *Holyfield* the Supreme Court held that a state court was not a court of competent jurisdiction to accept a voluntary termination of parental rights executed by a reservation-domiciled Indian. Therefore, for a state court to be a court of competent jurisdiction under the provisions of Section 1913(a) the state court should have jurisdiction under the provisions of Section 1911.

If the parent and child are domiciled off the reservation, the state court and possibly the tribal court would have the authority to accept a consent to foster care placement or termination of parental rights. Under the tribe's governing ordinances, including its constitution and code, it may continue to exercise jurisdiction over its members when they venture off the reservation.[126] An inquiry with the tribal court would be a possible manner of finding out this information.

TYPE OF CONSENT The consent form in Appendix G, Form 5, is a typical form used both for the consent to foster care placement and to termination of parental rights. It not only explains the consequences of the act of the parent or custodian but also clarifies the rights of the parent or custodian after execution of the consent form. It also gives the parent or custodian the option of recommending a foster care or adoptive placement. This recommendation, as discussed *infra* at 88–89, is entitled to a certain amount of deference by the court.[127]

It should be noted that in some tribal courts this type of consent form is not necessary because tribal law, and not ICWA, governs child custody proceedings on Indian reservations. Any time a voluntary consent is executed in the tribal court it is safe practice to assume that the child has become a ward of the tribal court and any future proceedings involving the child should be commenced in the tribal court.[128]

If the natural parent or custodian does not understand the English language, ICWA mandates that the state court provide translation into a language that the parent or custodian can understand. There are various persons, both on and off reservations, who still speak and write native languages. Certain federal agencies, including the Department of Interior and the Social Security Administration, may be helpful in locating translators of native languages.

Withdrawal of Consent

Section 1913(b) of ICWA permits an Indian parent or custodian to withdraw consent to a foster care placement and directs that upon said withdrawal the child shall be returned to the parent or custodian. There is no provision in Section 1913(b) allowing a court to refuse to return custody on the basis that it would not be in the best interest of the child to be returned. Section 1913(b) should be compared to Section 1916, discussed *infra* at 93–94, and Section 1920, both of which allow a state court to refuse to restore the custody of the child to the parent or custodian if certain conditions are met.

The rights secured an Indian parent or custodian under Section 1913(b) cannot, of course, be exercised if the state court has already entered an order terminating that parent or custodian's rights.[129] Before that time, however, Section 1913(b) permits a parent who has executed a consent to foster care placement to withdraw that consent and regain custody of the child.

Whereas Section 1913(b) governs the situation when a parent has lawfully placed a child in foster care pursuant to the provisions of

ICWA, Section 1920 controls when a party has obtained custody in violation of Section 1913(a) or has wrongfully kept custody after the termination of a voluntary placement. In that situation, ICWA directs the state court to decline to exercise jurisdiction over any petition filed by the party wrongfully obtaining custody and also directs the court to restore custody to the parent or guardian "unless returning the child. . . would subject the child to a substantial and immediate danger or threat of danger."[130] It is somewhat strange that ICWA mandates the unconditional return of custody to a parent who executed a lawful consent to a foster care placement but permits a party who unlawfully obtained custody to argue against a return of custody. This scheme seems to reward those entities that illegally gain custody of Indian children by providing them with a mechanism to avoid a return of custody, whereas parties that lawfully obtained custody must return the child upon demand without inquiry into whether return would be dangerous to the child.

Of course, if a public or private agency that was voluntarily vested with a foster care placement is desirous of avoiding a return of the child, an involuntary proceeding may be started by that agency, provided that the agency can satisfy the standards of proof discussed *supra* at 57–63. That option does not seem available to an agency that illegally obtained or retained custody because Section 1920 commands that the state court decline to exercise jurisdiction over any proceeding commenced by such a party.

There is no formal requirement for a revocation of consent to foster care placement, and it appears that even an oral notice of revocation would suffice under the statutory language of ICWA. The BIA guidelines, however, require the parent or Indian custodian to file a formal revocation of consent with the court where the consent form was filed.[131] Obviously, the existence of an absolute right to withdraw consent to foster care placement of an Indian child in the parent or custodian renders placements made pursuant to voluntary proceedings very insecure because they may be upset at any time. Congress chose this route, however, because of its grave concern over the abuses associated with "voluntary" placements that were in no sense voluntary. If state rules prohibit the return of custody of the child after the revocation of a voluntary placement, they are superseded by ICWA and are inapposite.[132]

Some state courts have avoided the application of Section 1913(b) by holding that the act of placing a child in a foster home or adoptive home constitutes abandonment under state law and that abandonment is *ipso facto* sufficient to sustain a finding of abuse and neglect. One court has held that a parent who has "abandoned" a child by placing the child after birth has lost the right even to object to an adoption.[133] That particular court seemed hostile to many provisions of ICWA, and its holding has been condemned by other courts that have held that the right to withdraw a consent to foster care placement is intact up to the point of the termination of parental rights.[134]

Voluntary Termination of Parental Rights Proceedings

The same provisions that govern voluntary foster care placements control the voluntary termination of an Indian parent's or custodian's parental rights. In no instance may the parental rights of an Indian parent or custodian be voluntarily terminated except in compliance with the requirements of Section 1913(a) and with any state law that requires a higher standard of proof. For example, in certain states the parental rights of a parent may not be voluntarily terminated except upon a showing that it would be in the best interest of the child. Such a standard prohibits a parent from terminating parental rights merely to avoid the obligations of parenthood. Arguably, this is a higher state standard, which the voluntary termination of an Indian parent's rights would be judged against.[135]

ICWA has elevated the rights of an Indian custodian to those of a parent, even though the Supreme Court has never recognized that the rights of extended family are synonymous with those of the parents.[136] Therefore, ICWA requires the voluntary termination of the parental rights of both parents and the Indian custodian, if one exists, before an adoptive placement can occur, even though Congress used the disjunctive "or" instead of "and" when discussing termination of parental rights. There is no indication that Congress intended to supplant the rights of natural parents to custody of their children by elevating the rights of Indian custodians to that of a parent. Even though the language of Section 1913 appears to require only the termination of the parental rights of the party with custody of the child, a more reasonable interpretation is that the parents' rights remain intact until a valid termination order is entered.[137] Before a valid adoption of an Indian child can take place, the parental rights as well as the rights of an Indian custodian, if applicable, must be terminated.

As with voluntary foster care placements, there are provisions under ICWA permitting parents to withdraw consent to a voluntary termination of parental rights or to an adoptive placement for any reason "prior to a final decree of termination or adoption, as the case may be, and the child shall be returned to the parent."[138] Unlike foster care placements, however, Section 1913(c) does not literally allow an Indian custodian to withdraw a consent and regain custody of a child. This appears to be another example of poor draftsmanship by the authors of ICWA because Section 1913(a), dealing with voluntary termination of parental rights, clearly pertains to both the parents and Indian custodian consenting to voluntary terminations of their respective rights. Yet Subsections (c) and (d) omit any reference to Indian custodians in conferring upon parents the right to withdraw consent. This appears to be inconsistent with Congress's intent, as expressed in the legislative history, to treat Indian custodians comparably.[139]

The right to withdraw a consent to termination of parental rights or to an adoptive placement expires upon the entry of either an order terminating parental rights or an order of adoption.[140] One court has refused to permit an Indian parent to withdraw a consent even though the child in question had not been adopted as of the date of the request to withdraw.[141] If the parent does withdraw consent before an order of termination or adoption, that parent has an unqualified right to regain custody of the child,[142] although at least one court has stated that the right to regain custody would be contingent upon the parent having custody before executing the consent.[143] Some courts have ignored the mandate of Section 1913(c) and concluded that a parent cannot revoke her or his consent to adoption and regain custody of the child because the act of consenting constitutes abandonment forfeiting the parent's rights to custody.[144] Other courts have questioned the logic behind such a ruling in finding to the contrary.[145]

Even when the consent to termination of parental rights is executed as part of an involuntary proceeding, the right to withdraw consent exists, although the right to reclaim custody of the child may not.

After the entry of a final decree of adoption an Indian parent cannot withdraw consent unless he or she can demonstrate that the consent was obtained through "fraud or duress."[146] Upon a showing of such the court can set aside an adoption unless it has been effective for more than two years, or longer if state law permits it to be invalidated even after two years. In light of the requirement that a parent appear before a judge of competent jurisdiction to execute a consent to termination or adoptive placement, it appears difficult to make the required showing of fraud or duress to set aside an adoption. This may explain the dearth of case law on this particular provision. One court has held that this provision cannot be used by a putative father to challenge an adoption that took place without his knowledge as such does not involve fraud or duress in the execution of a consent.[147]

Several courts have addressed the effect on involuntary proceedings of the discovery after the act of consent takes place that the child involved is Indian. Most have held that the consent to termination or adoption should be judged by the standards of state law and not ICWA, even when the mother suggested that she was of Indian heritage.[148] A more recent decision from Oregon, however, has held that a natural mother of an Indian child can revoke her consent to adoption, which had become irrevocable under state law, if the child becomes an Indian child before the finalization of an adoption.[149]

Full Faith and Credit

Tribal courts have a somewhat anomalous existence in the federalist scheme concocted by the framers of the Constitution, notwithstanding the framers' liberal use of the Iroquois Confederacy as a model for the United States' system of government. Tribal courts are not state courts for purposes of the constitutional full faith and credit clause.[150] Some state and federal courts have concluded that they are territorial courts for purposes of the federal full faith and credit statute,[151] but this point of view is clearly not a universal one.[152]

To eliminate any confusion over the deference a state court must grant a tribal court's judgment in a child custody proceeding, ICWA unequivocally provides at Section 1911(d) that the United States, every state and federal territory, and every Indian tribe must give full faith and credit to the "public acts, records, and judicial proceedings of any Indian tribe applicable to Indian child custody proceedings to the same extent that those entities give full faith and credit to the public acts, records, and judicial proceedings of any other entity."

Before a public act, record, or order from a judicial proceeding is entitled to full faith and credit under Section 1911(d) there must be a finding that the document is related to a child custody proceeding. In addition, several courts have held that Section 1911 does not mandate blind allegiance to a tribal court order but instead permits a state court to look beyond an order to determine whether the issuing court had jurisdiction over the subject matter and parties when it entered the order, much the same way state courts are permitted to examine the jurisdictional basis for a state court's entry of an order.[153]

If an Indian tribe makes a determination that a child is a member of that tribe, that finding is entitled to absolute allegiance even if the child in question has no Indian blood.[154] Granting full faith and credit to a document or court order should be distinguished from the question of whether a proper evidentiary foundation has been laid to admit a document or court order into evidence, the answer to which may lie in the state's rules of evidence and not in ICWA.[155] Most records of Indian tribes are admissible under the public records or business records exception to the hearsay rule, and most tribal court orders should be authenticated in a way that conforms to the state's recognition of foreign judgments act. One court, however, has ruled inadmissible an affidavit from a tribal official asserting that a child is eligible for membership.[156]

A tribal court judgment should be honored if it pertains to a child custody proceeding, provided that the tribal court had jurisdiction to enter the order when it did. Some tribes have apparently attempted to preempt a state court's exercise of its legitimate jurisdiction by making an Indian child a ward of the tribal court and arguing that such an order precludes state court jurisdiction under Section 1911(a). This practice has been spurned by some state courts, which have looked beyond the order to conclude that the tribal court lacked jurisdiction to act and have therefore declined to honor the particular order.[157] Certain states may have statutes governing the recognition of tribal court judgments that honor the judgments under the doctrine of comity.[158] Such statutes would appear to be preempted in ICWA child custody proceedings.

Interestingly, Section 1911(d) requires tribal courts to grant full faith and credit to other tribal court orders but not to state court orders. Some advocates have attempted to use the axioms set out in ICWA to argue for transfers of jurisdiction among tribal courts as well as from state to tribal courts. ICWA does not seem to create a mechanism for such transfers, although, again, tribal law may allow such transfers. A tribal court need not defer to a state court's findings with respect to a child custody proceeding made before the case is transferred to a tribal court as ICWA does not require such. The tribal court should recognize the state court's proceedings before transfer because the failure to do so could negatively influence tribal court transfer requests in future proceedings.

This chapter has examined the various procedural requirements of ICWA. The next chapter will explore the second objective of Congress in enacting ICWA—the placement of Indian children in homes that reflect their unique cultural and traditional heritages.

Notes

1. *See* In Interest of H.D., 729 P.2d 1234 (Kan. App. 1986) (failure to give tribe notice of termination proceeding renders the proceeding null and void).

2. 94 Stat. 500, 42 U.S.C. §§ 620–28, §§ 670–79a.

3. 25 U.S.C. § 1921. *See* Matter of Welfare of B.W., 454 N.W.2d 437 (Minn. App. 1990) (Minnesota courts must apply more heightened standard for "qualified expert witness" than what is contained in BIA guidelines because of enactment of state guidelines); *In re* Interest of D.S.P., 166 Wis.2d 464, 480 N.W.2d 234 (Wis. 1992) (court holds that state must not only prove serious emotional or physical harm may befall child if termination is not ordered, but also abandonment under state law, although abandonment may be demonstrated by clear and convincing evidence only).

4. For example, Minnesota seems to have adopted a standard for qualified expert testimony that is more onerous than most states. *See* Matter of Custody of S.E.G., 507 N.W.2d 872 (Minn. App. 1993); *rev'd on other grounds,* 521 N.W.2d 357 (Minn. 1994) *cert denied sub nom Campbell v. Leech Lake Band of Chippewa Indians,* 63 U.S.L.W. 3560 (1995).

5. *See* SDCL § 26-8A-21, requiring the provision of remedial and rehabilitative services to a family before removal of a child from the home.

6. 42 U.S.C. § 671(a)(3)(15).

7. *See Holyfield* at 49.

8. 25 U.S.C. § 1911(c).

9. 25 U.S.C. § 1911(b).

10. *See* note 1.

11. 25 U.S.C. § 1912(a).

12. *In re K.A.B.E.,* 325 N.W.2d 840 (S.D. 1982); *In re M.C.P.,* 571 A.2d 627 (Vt. 1989); *In re Kahlen* W., 233 Cal. App. 3d 1414, 285 Cal. Rptr. 507 (Cal. App. 5 Dist. 1991). If, however, it is determined that the tribe which claims entitlement to notice is not the "Indian child's tribe" a failure to give notice does not deprive the tribal court of jurisdiction. *See In re M.C.P., supra; People ex rel. Dept of Social Services in Interest of C.H.,* 510 N.W.2d 119 (S.D. 1993). A California court has also held that a tribe which, although it received notice by first class mail only, appeared to assert its interests waived the lack of proper notice by appearing. *In re Krystle D.,* 37 Cal.Rptr.2d 132, 30 Cal. App. 4th 1778 (Cal. App. 6th Dist. 1994).

13. *In re* Dependency of Colnar, 757 P.2d 534 (Wash. App. 1988); Matter of Baby Boy Doe, 849 P.2d 925 (Idaho 1993); People in Interest of C.H, S.H., S.H., C.H., M.H., S.H., and C.H., No. 18230 Supreme Court of South Dakota, Dec. 22, 1993.

14. BIA Guidelines, B.5, at 67588. The burden of bringing forward sufficient evidence to believe that an Indian child is involved, however, seems to rest with the proponent of applying ICWA. *See In re* Custody of C.C.R.S., 872 P.2d 1337 (Colo.

App. 1993) (naked allegation by mother that she is one-half Indian not sufficient to invoke notice); Matter of Adoption of Baby Boy W., 831 P.2d 643 (Okla. 1992) (mere fact that father was listed in school records as Indian did not warrant finding that ICWA applied); *In re* Interest of A.M., 235 Neb. 506, 455 N.W.2d 572 (Neb. 1990) (burden rests with parents to prove they are Indian).

15. BIA Guidelines, B.1(c), at 67586.

16. *See* note 13. *See also In re* Kahlen W., 285 Cal. Rptr. 507 (Cal. App. 5 Dist. 1991).

17. BIA Guidelines, B.2(e).

18. BIA Guidelines, B.1 Commentary, at 67586.

19. People in Interest of J.J., 454 N.W.2d 317 (S.D. 1990).

20. In Matter of J.R.S., 690 P.2d 10 (Alaska 1984), the Alaska Supreme Court held that ICWA does not mandate the granting of an intervention request by a tribe in an adoptive placement proceeding, but that the tribe could intervene under state law.

21. *See* Catholic Social Services, Inc. v. C.A.A., 783 P.2d 1159 (Alaska 1989), *cert. denied,* 495 U.S. 948 (1990); People In Interest of J.J., 454 N.W.2d 317 (S.D. 1990); Duncan v. Wiley, 657 P.2d 1212 (Okla. App. 1982).

22. 25 U.S.C. § 1911(c). A tribe is also entitled to intervene in a custody dispute between a grandparent and parent. *In re* Custody of A.K.H., 502 N.W.2d 790 (Minn. App. 1993).

23. 25 U.S.C. § 1912(a). In a recent California decision the California Court of Appeals held that an Indian tribe was entitled to intervene in a declaratory judgment action filed by an Indian mother who had been raised in a non-Indian adoptive home who was seeking a judgment that ICWA did not apply to her attempts to place her child in a non-Indian home for adoption. The court, however, suggested that the tribe there was not entitled to notice and that the mother could determine the child's fate notwithstanding the wishes of the tribe. *In re* Baby Girl A., 230 Cal. App. 3d 1611, 282 Cal. Rptr. 105 (Cal. App. 4 Dist. 1991).

24. *But see* Matter of Baby Girl Doe, 865 P.2d 1090 (Mont. 1993).

25. *See* 25 U.S.C. § 1914.

26. *See* note 24. *But see* BIA Guidelines, F.3, at 67594. The guidelines state that a parent's request for anonymity takes precedence over the tribe's right to notice of the placement.

27. 25 U.S.C. § 1912(a); BIA Guidelines, B.5(b), at 67588. The amended regulations, enacted February 14, 1994, now require that notice be sent to the Department of Interior in all cases, not just when tribal identity cannot be assertained. *See* 25 C.F.R. § 23.11(a).

28. BIA Guidelines, B.5(e).

29. 25 U.S.C. § 1912 (a).

30. BIA Guidelines, B.5(b), at 67588

31. *See* Matter of N.A.H., 418 N.W.2d 310 (S.D. 1988); Matter of B.J.E., 422 N.W.2d 597 (S.D. 1988); Matter of S.Z., 325 N.W.2d 53 (S.D. 1982).

32. *See* B.J.E., note 31.

33. Matter of Adoption of Crews, 825 P.2d 305 (Wash. 1992); People in Interest of A.E., 749 P.2d 450 (Col. App. 1987). Of course, if the state court or the parties involved should have known that the child involved was an Indian but still failed to provide notice, the proceedings would be invalid.

34. *See* 25 U.S.C. § 1911(c); People in Interest of J.J., 454 N.W.2d 317,331 (S.D. 1990); In Matter of Adoption Petition of Begay, 765 P.2d 1178 (N.M. App. 1988).

35. *See* Matter of J.R.S., 690 P.2d 10 (Alaska 1984) (permitting an Indian tribe and extended family members to intervene in an adoptive placement proceeding); A.B.M. v. M.H. and A.H., 651 P.2d 1170 (Alaska 1982); *In re* Custody of A.K.H., 502 N.W.2d 790 (Minn. App. 1993); *In re* Baby Girl A., 230 Cal. App. 3d 1611, 282 Cal. Rptr. 105 (Cal. App. 4 Dist. 1991).

36. BIA Guidelines, B.2 Commentary, at 67587.

37. People in Interest Of J.J., 454 N.W.2d 317 (S.D. 1990). Cases may also arise where the siblings in a particular case are members of different tribes so that several tribes may have a mandatory right of intervention.

38. If local rules of court prohibit appearances by a person other than an attorney for a tribe, those local rules would be superseded by the policy of ICWA allowing tribes the right to participate in ICWA cases. State *ex rel.* Juvenile Dep't of Lane County v. Shuey, 119 Or. App. 185, 850 P.2d 378 (Or. App. 1993) (ICWA preempts state rule that group of person may only appear in court through counsel).

39. 25 U.S.C. § 1912(c).

40. 25 U.S.C. § 1912(b). Failure to appoint counsel is the basis for a reversal of any action taken by a trial court. *See* Matter of J.W., 742 P.2d 1171 (Okla. App. 1987).

41. *Id.*

42. *Id.* The statute provides that appointment of counsel for the child depends on the best interest of the child. One court has held that ICWA does not mandate the appointment of a guardian ad litem for an incompetent Indian parent, however. *In re* Interest of D.S.P., 458 N.W.2d 823, *aff'd,* 480 N.W.2d 234 (Wis. 1993).

43. 25 C.F.R. § 23.13 speaks of the appointment of counsel in any child custody proceeding, not just those initiated by the state.

44. 455 U.S. 745 (1982). The Supreme Court has, however, refused to find that the right to counsel is a due process right in a termination proceeding. Lassiter v. Dep't of Social Services, 452 U.S. 18 (1981).

45. The procedure for seeking reimbursement from the Department of Interior is set out in 25 C.F.R. § 23.13.

46. An August 1994 report of the Office of Inspector General for the Department of Health and Human Services reveals that in 1993 only 59 of the eligible 542 Indian tribes received any federal funding under Title IV-B of the Social Security Act. *See* Department of Health and Human Services, Office of Inspector General Report, *Opportunities for ACF to Improve Child Welfare Services and Protections for Native American Children,* August 1994, at 7.

47. *In re* Petition of R.D.C. on behalf of C.E.D., 8 Indian Law Rptr. 5071 (1981).

48. *See* 25 C.F.R. § 23.13(b)(3).

49. For instance, both ICWA and Title IV-E require the state to make reasonable efforts to avoid a removal of a child from his or her home. 42 U.S.C. § 671(a)(13).

50. *In re* Interest of D.S.P., 166 Wis. 2d 464, 480 N.W.2d 234 (Wis. 1992) (trial court must not only apply ICWA standard in termination proceeding but must also apply relevant state law, which is not superseded by ICWA); People in Interest of E.M., 466 N.W.2d 168 (S.D. 1991) (state court must not only demonstrate that ICWA standards are met but also that termination is the least restrictive alternative).

51. 25 U.S.C. § 1912(d).

52. 25 U.S.C. § 1912(e).

53. *See* note 46.

54. 1977 Senate Hearings at 117–18.

55. *See* State *ex rel.* Juv. Dep't v. Charles, 688 P.2d 1354 (Or. App. 1984).

56. *See* B.R.T. v. Executive Director, 391 N.W.2d 594 (N.D. 1986).

57. *See* Matter of Kreft, 384 N.W.2d 843 (Mich. App. 1986) (beyond a reasonable doubt standard applicable to showing of whether remedial services provided in a termination proceeding); Matter of Welfare of M.S.S., 465 N.W.2d 412 (Minn. App. 1991) (state failed to demonstrate beyond reasonable doubt that remedial services had been provided when the state failed to place Indian child with a relative who could care for the child). *Accord,* People in Interest of E.M., 466 N.W.2d 168 (S.D. 1991); Matter of Morgan, 364 N.W.2d 754 (Mich. App. 1985); People In Interest of P.B., 371 N.W.2d 366 (S.D. 1985); *In re* L.N.W., 457 N.W.2d 17 (Iowa App. 1990). Other courts have not addressed the burden of proof issue. *See* C.E.H. v. L.M.W., 837 S.W.2d 947 (Mo. App. W.D. 1992); Long v. State Dep't of Health and Human Services, 527 So.2d 133 (Ala. Civ. App. 1988).

58. The Alaska Supreme Court has held that a mere preponderance of the evidence standard applies to the showing of whether remedial services were provided before termination in K.N. v. Alaska, 856 P.2d 468 (Alaska 1993), whereas the Maine Supreme Court has held that the showing must be made by clear and convincing evidence. *In re* Annette P., 589 A.2d 924 (Me. 1991).

59. BIA Guidelines, D.2, at 67592.

60. BIA Guidelines, D.2 Commentary, at 67592.

61. *See* note 57.

62. 25 U.S.C. § 1912(e).

63. House Report at 22.

64. BIA Guidelines, D.4 Commentary, at 67593.

65. BIA Guidelines, D.4(b), at 67593.

66. *See* note 4.

67. Matter of Custody of S.E.G., 507 N.W.2d 872,844 (Minn. App. 1993).

68. BIA Guidelines, D.4(b)(ii), at 67593.

69. *See, e.g., In re* Interest of Birdhead, 331 N.W.2d 785 (Neb. 1983).

70. State *ex rel.* Juvenile Dep't v. Charles, 688 P.2d 1354 (Or. App. 1984).

71. State *ex rel.* Children's Services Div. v. Campbell, 122 Or. App. 371, 857 P.2d 888 (Or. App. 1993) (expert testimony not necessary when the nature of the neglect suffered by child is due to mental illness of the mother and not cultural bias); *see also* Long v. State Dep't of Human Services, 527 So.2d 133 (Ala. Civ. App. 1988).

72. State *ex rel.* Juvenile Department v. Tucker, 710 P.2d 793 (Or. App. 1985).

73. *See, e.g., In re* Krystle D., 37 Cal.Rptr2d 132, 30 Cal. App. 4th 1778 (Cal. App. 6th Dist. 1994) (qualified expert witness requirement met even though some experts testified against termination because others testified for termination; *In re* Interest of C.W., 479 N.W.2d 105 (Neb. 1991) (psychologist with little experience working with Indian children qualified as expert); In Interest of S.M., 508 N.W.2d 732 (Iowa App. 1993) (social worker who worked with Indian families and who had training in native cultures qualified); State *ex rel.* Juvenile Dept. v. Woodruff, 108 Or. App. 352, 816 P.2d 623 (Or. App. 1991) (Indian psychologist qualified); *In re* L.N.W., 457 N.W.2d 17 of cases were Indian children and Indian friends qualified); Cf. C.E.H. v. L.M.W., 837 S.W.2d 947 (Mo. App. 1993); Matter of Custody of S.E.G., 507 N.W.2d 872 (Minn. App. 1993); Matter of Custody of S.E.G., 507 N.W.2d 872 (Minn. App. 1993); *In re* Interest of D.S.P., 480 N.W.2d

234 (Wis. 1992); Matter of D.S., 577 N.E.2d 572 (Ind. 1991); *In re* T.J.J., 366 N.W.2d 651 (Minn. App. 1985).

74. *But see* Matter of Welfare of B.W., 454 N.W.2d 437 (Minn. App. 1990) (court-appointed psychologist not an expert under Minnesota's more restrictive guidelines); Matter of Welfare of M.S.S., 465 N.W.2d 412 (Minn. App. 1991) (merely because social worker works with Indian families does not qualify her as an expert).

75. In Interest of R.L.F., 437 N.W.2d 599 (Iowa App. 1989); *In re* Riva M., 235 Cal. App. 3d 403, 286 Cal. Rptr. 592 (Cal. App. 4 Dist. 1991).

76. 25 U.S.C. § 1912(e).

77. BIA Guidelines, D.3, at 67593.

78. BIA Guidelines, D.3 Commentary, at 67593.

79. *See* 25 U.S.C. § 1921.

80. House Report at 10.

81. BIA Guidelines, D.3 Commentary, at 67593.

82. *See* Matter of Appeal in Coconino County Juvenile Action J-10175, 736 P.2d 829 (Ariz. App. 1987); Matter of Adoption of Baade, 462 N.W. 2d 485 (S.D. 1990).

83. *See, e.g.,* Matter of Adoption of D.M.J., 741 P.2d 1386 (Okla. 1985).

84. Matter of Adoption of a Child of Indian Heritage, 543 A.2d 925 (N.J. 1988); *In re* Jacobs, 433 Mich. 24, 444 N.W.2d 789 (Mich. 1989) (over stinging dissent court holds that an Indian mother who suffered stroke would represent a danger to her child if returned).

85. *See* A.H. v. State, 779 P.2d 1229 (Alaska 1989) (abuse inflicted upon children by custodial parent can be used to find that children are in danger of serious emotional or physical harm if returned to noncustodial parent); Matter of Adoption of Baby Boy D., 742 P.2d 1059 (Okla. 1985) (father's rights terminated before birth of child on theory that child had been abandoned by father).

86. 455 U.S. at 753 (1982).

87. *Id.* at 769.

88. *Id.*

89. *Id.*

90. *See* C.E.H. v. L.M.W., 837 S.W.2d 947 (Mo. App. W.D. 1992) (finding that child would be psychologically harmed by removal from foster home grounds for termination); K.N. v. State, 856 P.2d 468 (Alaska 1993) (mental illness prevented father from providing appropriate parenting skills); D.W.H. v. Cabinet for Human Resources, 706 S.W.2d 840 (Ky. App. 1986) (nomadic lifestyle of parents and the child's need for stability justified termination); Matter of S.D., 402 N.W.2d 346 (S.D. 1987) (failure to cooperate in case service plan and to address alcohol problem grounds for termination); Matter of Blue Bird, 411 S.E.2d 820 (N.C. App. 1992) (mother's move to another state coupled with bonding between child and foster parents justified termination).

91. Matter of Morgan, 364 N.W.2d 754 (Mich. App. 1985); People in Interest of P.B., 371 N.W.2d 366 (S.D. 1985); *In re* Smith, 731 P.2d 1149 (Wash. App. 1989); Matter of Welfare of W.R., 379 N.W.2d 544 (Minn. App. 1985).

92. *In re* Interest of D.S.P., 166 Wis. 2d 464, 480 N.W.2d 234 (Wis. 1992); *In re* Dependency of Roberts, 732 P.2d 528 (Wash. App. 1987); Matter of Blue Bird, 411 S.E.2d 820 (N.C. App. 1992). In these cases the courts seem to use a hybrid burden of proof scheme, with state grounds having to be proven by clear and convincing evidence but evidence beyond a reasonable doubt being required for a showing of

serious emotional or physical harm. *See also* New York City Dep't of Social Services on Behalf of Oscar C., Jr. v Oscar C., 192 A.D.2d 280, 600 N.Y.S.2d 957 (N.Y.A.D. 2 Dep't 1993) (court holds that at adjudication preponderance of the evidence standard for court findings of fact did not conflict with ICWA).

93. 25 U.S.C. § 1912(f).

94. *See* People In Interest of A.R.P., 519 N.W.2d 56 (S.D. 1994); *In re* L.N.W., 457 N.W.2d 17 (Iowa App. 1990); Matter of Welfare of M.S.S., 465 N.W.2d 412 (Minn. App. 1991); Matter of Morgan, 364 N.W.2d 754 (Mich. App. 1985).

95. K.N. v. State, 856 P.2d 468 (Alaska 1993).

96. *See* note 92.

97. BIA Guidelines, D.3(c) and Commentary, at 67593.

98. BIA Guidelines, D.3(c).

99. In Matter of S.D., 402 N.W.2d 346 (S.D. 1987).

100. Matter of Blue Bird, 411 S.E.2d 820 (N.C. App. 1992).

101. K.N. v. State, 856 P.2d 468 (Alaska 1993).

102. People In Interest of J.J., 454 N.W.2d 317 (S.D. 1990).

103. Matter of Adoption of Baade, 462 N.W.2d 485 (S.D. 1990).

104. People in Interest of P.B., 371 N.W.2d 366 (S.D. 1989); People In Interest of A.R.P., 519 N.W.2d 56 (S.D. 1994); *In re* Annette P., 589 A.2d 924 (Me. 1991).

105. *See* note 95.

106. *In re* T.J.J., 366 N.W.2d 651 (Minn. App. 1985).

107. K.N. v. State, 856 P.2d 468 (Alaska 1993).

108. Matter of Adoption of D.M.J., 741 P.2d 1386 (Okla 1985).

109. *See* note 100.

110. *In re* Riva M., 286 Cal. Rptr. 592 (Cal. App. 4 Dist. 1991) (failure of father to raise issue below precludes review of court's standard of proof).

111. *See* note 92.

112. House Report at 10.

113. *See* Doe v. Hughes, 838 P.2d 804 (Alaska 1992) (court holds that it is malpractice for an attorney representing adoptive parents not to obtain consent under ICWA by natural mother even in case where child born by artificial insemination).

114. *See* Catholic Social Services v. C.A.A., 789 P.2d 1159 (Alaska 1989).

115. *See* 25 U.S.C. § 1903(1)(i).

116. *See, e.g., In re* Adoption of K.L.R.F., 515 A.2d 33 (Pa. Super. 1986). Of course, if the foster care placement is preceded by the filing of a petition alleging abuse and neglect by the custodian, the fact that the parent or custodian admits to the petition does not render that a "voluntary" placement. C.E.H. v. L.M.W., 837 S.W.2d 947 (Mo. App. W.D. 1992) (mother not entitled to regain custody by withdrawing consent made in an involuntary removal proceeding).

117. *See* C.E.H. v. L.M.W., 837 S.W.2d 947 (Mo. App. W.D. 1992); *but see* Matter of J.R.S., 690 P.2d 10 (Alaska 1984) (parent could revoke consent to foster care placement entered in an involuntary proceeding).

118. *See* Matter of J.R.S., 690 P.2d 10 (Alaska 1984); *see also* Quinn v. Walters, 845 P.2d 206 (Or. App. 1993), *rev'd,* 881 P.2d 795 (Or. 1994) (Oregon Supreme Court rejects lower court finding that child involved was Indian child). The fact that a parent withdraws a consent to termination does not, however, entitle the parent to the automatic return of the custody of the child. *See* Harvick v. Harvick, 828 P.2d 769

(Alaska 1992) (mother who withdraws consent to termination not entitled to return of custody from natural father who had been vested with custody).

119. 25 U.S.C. § 1913(a).

120. This is not, however, true for a termination of parental rights.

121. *Id.*

122. House Report at 23.

123. 25 U.S.C. § 1903(1)(i).

124. *See In re* Adoption of K.L.R.F., 515 A.2d 33 (Pa. Super. 1986). Obviously, a party who has gained custody of a child in violation of ICWA should not have more superior rights to the child than a party who has obtained the custody of the child in violation of ICWA.

125. D.E.D. v. State, 704 P.2d 774 (Alaska 1985).

126. *See* Matter of D.L.L. and C.L.L., 291 N.W. 2d 278 (S.D. 1980) (tribal court retains exclusive jurisdiction over minor Indian children who are wards of the tribal court even though they live off the reservation); Matter of M.R.D.B., 241 Mont. 455, 787 P.2d 1219 (Mont. 1990) (tribal court has exclusive jurisdiction over adoption proceeding after natural mother withdraws consent to adoption in state court and tribal court makes child ward of court).

127. *See, e.g.,* Matter of Adoption of F.H., 851 P.2d 1361 (Alaska 1993) (court states that a parent's preference for placement is good cause for deviating from placement preference provisions of ICWA).

128. *See* 25 U.S.C. § 1911(a).

129. *See* Matter of Kiogma, 472 N.W.2d 13 (Mich. App. 1991), *cert. denied,* 112 S.Ct. 952 (1992); B.R.T. v. Executive Director, 391 N.W.2d 594 (N.D. 1986); Matter of J.R.S., 690 P.2d 10 (Alaska 1984).

130. 25 U.S.C. § 1920.

131. BIA Guidelines, E.3, at 67594.

132. *But see* Matter of Adoption of Infant Boy Crews, 825 P.2d 305 (Wash. 1992) (if termination becomes final under state law prior to mother becoming member of tribe, she cannot revoke consent).

133. *See* Matter of Adoption of T.R.M., 525 N.E.2d 298 (Ind. 1988), *cert. denied,* 490 U.S. 1069 (1989).

134. Matter of Adoption of Child of Indian Heritage, 543 A.2d 925 (N.J. 1988); *see also* Matter of M.R.D.B., 241 Mont. 455, 787 P.2d 1219 (Mont. 1990).

135. *See* 25 U.S.C. § 1921.

136. *See* Moore v. City of East Cleveland, 431 U.S. 494 (1977).

137. Such would appear to violate the due process rights of parents recognized in Santosky v. Kramer, 455 U.S. 745 (1982).

138. 25 U.S.C. § 1913(c).

139. *See* A.B.M. v. A.H. and M.H., 651 P.2d 1170 (Alaska 1982).

140. *See* note 129.

141. *See* note 133.

142. *See* Quinn v. Walters, 845 P.2d 206 (Or. App. 1993), *rev'd on other grounds,* 881 P.2d 795 (Or. 1994) (appellate court's order setting aside adoption because natural mother withdrew consent prior to adoption reversed on ground that natural mother's use of an affidavit from tribe alleging that she was enrolled member was inadmissible hearsay and therefore mother failed to show that child was eligible for membership with tribe).

143. *In re* Custody of S.B.R., 719 P.2d 154 (Wash. App. 1986); *see also* Harvick v. Harvick, 828 P.2d 769 (Alaska 1992) (mother not entitled to return of custody from father merely because she revoked a consent to adoption).

144. *See* note 133.

145. *See* note 134.

146. 25 U.S.C. § 1913(d).

147. *See* note 134.

148. Matter of Adoption of Infant Boy Crews, 825 P.2d 305 (Wash. 1992).

149. *See* note 142. The Oregon Supreme Court reversed the appellate court's finding that ICWA applied to the adoption, but it did not address the propriety of the court's ruling on the right to withdraw consent.

150. Dement v. Oglala Sioux Tribal Court, 874 F.2d 510 (8th Cir. 1989).

151. *See* 28 U.S.C. § 1738.

152. *See* Sheppard v. Sheppard, 655 P.2d 895 (Idaho 1982); *In re* Adoption of Buehl, 555 P.2d 1334 (Wash. 1976).

153. *See* Application of Defender, 435 N.W.2d 717 (S.D. 1989) (state court can determine whether tribal court had personal jurisdiction over mother before granting comity to tribal court custody order); *see also* Matter of Welfare of R.I., 402 N.W.2d 173 (Minn. App. 1987) (state court need not defer to tribal court order finding that child is ward of tribal court in situation where tribal court had no jurisdiction).

154. Matter of Dependency and Neglect of A.L., 442 N.W.2d 233 (S.D. 1989).

155. *See* Quinn v. Walters, 881 P.2d 795 (Or. 1994), *reversing* 845 P.2d 206 (Or. App. 1993).

156. *Id.*

157. *See* Matter of Adoption of T.R.M., 525 N.E.2d 298 (Ind. 1988), Matter of Welfare of R.I., 402 N.W.2d 173 (Minn. App. 1987), Matter of W.L., 260 Mont. 325, 859 P.2d 1019 (Mont. 1993) (state court does not lose jurisdiction under ICWA because of mother's move to reservation); *but see* Matter of M.R.D.B., 241 Mont. 455, 787 P.2d 1219 (Mont. 1990) (tribal court has exclusive jurisdiction over adoption proceeding when natural mother withdraws consent to adoption in state court and tribal court has made child ward of tribal court).

158. *See, e.g.*, SDCL 1-1-25.

CHAPTER • V

Placement Provisions of ICWA

A second, and equally important, goal of Congress in implementing ICWA was to ensure the placement of Indian children in homes "which will reflect the unique values of Indian culture."[1] As the Supreme Court stated in *Holyfield* "the most important substantive requirements imposed upon state courts" are the placement preferences expressed in Section 1915 of the act.[2] Those provisions reflect congressional realization that even if the Indian child's bond to the parents or Indian custodian is severed, state courts must make every effort not to dissolve that tie between the child and his or her tribe because it is that association that will protect the integrity and future viability of the tribe itself.[3]

Many times it is the child's tribe that will most fervently advocate for the placement of an Indian child in accord with the provisions of Section 1915, sometimes in the face of a parental effort to avoid such a placement.[4] In adoptive placement issues the Indian child's tribe becomes the primary benefactor of the placement provisions of ICWA as the parents and Indian custodians have left the scene by way of a parental rights termination. The tribe's rights then become paramount to the parents, whereas in foster care placement and termination proceedings the parent's rights prevail over tribal wishes. An interesting illumination of this principle is a Montana Supreme Court decision holding that the right of the tribe to be notified of an adoptive placement supersedes a parent's request for anonymity.[5]

Unfortunately, Congress's aspiration to maintain Indian children in foster and adoptive homes that adequately reflect their unique cultural heritage has not borne fruit in many states where Indian children continue to be placed overwhelmingly in non-Indian homes, especially foster homes. This failure does not necessarily reflect state disregard of ICWA commands but may more likely mirror the difficulties associated with recruiting Indian foster homes, especially in urban areas with small Indian populations. Nevertheless, the placement provisions of ICWA should never become subservient to the provisions regarding the removal of Indian children from their homes, as both areas were of equal importance to Congress.

Foster Care Placements

The placement preference provisions for foster care placements are set out at Section 1915(b) of ICWA. These provisions apply to both voluntary and involuntary foster care placements and preadoptive placements as well as placements made in contemplation of the termination of parental rights. Although mandated by ICWA, at least one court has held that failure to follow the placement provisions will not vitiate an otherwise valid termination of parental rights.[6] However, if the Indian child becomes bonded to foster parents, failure to follow the foster care placement preference provisions should not constitute good grounds to deviate from the adoptive placement preference provisions.[7]

Section 1915(b) directs a state court, state agency, or private agency to place an Indian child in the least restrictive setting that closely approximates his or her family and that is within a reasonable proximity to his or her home. The standard for evaluating whether a placement conforms to this directive by Congress is the "prevailing social and cultural standards of the Indian community in which the parent or extended family resides or with which the parent or extended family members maintain social and cultural ties."[8] Applying such a directive becomes awkward in situations in which the Indian child has not resided in an Indian family. Even in that context, however, the majority of courts have stated that the foster care placement preference provisions must be followed and the child must be introduced into his or her Indian culture, provided that good cause to the contrary does not exist.[9] An Arizona appeals court explicitly rejected as a ground for deviating from the placement preference provisions a trial court's determination that introducing an Indian child into an Indian family would cause cultural shock to the child because of the child's upbringing in non-Indian families.[10]

A primary objective of Section 1915(d) is to prohibit state courts from imposing value judgments on proposed foster care placements based on the prevailing social and cultural standards of the non-Indian community, much in the same way state courts are prohibited from removing Indian children from their homes based on the prevailing child-rearing norms in the non-Indian community. An example cited in the BIA guidelines is the bias against placement of children in single-parent homes in the non-Indian community.[11] The guidelines expressly pronounce that single-family homes should be considered as placements, notwithstanding any preconceived notions of the proper composition of a foster family. Other factors, such as apparently overcrowded living conditions or residing in an impoverished area, also appear to be illegitimate bases for denial of placements.[12] One of the major problems confronting social workers who attempt to comply with the placement preference provisions for foster care, however, is the eligibility of the family for foster care payments under Title IV-E of the Social Security Act. To be eligible for payments, oftentimes the family must be licensed as a foster home by the state.[13] The very conditions that are illegitimate considerations to deny placement under ICWA may very well disqualify the family from licensing. However, Section 1931(b) seems to eliminate this problem by stating that "for purposes of qualifying for assistance under a federally-assisted program" licensing by a tribal entity should be deemed the equivalent of licensing by the state. This provision of ICWA has to be reconciled with the provisions of Title IV-E by those entities that provide foster care subsidies for Indian children, especially in areas where tribes are active in the licensing of foster homes and institutions. It appears that a state must provide foster care subsidies and any other federal benefits it administers to a child in a home licensed by the tribe, provided that a cooperative agreement between the tribe and the state has been entered into. Some tribes and states are attempting a reciprocal recognition of licensing standards so more Indian families can be recruited as foster homes. Such agreements are specifically contemplated by ICWA, and in the long run may be more beneficial than litigation of these issues.[14]

Preferences

In the absence of good cause to the contrary, discussed *infra* at 88–92, in any foster care or preadoptive placement an Indian child shall be placed with

i. a member of the Indian child's extended family;

ii. a foster home licensed, approved, or specified by the Indian child's tribe;

iii. an Indian foster home licensed or approved by an authorized non-Indian licensing authority; or

iv. an institution for children approved by an Indian tribe or operated by an Indian organization which has a program suitable to meet the Indian child's needs.[15]

A few things are apparent from this ICWA provision. First, an Indian tribe plays a vital role in the implementation of the foster care placement preferences, not only because many of the preferences refer to homes or institutions licensed by the tribe but also because an Indian tribe may be in possession of information about the child's extended family members that is otherwise unavailable to the state court.[16] Notwithstanding the vital role tribes play in placement issues, many courts have held that Indian tribes are not entitled to notice of voluntary foster care or termination proceedings.[17] The failure to receive notice inhibits a tribe's ability to assist in achieving a placement in compliance with the law.[18]

Second, ICWA does not prefer an Indian relative over a non-Indian relative under Subsection (i) of Section 1915(b). A review of the definition of "extended family member," contained at Section 1903(2), reveals that the definition encompasses various relatives of the child without regard to race, unless the tribe defines the term in another manner. Therefore, a state court would be in compliance with ICWA by placing the child in a non-Indian relative's home, provided that placement meets the requirement of approximating as closely as possible the prevailing social and cultural standards of the Indian community where the parent has resided.[19]

Third, the foster care placement preference provisions seem to beg the question of whom is to pay for the foster care placement. If the placement is with a relative, payment may not be a problem because the relative may be eligible for either AFDC payments or some type of other cash assistance from the state.[20] If the child is placed in a home licensed as a foster home by the tribe and the state does not recognize that license, however, the state may balk at payment because of state requirements enacted to comply with Title IV-E of the Social Security Act. ICWA seems to address this problem at Section 1931(b) by stating that "for purposes of qualifying for assistance under a federally assisted program, licensing or approval of foster or adoptive homes or institutions by an Indian Tribe shall be deemed equivalent to licensing or approval by a State." It appears, however, that some states do not recognize tribal licensing and insist that a foster care placement be arranged by the state before Title IV-E foster care subsidies are payable.[21] In addition some tribes lack the resources to license foster homes in urban areas because of the meager amount of money appropriated by Congress under Title II of ICWA for tribal ICWA programs. All these areas appear suitable for cooperative agreements between tribes and states to resolve any conflicts.

The legislative history and the BIA guidelines make it clear that the foster care preferences are listed in order of their preference and not as equal alternatives.[22]

Tribal Designation of Different Preferences

ICWA permits the Indian child's tribe to change the order of preference by resolution and requires the state court to adhere to the tribe's resolution, provided that the resolution complies with the prefatory language in Section 1915(b) pertaining to least restrictive alternative for the child.[23] There does not appear to be a good cause exception for deviating from a tribal resolution altering the preferences, and the courts that have addressed this issue have held that the tribal resolution is binding on the state court.[24]

Section 1915(c) seems to permit the tribe to change the order of the preferences and not necessarily to interject or omit preferences. Thus a tribe may pass a resolution amending the placement preference provisions by requiring that its children be placed, as a first option, in an institution operated by the tribe rather than with an extended family member and this must be respected by the state court. This right of the tribe to alter preferences also extends to adoptive placements, discussed *infra* at 91.

To avoid a state court finding good cause to deviate from the placement preference provisions, it appears that a tribe can merely pass a resolution altering the placement scheme and such action apparently eliminates the good cause exception. To date, however, the only court to address this issue, the Indiana Supreme Court, has refused to abide by a tribal resolution prohibiting the adoption of tribal members by non-Indians in an opinion that appears to whitewash the meaning of Section 1915(c).[25]

Parental Preference for Placement

ICWA attempts to balance the rights of the parents of Indian children and the children's tribe by requiring state courts to consider the preference of the parent, where appropriate, in effecting both foster care and adoptive placements.[26] ICWA also states that if the consenting parent requests anonymity the court shall consider such request in applying the preferences.[27] The BIA guidelines state that in a case where the parent requests anonymity that request "takes precedence over efforts to find a home consistent with the Act's priorities."[28]

The BIA guidelines were expressly overridden in a recent Montana decision, wherein the Montana Supreme Court held that the tribe's right to be notified of the identity of the parent of an Indian child to enable the tribe to find a relative placement prevails over the right of the parent to anonymity.[29] In so holding the court relied extensively on the Supreme Court's decision in *Holyfield* that the parents of an Indian child cannot defeat the tribe's interest in the fate of a child by placing the child off the reservation.[30] The court analogized the *Holyfield* scenario to the situation in which a parent was attempting to avoid tribal input on the issue of placement by requesting anonymity in finding that *Holyfield* prevented such.[31]

Most courts that have addressed this issue have held that the parental preference is entitled to deference but does not absolutely bar application of the preference provisions, nor does it bar input from the tribe.[32] Once again, however, the reader should remember that certain courts have held that Indian tribes are not entitled to notice of voluntary proceedings, which in effect renders the tribe's right to participate in placement proceedings very tenuous in those states.[33] One of the states holding such has held that the tribe is nonetheless entitled to intervene to assert its interests if it does find out about a proceeding.[34]

Good Cause to Deviate from Placement Preferences

Just as with a transfer request to tribal court, ICWA gives state courts and state agencies the discretion to deviate from both the foster care and adoptive placement preferences upon a showing of "good cause to the contrary." The BIA guidelines cite to several examples of what would constitute good cause to the contrary and, predictably, numerous state courts have cited these examples in support of placement decisions that deviate from placement preferences.[35]

Burden of Proof

The BIA guidelines state that the burden of proving that good cause exists to deviate from the placement preference provisions rests with the party requesting deviation.[36] There is a conflict among the courts on the required level of evidence to carry that burden, with the Alaska Supreme Court holding that a mere preponderance of the evidence is sufficient[37] and the Minnesota Court of Appeals holding that clear and convincing evidence is necessary.[38] Another court has suggested that a parent waives the right to demand compliance with the placement provisions by agreeing to a placement that deviates from those provisions.[39] All courts seem to be in agreement that the question of whether good cause exists lies within the discretion of the trial court and will not be disturbed on appeal absent an abuse of that discretion.[40]

BIA Guidelines Grounds

The BIA guidelines give several illustrations of situations that may constitute good cause to deviate from either the foster care or adoptive placement provisions of ICWA. The list does not appear to be exhaustive but merely illustrative.

i. The request of the biological parents or the child when the child is of sufficient age.

ii. The extraordinary physical or emotional needs of the child as established by testimony of a qualified expert witness.

iii. The unavailability of suitable families for placement after a diligent search has been completed for families meeting the preference criteria.[41]

The first good cause exception is an apparent attempt to implement that section of ICWA, Section 1915(c), directing a state court to consider the wishes of the parent, when appropriate, in making placement decisions. The request of the parent, of course, would carry more weight in a foster care placement than in an adoptive placement because the parent arguably possesses no rights after parental rights have been terminated.[42] Thus, the parent's desire to control the placement of the child should not supersede the right of the tribe or extended family members to assert a placement that would serve the overall purpose of ICWA.[43] Nonetheless, many courts have cited to the preference of the parent as a ground for deviating from the adoptive placement preferences of ICWA.[44]

Most courts have held that the right of the parent to suggest a foster care placement should not prevail over the right of a natural parent to assert custodial rights.[45] Typically, the cases in which a parent requests a placement not in accordance with ICWA arise in situations in which a non-Indian parent attempts to place an Indian child in a home where the Indian parent and family cannot gain access to the child. That does not appear to be Congress's intent in directing state courts to pay heed to the wishes of the natural parent in a foster care placement.[46]

The guidelines literally state that the request must be from both parents before it can be used as a ground for deviating. This appears to be poor draftsmanship of the guidelines, and most courts have held that the preference of either parent can serve as a ground to deviate.[47] When a parent requests a placement that violates the intent of ICWA (e.g, placement of an Indian child in a non-Indian home when suitable relative placements are available), applying the guidelines raises contentious issues. One could argue that the requirement that a court respect a parent's wishes as to placement merely requires that the court heed the suggestion of the parent as to a placement within a particular preference, such as one relative over another, although no court has apparently adopted that logic. *Holyfield* teaches that a parent should not be able to defeat the intent of the act unilaterally by her or his own interests. If that admonishment is adhered to in the context of placement preferences they should be observed, unless carrying out the parent's wishes would further the purposes of ICWA. A recent decision from Alaska, however, expressly rejects the use of *Holyfield* in this context.[48]

The inclusion of the wishes of an older child by the drafters of the BIA guidelines is not explained other than the statement that "the wishes of an older child are important in making an effective placement."[49] "Older child" is not defined, although it would not be inappropriate to use the age of twelve, as this is the age that the drafters chose to allow a child's objection of transfer of jurisdiction to tribal court to be considered as a ground for denying transfer.[50]

The second BIA guideline ground is to be considered when the child is in need of "highly specialized treatment services that are unavailable in the community where the families who meet the preference criteria reside."[51] There appears to be only one case discussing this exception, wherein the Minnesota Court of Appeals found that the children therein did have extraordinary emotional and physical needs that could not be met by placement elsewhere.[52] The court seemed to tie the requirement of extraordinary emotional and physical needs of the children in with the issue of permanency in a way that makes it appear that the court held that permanency is an extraordinary emotional need of children.[53] On appeal of this decision the Minnesota Supreme Court reversed the appellate court's finding of good cause and held that the appellate court had actually applied a best interest standard that was inappropriate.[54]

The requirement of qualified expert testimony to support this ground for deviating from the placement preferences mirrors the language pertaining to the need of that type of testimony to support an involuntary foster care placement or termination of parental rights, discussed at 59–61 *supra.*

The last ground cited by the guidelines is the inability to comply with the placement criteria after a diligent search has been conducted.[55] A diligent attempt is defined in the guidelines as "at a minimum, contact with the child's tribal social services program, a search of all county or state listings of available Indian homes, and contact with nationally known Indian programs with available placement resources."[56] This is a substantial requirement and, not surprisingly, in most cases where good cause to the contrary is asserted this ground is not put forth by the petitioning party.[57]

In addition to the BIA guideline grounds for finding good cause to the contrary to deviate from the placement preference provisions, courts have found that other circumstances qualify as good cause to the contrary. They include bonding with the proposed adoptive parents,[58] the need for stability,[59] the willingness of the adoptive family to expose the child to his or her Indian culture and traditions,[60] the best interest of the child,[61] and the child's lack of ties to the tribe.[62] Certain courts have expressly rejected the last ground as a reason to deviate.[63]

Adoptive Placements

ICWA has different placement preference criteria for adoptive placements. The same provisions discussed with respect to foster care placements—including the right of the tribe to alter the preference provisions by resolution, the right of the parent to request anonymity and to suggest a placement, and the good cause to the contrary grounds for deviating from the placement preference provisions—apply equally to adoptive placements. In fact, the majority of the cases discussing deviation from the placement preferences focus on adoptive placements.

In the absence of good cause to the contrary, a preference shall be given for the adoption of an Indian child to (1) a member of the Indian child's extended family; (2) other members of the Indian child's tribe; or (3) other Indian families.[64] This is the order of preference a state court must follow, unless the tribe has altered it by resolution or if good cause exists to deviate. Once again, it should be noted that ICWA does not bar the adoption of an Indian child by a non-Indian couple, unless the tribe adopts a resolution banning such adoptions, which one court has ruled even then is not binding.[65] The first preference for adoption may in fact be a non-Indian family because interracial marriages between Indians and non-Indians are becoming increasingly common, and therefore a non-Indian family may be a member of the child's extended family.

However, in the absence of non-Indian extended family members, it is apparent that the drafters of ICWA frowned upon adoptions of Indian children by non-Indian families not because of some evil intent of the adoptive family but because of the potential effect that the removal of the Indian child from his or her culture has on both the child and the tribe.[66] Congress, after long hours of testimony and investigation, concluded that in the overwhelming majority of cases in which the adoption of an Indian child became necessary it would be in the child's best interest to be adopted by a family that would preserve the child's unique Indian culture and heritage. Although some may disagree with this finding,[67] state courts are bound to follow the dictates of Congress in this arena unless Congress amends ICWA to acknowledge the contrary point of view.

Post Placement Issues

ICWA continues to play a role in child custody proceedings involving Indian children even after a placement, either foster care or adoptive, has been effected. The continued role assures that if the placement goes awry the intent of Congress will once again be realized in the post-placement proceedings.

Removal from Foster Home

If an Indian child is removed from a foster home or other institution, the placement preference criteria apply to any future placement, unless the removal from the foster home is for the purpose of returning the child to his or her parent or Indian custodian.[68] This provision of ICWA prevents state courts from initially effecting a placement in compliance with ICWA and then removing the child from that home for placement in one that may not comply with the placement provisions. Every placement of an Indian child must be made in accordance with the placement preference provisions.[69] ICWA does not seem to address the situation in which an Indian child is being removed from an Indian custodian and returned to a natural parent. One could argue that because ICWA has elevated the custodian to the position of parent she or he is entitled to all the procedural and substantive protections of ICWA, including the requirement that clear and convincing evidence be produced to show that serious emotional or physical harm will result if the child remains in the home of the custodian. This perhaps explains the reluctance of some state courts to grant Indian custodian status to Indian extended family members who are chosen as foster care placements for children, as such would entail formal proceedings to change the placement.[70]

Vacation of Adoption Decree

If an adoption decree is set aside under state law or the adoptive parents voluntarily terminate their parental rights, the biological parent or prior Indian custodian may petition the court for a return of custody and shall be restored custody unless there is a showing that return would not be in the best interest of the child.[71] If the return of custody is opposed, the hearing held to determine whether custody shall be returned shall comply with Section 1912.

This is a very interesting provision of ICWA that has been discussed infrequently.[72] It grants rights only to the biological parent of the child and to the prior Indian custodian and not to an Indian who previously adopted the child, who would be a parent under ICWA. The provision also makes reference to the "best interest of the child" standard, a rarity in ICWA. The unique thing about this provision is that it seems to require the state court to recommence a proceeding, which would then be governed by all the provisions of Section 1912, including the right to appointed counsel and the obligation to notify the tribe. In effect, the state court would be bound to conduct another adjudicatory hearing consistent with ICWA. It is unclear what the standard would be at that hearing—the serious emotional or physical harm standard or the best interest of the child standard. Because the provision makes reference to the best interest of the child, most likely this would be the standard adopted by the court.

Record of Placements

Each state that places an Indian child in either foster care or in an adoptive placement shall keep records of each placement along with efforts exerted by the state agency to comply with the placement preference provisions of ICWA.[73] Such records will be made available to either the Indian child's tribe or the Department of Interior upon request, notwithstanding any state law requiring the confidentiality of such proceedings. This requirement would appear to extend to private agency placements, provided that the state court plays some role in the placement of the Indian child. The provision does not require the records to be maintained at a central location, but other federal law may mandate such.[74] The existence of this requirement imposed on the state may prove useful to any Indian tribe or ICWA advocate wishing to demonstrate a systematic violation of the placement provisions of the law.

Right of Indian Child to Discover Tribal Affiliation

A miscellaneous provision of ICWA, but one that would be of great importance to an Indian child adopted by a non-Indian family, is the provision allowing an adult adopted child to apply to the state court where he or she was adopted for information relating to the tribal affiliation of his or her parents and any other information assisting the child in establishing the child's relationship with an Indian tribe.[75] If the child is not aware of which court granted the adoption, the child should inquire with the BIA because that agency is charged with the responsibility of keeping a central registry of adoptions involving Indian children.[76] This provision seems to apply even to adoptions that took place before the enactment of ICWA in 1978, although states may not have maintained the records required under ICWA back to that date.[77]

Notes

1. 25 U.S.C. § 1902.
2. *Holyfield* at 36.
3. *Id.*

4. *See, e.g.*, Matter of Baby Girl Doe, 865 P.2d 1090 (Mont. 1993) (mother's desire to see that child is placed with non-Indian family does not override tribe's efforts to gain placement of child with Indian family).

5. *Id.*

6. State *ex rel.* Juv. Dep't v. Woodruff, 816 P.2d 623 (Or. App. 1991) (violation of foster care placement requirements is not a ground for dismissal of a termination petition).

7. In B.R.T. v. Executive Director, 391 N.W.2d 594, 601 n.10 (N.D. 1986), the North Dakota Supreme Court suggested that the state could not rely on the bonding that took place between a foster home and Indian child as grounds for deviating from the adoptive placement requirements if the state did not make an effort to comply with the foster care placement preferences.

8. 25 U.S.C. § 1915(d).

9. *See, e.g., In re* Junious M., 193 Cal. Rptr. 40 (Ct. App. 1 Dist. 1983); *In re* Adoption of M.T.S., 489 N.W.2d 285 (Minn. App. 1992).

10. Matter of Appeal in Coconino Juvenile Action No. J-10175, 736 P.2d 829 (Ariz. App. 1987).

11. BIA Guidelines, F.1 Commentary, at 67594.

12. The BIA Guidelines, at D.3(c), clearly do not permit these factors to be considered in deciding whether a child will suffer serious physical or emotional harm while in the home of the parents or Indian custodian. The guidelines are silent, however, on the question of whether the presence of any of these conditions will disqualify a home from consideration as a placement. In Interest of J.R.H., 358 N.W.2d 311 (Iowa 1984), the Iowa Supreme Court, in rejecting a lower court's rationale for denying a placement with a natural mother on the reservation because of socioeconomic conditions there, stated that factors that cannot be used to justify a removal of an Indian child are equally illegitimate considerations in determining where to place a child. At 322.

13. *See* 42 U.S.C. § 672.

14. *See* 25 U.S.C. § 1919(a).

15. 25 U.S.C. § 1915(b).

16. In Matter of J.R.S., 690 P.2d 10 (Alaska 1984), the Alaska Supreme Court, in reversing a lower court ruling denying a tribe's motion to intervene in an adoptive placement proceeding, discussed the importance of allowing a tribe to participate in an adoptive placement proceeding even if ICWA does not permit intervention by right. The court held that intervention should be granted under state law, especially since the tribe would not be able to use 25 U.S.C. § 1914 to assert a violation of the adoptive placement preferences because Section 1914 does not permit such an attack; *see also In re* Custody of A.K.H., 502 N.W.2d 790 (Minn. App. 1993) (tribe entitled to intervene in custody dispute between grandparent and parent).

17. *See* Chapter 4, note 21.

18. *But see* Matter of Baby Girl Doe, 865 P.2d 1090 (Mont. 1993). The Montana Supreme Court seemed to assume that a tribe was otherwise entitled to notice in a voluntary proceeding and instead addressed the issue of whether a parent's request for anonymity could override that right to notice; *see also In re* Baby Girl A., 230 Cal. App. 3d 1611, 282 Cal. Rptr. 105 (Cal. App. 4 Dist. 1993) (tribe entitled to intervene in declaratory judgment action brought by Indian mother seeking to place Indian child with non-Indian adoptive home although court suggests that tribe is not entitled to notice).

19. 25 U.S.C. § 1915(d).

20. *See* 42 U.S.C. § 602.

21. In Native Village of Stevens v. Smith, 770 F.2d 1486 (9th Cir. 1985), the Ninth Circuit upheld a refusal by the state of Alaska to provide foster care payments for tribally arranged placements absent an agreement between the state and tribe.

22. BIA Guidelines, F.2, at 67594.

23. *See In re* Guardianship of Q.G.M., 808 P.2d 684 (Okla. 1991). There, the Oklahoma Supreme Court held that the tribe could change the order of preference without a showing of good cause as long as the proposed placements were the least restrictive alternative for the child.

24. *Id.*

25. Matter of Adoption of T.R.M., 525 N.E.2d 298 (Ind. 1988), *cert. denied,* 490 U.S. 1069 (1989). The *T.R.M.* court seemed to imply that the provision of ICWA relating to the right of the tribe to alter the placement preference criteria did not apply in state court, as that court permitted an adoption of an Indian child in direct contravention of a tribal resolution prohibiting such.

26. 25 U.S.C. § 1915(c). The preference of the parent can either be expressed while the parent is alive or through a testamentary appointment. *See* Adoption of N.P.S., 868 P.2d 934 (Alaska 1994) (mother's appointment of live-in boyfriend as guardian in will entitled to deference in determining adoptive placement of Indian child).

27. *Id.*

28. BIA Guidelines, F.1 Commentary, at 67594.

29. Matter of Baby Girl Doe, 865 P.2d 1090 (Mont. 1993).

30. *Id.* at 1094–95.

31. *Id.*

32. *See* Matter of Adoption of F.H., 851 P.2d 1361 (Alaska 1993); Matter of M.E.M., 725 P.2d 212 (Mont. 1986); *In re* Baby Girl A., 230 Cal. App. 3d 1611, 282 Cal. Rptr. 105 (Cal. App. 4 Dist. 1991).

33. *See* Chapter 4, note 21.

34. In Matter of J.R.S., 690 P.2d 10 (Alaska 1984).

35. *See, e.g.,* Matter of Custody of S.E.G., 507 N.W.2d 872 (Minn. App. 1993), *rev'd* 521 N.W.2d 357 (Minn. 1994) *cert denied sub nom Campbell v. Leech Lake Band of Chippewa Indians,* 63 U.S.L.W. 3560 (1995), (appellate court's decision to allow non-Indian family to adopt Indian child over the objection of the tribe, which was recommending an Indian family, reversed by the Minnesota Supreme Court, which concluded that the appellate court erred in going beyond the BIA guidelines to allow deviation based on the best interest of the child); *see also* Matter of Adoption of F.H., 851 P.2d 1361 (Alaska 1993); *In re* Robert T., 246 Cal. Rptr. 168 (Ct. App. 6 Dist. 1988); *In re* Baby Girl A., 282 Cal. Rptr. 105 (Cal. App. 4 Dist. 1991).

36. BIA Guidelines, F.3(b), at 67594.

37. *See* Adoption of N.P.S., 868 P.2d 934 (Alaska 1994); Matter of Adoption of F.H., 851 P.2d 1361, 1363 (Alaska 1993).

38. Matter of Custody of S.E.G., 507 N.W.2d 872, 878 (Minn. App. 1993), *rev'd on other grounds,* 521 N.W.2d 357 (Minn. 1994) *cert denied sub nom Campbell v. Leech Lake Band of Chippewa Indians,* 63 U.S.L.W. 3560 (1995).

39. *In re* Interest of C.W., 239 Neb. 817, 479 N.W.2d 105 (Neb. 1992).

40. *See* notes 36 and 37; *see also In re* Interest of Bird Head, 331 N.W. 2d 785, 791 (Neb. 1983); *In re* Adoption of M., 832 P.2d 518,522 (Wash. App. 1992); *In re*

Appeal in Maricopa County Juvenile Action No A-25525, 667 P.2d 228, 234 (Ariz. App. 1983).

41. BIA Guidelines, F.3, at 67594.

42. *See, e.g.,* Santosky v. Kramer, 455 U.S. 745 (1982).

43. *See* Matter of Baby Jane Doe, *supra.*

44. *See, e.g., In re* Baby Girl A., 282 Cal. Rptr. 105 (Cal. App. 4 Dist. 1991); Matter of Adoption of F.H., *supra.*

45. *See In re* Custody of S.B.R., 719 P.2d 154 (Wash. App. 1986) (non-Indian mother cannot defeat rights of father by asserting a preference for placement with her parents); *see also In re* Guardianship of Q.G.M., 808 P.2d 684 (Okla. 1991).

46. *Id.*

47. *See* Matter of Adoption of F.H., *supra.*

48. Matter of Adoption of F.H., *supra; see also* Adoption of N.P.S., 868 P.2d 934 (Alaska 1994).

49. BIA Guidelines, F.3 Commentary, at 67594.

50. BIA Guidelines, at C.3(a)(ii).

51. BIA Guidelines, F.3 Commentary.

52. Matter of Custody of S.E.G., 507 N.W.2d 872 (Minn. App. 1993). A New York court has also referred to the "special needs of a child" as grounds for deviating from the placement preferences in Matter of Oscar C., Jr., 559 N.Y.S.2d 431 (Fam. Ct. 1990), although the child there did not seem to have any extraordinary physical or emotional needs.

53. *S.E.G.* at 882.

54. In Matter of Custody of S.E.G., 521 N.W.2d 357 (Minn. 1994) *cert denied sub nom Campbell v. Leech Lake Band of Chippewa Indians,* 63 U.S.L.W. 3560 (1995), (Minn. Aug. 31, 1994), No. C4-93-1054.

55. BIA Guidelines, F.3(a)(iii), at 67594.

56. *Id.* at F.3 Commentary.

57. In *In re* Robert T., 246 Cal. Rptr. 168 (Cal. App. 6 Dist. 1988) the Court seemed to imply that the burden of coming forward with relative placements and Indian home placements rested with the Indian tribe involved therein and the failure of the tribe to find placements in compliance with ICWA justified a deviation from ICWA adoptive placement requirements. *See also In re* Krystle D., 37 Cal.Rptr.2d 132, 30 Cal. App. 4th 1778 (Cal. App. 6 Dist. 1994).

58. *See, e.g.,* Matter of Custody of S.E.G., 507 N.W.2d 872 (Minn. App. 1993), *rev'd,* 521 N.W.2d 357 (Minn. 1994) *cert denied sub nom Campbell v. Leech Lake Band of Chippewa Indians,* 63 U.S.L.W. 3560 (1995). In that case the appellate court found that the children had special needs for permanency as well as finding that suitable homes were not available in compliance with ICWA's placement provisions. Lastly, the court held that it would be in the best interest of the children for the non-Indian couple there to adopt because of the bonding that had taken place. The Minnesota Supreme Court reversed and held that the court had erred by going beyond the good cause exceptions listed in the BIA guidelines and by accepting the testimony of certain witnesses as experts. *See also* Matter of Adoption of F.H., 851 P.2d 1361 (Alaska 1993).

59. Matter of Adoption of F.H., 851 P.2d 1361 (Alaska 1993). *See also In re* Interest of Birdhead, 331 N.W.2d 785 (Neb. 1983); Matter of N.L., 754 P.2d 863 (Okla. 1988).

60. *See, e.g., In re* Robert T., 246 Cal. Rptr. 168 (Ct. App. 6 Dist. 1988); Matter of Custody of S.E.G., 507 N.W.2d 872, 883 (Minn. App. 1993), *rev'd,* 521 N.W.2d 357 (Minn. 1994) *cert denied sub nom Campbell v. Leech Lake Band of Chippewa Indians,* 63 U.S.L.W. 3560 (1995).

61. *See* Custody of S.E.G., *supra;* Matter of Adoption of F.H., *supra.*

62. In *In re* Baby Girl A., 282 Cal. Rptr. 105 (Cal. App. 4 Dist. 1991), a California court implied that Indian tribes have less of an interest in off-reservation-domiciled Indian children and therefore the good cause standard should be liberally applied in the decision to place off-reservation-domiciled Indian children. This seems inconsistent with ICWA because the placement provisions of ICWA apply predominately to off-reservation children rather than reservation-domiciled children. The mother in that case, however, was also advocating for placement with a non-Indian family. *See also* Matter of Adoption of F.H., *supra.*

63. *See* Matter of Appeal in Coconino County Juvenile Action No. J-10175, 736 P.2d 829 (Ariz. App. 1989); *In re* Adoption of M.T.S., 489 N.W.2d 285 (Minn. App. 1992) (court holds that it is "presumptively" in the best interest of Indian child to be placed with Indian relative over a non-Indian couple seeking to adopt).

64. 25 U.S.C. § 1915(a).

65. Matter of Adoption of T.R.M., 525 N.E.2d (Ind. 1988), *cert. denied,* 490 U.S. 1069 (1989).

66. *See, e.g.,* Matter of Custody of S.E.G., 507 N.W.2d 872, 887 (Minn. App. 1993) (Schumacher, J., dissenting), *rev'd,* 521 N.W.2d 357 (Minn. 1994) *cert denied sub nom Campbell v. Leech Lake Band of Chippewa Indians,* 63 U.S.L.W. 3560 (1995); *In re* Adoption of M.T.S., 489 N.W.2d 285 (Minn. App. 1992).

67. *See, e.g.,* Barsh, *The Indian Child Welfare Act of 1978: A Critical Analysis,* 31 HASTINGS L.J. 1287 (1980).

68. 25 U.S.C. § 1916(b).

69. *See* People in Interest of J.L.G., 687 P.2d 477 (Colo. App. 1984).

70. *See, e.g., In re* Interest of Birdhead, 331 N.W.2d 785 (Neb. 1984).

71. 25 U.S.C. § 1916(a).

72. *See* Matter of Adoption of a Child of Indian Heritage, 543 A.2d 925 (N.J. 1988).

73. 25 U.S.C. § 1915(e).

74. *See* 42 U.S.C. § 671.

75. 25 U.S.C. §1917. In Matter of Adoption of Rebecca, 158 Misc.2d 644, 601 N.Y.S.2d 682 (N.Y. Surr. 1993), the court held that the child there had a right to discover her tribal affiliation but that the information regarding the adoption would only be released to the Oneida Nation, the tribe that she was attempting to get enrolled with.

76. 25 U.S.C. § 1951.

77. *See* Matter of Hanson, 470 N.W.2d 669 (Mich. App. 1991) (a request to examine adoptive records is a subsequent proceeding under 25 U.S.C. § 1923; therefore ICWA applies). *Concur,* Matter of Adoption of Rebecca, 158 Misc.2d 644, 601 N.Y.S.2d 682 (N.Y. Surr. 1993).

CHAPTER • VI

Collateral Challenges to ICWA Determinations

A review of the cases involving ICWA reveals quite a divergence of opinion on the proper application of the act. Some of the more stark examples are the courts that have carved out an existing Indian family exception to the applicability of ICWA versus the courts that have rejected the exception[1] and the courts that have used the "best interest of the child" standard to deny a transfer of jurisdiction to a tribal court versus those denouncing that ground.[2]

Obviously, with so many conflicting opinions regarding ICWA, we are reaching the point where the Supreme Court's admonishment that ICWA, because it is a federal law, should be applied uniformly is being ignored and the application of the act will depend in many circumstances on where a child custody proceeding is commenced.[3] The remedy for this problem appears to lie in ICWA's Section 1914, which permits any Indian child, tribe, parent, or Indian custodian to petition a court of competent jurisdiction to invalidate a child custody proceeding if it violates Section 1911, Section 1912, or Section 1913 of the act.[4] This provision seems to grant those parties, either alone or in concert, a federal court cause of action to attack collaterally an order that violates ICWA. The availability of that remedy has proven to be illusory, however. There are numerous provisions of ICWA granting various parties the right to challenge state court proceedings after their culmination. For example, Section 1913(d) allows a parent who consented to an involuntary termination of parental rights to withdraw that consent and to regain custody of the child upon a showing that the consent was obtained through fraud or coercion. Section 1914 is a broader remedy vested in the tribe, parents, Indian custodian, or the child to attack collaterally a state court order entered in violation of three sections of ICWA. It should be noted that Section 1914 is not available to a party who wishes to challenge a placement issue collaterally.

There are several obstacles that have been encountered by litigants who have attempted to use Section 1914 in federal court. First, Section 1914 does not explicitly confer on the federal courts subject matter jurisdiction to review state court ICWA decisions, unlike other provisions of federal law that do.[5] It is apparent from the legislative history that Congress did intend to allow some type of collateral review of ICWA decisions,[6] but the language of Section 1914 certainly does not unambiguously express that federal courts would have that authority. The courts that have addressed this issue have found that jurisdiction may still lie under 28 U.S.C. Section 1331, although that also is a contentious issue.[7]

Second, and more problematic, is the requirement that a federal court grant full faith and credit to the judgment of state courts.[8] In the cases that have been decided regarding the application of Section 1914 this provision of federal law has proved to be the biggest obstacle to meaningful federal court review.[9] 28 U.S.C. Section 1738 clearly requires that a federal court grant preclusive effect to a state court decision, provided that there is identity of parties and the issues sought to be litigated in federal court were litigated in the state forum. One court has even suggested that a tribe may not forego its appellate remedies in state court to commence a federal court action in an attempt to challenge the state court's determination.[10] Thus, it appears that any case brought in federal court to review a state court's application and disposition of a child custody proceeding under ICWA may be barred by *res judicata,* provided that the issues were litigated in state court.

There are several potential ways to derail the use of full faith and credit, but they are risky. One would be for a party to seek federal court intervention before the state court acts, possibly under federal question jurisdiction or even under 42 U.S.C. Section 1983, seeking to enjoin the state court from taking action in violation of ICWA. Such an action would obviously be met with an argument that the Anti-Injunction Act prohibits a federal court from enjoining a state court from taking action on a matter clearly within its jurisdiction.[11] There are numerous exceptions to the Anti-Injunction Act, including actions brought under Section 1983, but no court has ruled that an action brought to enjoin a state court from adjudicating an ICWA case is an exception.[12]

A second mode of operation would be for an interested party with standing, such as a tribe, to intentionally not participate in the state court proceeding to avoid the identity of parties requirement for the application of the full faith and credit clause. Choosing this route is dangerous, however, especially because the failure of the tribe to participate in the state court proceedings may translate into the loss of input into important decisions, including placement decisions.

Of course, a federal court may not be the only court of competent jurisdiction to bring an action under Section 1914. If the child in question was domiciled on a reservation at the time of the commencement of some child custody proceeding in state court and the state court nonetheless exercised jurisdiction, the tribal court may be an available forum to bring an action to invalidate the state court order.[13] Obtaining the tribal court order and having it enforced are two different matters, however, and some type of federal court intervention, possibly under 28 U.S.C. Section 1331 (federal question jurisdiction), to declare that the tribal court order is entitled to deference may be necessary.[14] A recent federal court decision from the Western District of Oklahoma recognizes that a federal court may exercise jurisdiction under Section 1331 to declare that a tribal court has exclusive jurisdiction over an Indian child.[15]

Additionally, if new evidence becomes available that was not reasonably obtainable at the time of the state court proceeding, even a state court may be a possible forum for an invalidation action. For example, if a state agent knows that the child in question is possibly Indian but suppresses that information from the court, the parent, child, or tribe may be able to use Section 1914 to invalidate all proceedings held in state court in violation of ICWA, although one court has held that such jurisdiction does not lie.[16]

There does not appear to be any statute of limitations associated with the use of Section 1914, as compared to Section 1913(d), which does not permit a collateral attack on an adoption obtained through fraud or duress after the adoption has been effective for more than two years. However, the violation of Section 1913 gives rise to an action to invalidate under Section 1914; thus, those provisions have to be read in *pari materia.*

Federal court jurisdiction does seem to lie to challenge tribal court determinations in child custody proceedings if the litigants challenge the tribal court's jurisdictional authority.[17] One court has even held that a federal court can intervene to remove from a tribal court's jurisdiction a child who had been wrongfully transferred to the tribal court's jurisdiction without the natural parents' notice.[18]

Notes

1. *See* Chapter II, notes 15–39.

2. Chapter III, notes 62 and 67.

3. *Holyfield,* 490 U.S., at 49. One of the grounds cited by the *Holyfield* court for rejecting Mississippi law on the definition of domicile was that it would subject the intent of Congress to different interpretations depending on which state an ICWA case arose in. Obviously, there are numerous provisions of ICWA that have been interpreted differently by various state courts, which produces the result the Court sought to avoid in *Holyfield.*

4. Placement provisions, governed by Section 1915, cannot be challenged under Section 1914.

5. For example, federal courts are explicitly vested with habeas corpus jurisdiction to review violations of the Indian Civil Rights Act. *See* 25 U.S.C. § 1303.

6. House Report at 23.

7. *See* Roman Nose v. New Mexico Dep't of Human Resources, 967 F.2d 435 (10th Cir. 1992).

8. *See* 28 U.S.C. § 1738.

9. *See, e.g.,* Navajo Nation v. District Court, 624 F.Supp. 130 (D.Utah 1985), *dismissed as moot,* 831 F.2d 929 (10th Cir. 1987); Kiowa Tribe of Oklahoma v. Lewis, 777 F.2d 587 (10th Cir. 1985); Kickapoo Tribe of Oklahoma v. Rader, 822 F.2d 1493.

10. *See* Kickapoo Tribe of Oklahoma v. Rader, *supra.*

11. *See* 28 U.S.C. § 2283.

12. *See, e.g.,* Mitchum v. Foster, 407 U.S. 225 (1972).

13. The Supreme Court in *Holyfield, supra,* stated that when a reservation-domiciled child is involved the tribal court is the only court with jurisdiction. At 51 n. 26.

14. The Supreme Court has recognized that the extent of a tribal court's jurisdiction is a matter of federal law and raises a federal question under 28 U.S.C. § 1331. National Farmers Union Insurance Co. v. Crow Tribe of Indians, 105 S.Ct. 2447 (1985). The U.S. Court of Appeals for the Eighth Circuit has also held that a federal court may properly exercise jurisdiction over a dispute between parties with conflicting tribal and state court custody orders, provided that tribal court remedies are exhausted. *See* Dement v. Oglala Sioux Tribal Court, 874 F.2d 510 (8th Cir. 1989).

15. *See* Comanche Indian Tribe of Oklahoma v. Hovis, 847 F.Supp. 871 (W.D. Okla. 1994); *but see* Fletcher v. Florida, 858 F. Supp. (M.D. Fla. 1994) (court dismisses claims of Indian mother against various state and private officials brought under various federal civil rights statutes for alleged violations of ICWA).

16. In Slone v. Inyo County Juvenile Court, 230 Cal. App. 3d 263, 282 Cal. Rptr. 126 (Cal. App. 4 Dist. 1991), the court rejected an attempt to invoke the superior court's jurisdiction to reverse a juvenile court's application of ICWA.

17. *See* LaBeau v. Dakota, 815 F. Supp. 1074 (W.D. Mich. 1993) (habeas corpus jurisdiction lies in federal court to challenge tribal court's assumption of jurisdiction); Sandman v. Dakota, 816 F. Supp. 448 (W.D. Mich. 1992).

18. Brown on Behalf of Brown v. Rice, 760 F. Supp. 1459 (D. Kan. 1991).

CHAPTER • VII

Funding of ICWA Programs

Funding for tribes and tribal organizations to operate ICWA programs has been of utmost concern to those entities since the enactment of ICWA. In the 1984 Senate Select Committee on Indian Affairs Oversight Committee hearings on the implementation of ICWA,[1] one of the most frequently cited obstacles raised by tribes and tribal organizations attempting to implement ICWA was the lack of funding. Indian tribes and organizations need funding to provide the variety of services needed to establish and maintain an effective child welfare assistance program. The types of services expected of Indian tribes are listed in the Code of Federal Regulations governing the award of grants under Title II of ICWA[2] to Indian tribes and organizations.[3] A review of these regulations reveals that Indian tribes are charged with the licensing of foster homes; the delivery of services to families to avoid displacement of children; the provision of legal services and advice for both the tribe and entities involved in ICWA proceedings; and the education and training of tribal court personnel to implement ICWA. This is a very ambitious agenda for any tribe delving into the ICWA arena.

Unfortunately, the funding for tribal ICWA programs has not been as ambitious.[4] Currently there are three sources of federal funding that a tribe or tribal organization may access to operate ICWA programs, exclusive of any money the tribe may provide from other sources. First, under Title II of ICWA the secretary of interior is authorized to make grants to Indian tribes and organizations, including off-reservation programs, for the establishment and operation of child welfare programs and implementation of child welfare codes.[5] The grants for on-reservation programs are directed at the delivery of services to reservation families or near-reservation families, while the off-reservation grants are geared toward allowing the payment of foster care subsidies in a manner comparable to the state's.

One of the past problems confronting tribes and organizations that applied for grants under Title II, other than the scarcity of funding, was that the applications were scored competitively.[6] Thus, in a given year a program may have been funded for a certain amount of money and in the next year completely defunded if the Department of Interior believed that another applicant was more worthy of funding. In fact, in one recent year the nation's largest tribe, the Navajo Nation, received no money under Title II of ICWA, even though, perhaps more than any other tribe, it must handle the brunt of the responsibility bestowed on it by the enactment of ICWA.[7]

This process did not lead to stability in many tribal social services programs. Resultantly, the Department of Interior has enacted new regulations that award funding to tribes on a noncompetitive basis, although nontribal entities must still compete for Title II funding.[8]

Exacerbating the crisis in funding for many Indian tribes is the ability of urban Indian programs to apply for Title II funds. Funding for urban Indian programs is just as sorely needed as funding for tribal programs. However, by having both entities eligible only for the same programs, the department has effectively made them adversaries in the solicitation for funding. Some consternation has also resulted from Section 1934's definition of Indian, which refers back to a section that defines Indian as including any terminated tribe's members.[9] This seems to conflict openly with ICWA's definition of Indian,[10] which excludes members of terminated Indian tribes, thereby creating the possibility of those tribes receiving funding under Title II although ICWA does not apply to them.

A second source of funding is Title IV-B of the Social Security Act,[11] which authorizes direct funding to "an Indian tribal organization which has a plan for child welfare services" under Title IV-B.[12] The types of services Title IV-B monies can be used for are more aptly described at Section 625 of the subchapter.

Title IV-B is unique in that it provides for the federal secretary of health and human services to provide direct funding for an Indian tribe's operation of a child welfare system, whereas most of the Title

IV programs only permit direct funding to state governments.[13] Title IV is a matching funds program, meaning that the entity that receives funding must provide a fiscal match to the amount provided by the federal government. Title II of ICWA specifically authorizes ICWA grants to be used as the match for a grant under Title IV-B.[14] That section also prohibits the secretary of health and human services from denying funding under Title IV-B because of the possibility of a tribe receiving funding under Title II of ICWA.[15]

Unfortunately, Title IV-B funding is not as enriching as the potential for funding under Title IV-E of the Social Security Act.[16] Tribes cannot receive funding under Title IV-E directly from the federal government to provide foster care payments and adoption assistance. Tribes can, however, enter into cooperative agreements with states whereby the states can pass through Title IV-E monies to the tribe for the provision of foster care and adoption assistance programs for reservation-domiciled children.[17] Tribes already possess the authority to license foster homes, which in turn renders that home eligible for any federally assisted program, which would include Title IV-E as well as medical assistance programs.[18] The only court to address this issue has concluded, however, that although a state must honor a tribe's licensing of a foster or adoptive home it is under no obligation to make foster care payments to that home under Title IV-E, unless and until the tribe and state enter into a cooperative agreement.[19] Unfortunately for tribes, the court there went on to hold that the state was under no affirmative obligation to attempt to enter into cooperative agreements with tribes for the pass-through of Title IV-E monies. This holding is contrary to a recent federal court decision on the need for cooperative agreements between states and tribes for the delivery of services mandated under another subparagraph of Title IV of the Social Security Act.[20]

Lastly, tribes are eligible for block grants from the federal government under Title XX of the Social Security Act[21] to operate social services programs. A list of programs for which Title XX monies are earmarked is contained in the statute.[22] Once again, an ICWA grant can be used as a match to any assistance provided by the federal government to a tribe under Title XX.[23]

It is apparent that Indian tribes and tribal organizations as well as urban Indian programs have to remain adept at grant applications to fund an ICWA program fully and carry out the huge responsibilities vested them by Congress when it enacted ICWA. Only with adequate funding for tribes will the problems that frequently lead to the removal of Indian children from their homes be redressed.

Notes

1. Senate Select Committee on Indian Affairs, Oversight Hearings on State Compliance with Indian Child Welfare Act, S. Hrg. 98–952, 98th Cong., 2nd Sess. (April 25, 1984).

2. 25 U.S.C. § 1931.

3. 25 C.F.R. § 23.22.

4. In an August 1994 report, the Office of Inspector General for the Department of Health and Human Services suggested numerous ways to expand tribal access to various federal programs for the delivery of services to children in need of protection. They include eliminating the requirement of state oversight and financial responsibility for tribally operated child protection programs under Title IV-E of the Social Security Act; eliminating the need for a tribal match to receive funding under Title IV-E; and eliminating some of the requirements to receive monies under Title IV-B of the Social Security Act. Department of Health and Human Services, Office of Inspector General, *Opportunities for ACF to Improve Child Welfare Services and Protections for Native American Children*, August 1994, OEI-01-93-00110.

5. 25 U.S.C. § 1931, § 1932.

6. The BIA recently promulgated regulations, published in 59 Fed. Reg. 2248 (January 13, 1994), that convert the competitive grant award process for Indian tribes into a noncompetitive funding process. However, nontribal entities, such as urban Indian programs, must still compete for ICWA grants.

7. The Navajo Nation sued over its defunding but was unsuccessful. *See* Navajo Nation v. Hodel, 645 F. Supp. 825 (D. Ariz. 1986).

8. 25 C.F.R. 23.25, as amended by 59 Fed. Reg. at 2248 (January 13, 1994).

9. *See* 25 U.S.C. § 1603(c).

10. 25 U.S.C. § 1903(8).

11. 42 U.S.C. § 620 *et seq.* There have been two recent amendments to Title IV-B which impact upon ICWA. The "Social Security Amendment Acts of 1994" (P.L. 103-432) require states to include in their Title IV-B plans a description of the specific measures the state has taken to comply with ICWA after consultation with tribal entities. The second, the "Multi-Ethnic Placement Act" (P.L. 103-382), enacted to prohibit the exclusion of a person as a foster or adoptive placement because of race, specifically exempts Indian children from its coverage. However, that act does contain language, amending Title IV-B, requiring states to make a more concerted effort to recruit minority foster families, which may assist in recruitment of Indian foster families.

12. 42 U.S.C. § 628.

13. Despite this opportunity for tribes, only 59 of the 542 federally eligible Indian tribes received any money under Title IV-B in 1993. *See* Department of Health and Human Services, Report of Inspector General, August 1994, at 7.

14. 25 U.S.C. § 1931(b).

15. *Id.*

16. 42 U.S.C. § 670 *et seq.*

17. There are two provisions of federal law that are instructive in the area of cooperative agreements. First, ICWA § 1919(a) authorizes states and tribes to enter into cooperative agreements respecting care and custody of Indian children. Second, a provision of Title IV-E, 42 U.S.C. § 672(a)(2), requires that before a state may make payment under Title IV-E the child's placement must be the responsibility of either the state agency or a public agency with which the state has an agreement. Read in *pari materia,* at least one court has construed these sections to mean that a state can pass through Title IV-E monies to a tribe with which it has a cooperative agreement. *See* Native Village of Stevens v. Smith, 770 F.2d 1486 (9th Cir. 1985).

18. *See* 25 U.S.C. § 1931(b).

19. Smith, *supra,* at 1489.

20. *See* Howe v. Ellenbecker, 8 F.3d 1258 (8th Cir. 1993), holding that a state must attempt to enter into cooperative agreements with Indian tribes to implement the provisions of Title IV-D of the Social Security Act.

21. *See* 42 U.S.C. § 1397 *et seq.*

22. 42 U.S.C. § 1397(a)(2)(A).

23. 25 U.S.C. § 1931(b).

CHAPTER • VIII

ICWA: Its Successes and Failures

Almost sixteen years have passed since the Indian Child Welfare Act became binding on all state courts and agencies in this country. In examining the present state of the law on ICWA, we oftentimes indulge ourselves in the minutiae of the law and neglect the ultimate inquiry of whether the law has served the best interest of Indian children and tribes in this country. After all, no one would disagree with the proposition that all persons working with Indian children desire to see that those children are raised in the least restrictive manner that preserves both their physical and emotional well-being as well as their unique cultural traditions. However, it has become apparent that the manner by which these objectives are reconciled is frequently the subject of much debate. One can look beyond that debate, however, and define certain benefits from the enactment of the law without necessarily subscribing to the belief that the law has been a resounding success.

ICWA has certainly been successful in many respects. First, it has served as an educational device for many state court judges and social services agencies in this country who perhaps never paused to reflect on the uniqueness of Indian children. Many lawyers representing the interests of Indian tribes and parents in ICWA cases will acknowledge that often the key to obtaining a fair application of ICWA is to educate the judge about the need for a special law applicable to Indian children and tribes. Most laws are universally applied without mention of the rationale behind the enactment of the law.

Implementing ICWA is part of a broader objective of educating predominately non-Indian judges about Indian tribes and children in a manner that promotes multicultural understanding and sensitivity. An examination of some ICWA decisions, ranging from those written by urban New Jersey judges to those by rural Alaska judges, pontificating on the cultural uniqueness of Indian children is perhaps the best evidence that ICWA has been a successful educational tool.

Second, ICWA has brought state and tribal judges and officials together in a dialogue that has extended beyond ICWA into other areas of mutual concern, such as recognition of each other's judgments and cooperative agreements to enhance the welfare of Indian children. In many states discussion regarding ICWA has been the lure for state and tribal court judges to convene to discuss the state of the law and working arrangements for its implementation. Those discussions have inevitably extended into other areas of concern and have led to state and tribal court fora in some states, where meetings are held on a regular basis to resolve matters of mutual concern that state legislatures and tribal councils often anguish over.

Third, ICWA has played a primary role in strengthening tribal courts and other tribal institutions, thereby increasing the esteem by which those entities are held in the eyes of the non-Indian community. Tribal courts play a critical role in the implementation of ICWA, and most tribes have accepted this role by upgrading their court systems and social service agencies in a manner that redounds to the benefit of all persons that appear before those entities. It is perhaps not coincidental that after the enactment of ICWA the federal courts began issuing decisions recognizing the role tribal courts play in the American system of jurisprudence by deferring to the authority of tribal courts.[1]

Other tribes have resurrected their court systems in response to the enactment of ICWA, which has led to an extension of those tribes' sovereign authorities as well as an examination of more traditional forms of dispute resolution.

Fourth, ICWA has proscribed many of the pernicious practices that had the potential to derail the survival of many unique tribal societies. Although adoptions of Indian children by non-Indian homes have not been eliminated, the practice has been circumscribed and the adoptions that do take place are often conditioned upon the child continuing to be exposed to his or her culture and traditions. More Indian children are placed with extended family members than was so before ICWA, resulting in children being raised aware of their roles in both the family and the tribe.

Indian foster home recruitment remains a problem, but with the advent of ICWA the problem has been identified and many strong Indian families have opted to bear the burden of helping with the rearing of Indian children, resulting in a decrease of placements in non-Indian homes. Similarly, many Native Americans have opted to become social workers in the desire to assist Indian tribes and children to overcome many of the social ills that led to the high placement of Indian children.

For all its successes, however, ICWA has its detractors. Critics point to Indian children being removed from non-Indian homes where they have closely bonded simply because the foster parents are not Indian. Although this probably happens less than ICWA dissidents would acknowledge, when these cases do occur they are often accompanied by much negative publicity and emotion, especially toward ICWA. Putting emotions aside, there are several criticisms of ICWA that are meritorious.

First, ICWA is a procedural statute for a substantive problem. The underlying problems that lead to the breakup of many Indian families are not, in many instances, the by-products of faulty state institutions but instead are the result of social ills in the family. These ills, many of which can be directly tied to the introduction of alcohol into the lives of Native Americans and the destruction of the lifestyle of Native Americans by non-Indians, must be redressed before the effects of present-day institutional racism can be assessed.

When confronted with the removal of Indian children, many state court judges have no benchmark to judge "traditional Native American culture" against except that particular judge's observations of that culture, which in many cases will not be positive. The concepts embodied in ICWA, of traditional Native American child-rearing practices preserving the unique values of Indian culture, are idealistic, perhaps even myopic, when considered in light of the panoply of social problems confronting Indian children. Those social problems receive little, if any, attention in ICWA, except in Title II where funding is made available for Indian tribes. That funding has barely been sufficient for some tribes to deal with the day-to-day problems associated with transferring state court cases and intervening in those cases, much less to confront family dysfunctions.

Quite naturally, in criticizing the law detractors of ICWA rely extensively on the social maladies confronting many Indian families. In defense of ICWA, the primary focus of the law was to eliminate state institutional practices that led to the breakup of Indian families and not to redress the social ills that led to family disintegration. However, some contend that Congress made states the scapegoats for the problems that confront Indian families and has not allocated sufficient federal resources or effort to attack the root causes for the displacement of Indian children.

Second, Indian children continue to be removed from their homes by state agencies at a disproportionately higher rate than other children.[2] This does not necessarily reflect states' disobedience to the mandates of ICWA but more likely reveals the exacting nature of the problems confronting Indian families in contemporary society. Unfortunately, there have been no statistical analyses regarding the pre-ICWA and post-ICWA removal rates of Indian children from their homes, but the present statistics on removal rates rival, in some states, the statistics cited by Congress when it enacted ICWA. Does this mean that the institutional racism cited by Congress has gone unabated or, perhaps, did Congress improperly link high removal rates with the improper actions of state courts and agencies? Most likely, the still-existent disparities between the removal rates for Indian children and other children is evidence that the problems confronting Indian families and children have become subservient to other legislative objectives of both Congress and state governments.

Whatever one's perspective is on ICWA, one has to marvel at the grand design and ambitious objective sought by its enactment. Its ultimate goal is to preserve a distinct culture by protecting the children of that culture. It is a recognition that cultural attachment is a right of Indian children worthy of congressional protection. It is the children who receive the protections of ICWA who will eventually decide the fate of Native American culture and traditions. Whether they embrace their traditions or ultimately reject them will be their decision and not the result of a system that alienates them from their culture.

Notes

1. *See, e.g.,* National Farmer's Union Insurance Co. v. Crow Tribe of Indians, 105 S.Ct. 2447 (1985); Iowa Mutual Insurance Co. v. LaPlante, 107 S.Ct. 971 (1987).

2. According to the most recent data compiled by the Administration for Children and Families, in conjunction with the BIA, about nine thousand Indian

children were in substitute care in 1986. This represents sixteen out of every one thousand Indian children, whereas in the non-Indian community only five out of every one thousand children is in substitute care. *See* INDIAN CHILD WELFARE ACT: A STATUS REPORT, FINAL REPORT OF THE SURVEY OF INDIAN CHILD WELFARE ACT AND SECTION 428 OF THE ADOPTION ASSISTANCE AND CHILD WELFARE ACT OF 1980, prepared by CSR, Inc., in Washington. D.C., and Three Feathers Associates in Norman, Oklahoma, April 18, 1988, at ES/3-1/26.

Table of Cases

A.B.M. v. M.H., 651 P.2d 1170 (Alaska 1982).
A.H. v. State, 779 P.2d 1229 (Alaska 1989).
Adoption of N.P.S., 868 P.2d 934 (Alaska 1994).
Application of Angus, 60 Or. App. 546, 655 P.2d 208 (1982), *cert denied*, 464 U.S. 830 (1989).
Application of Bertelson, 189 Mont. 524, 617 P.2d 121 (Mont. 1980).
Application of Defender, 435 N.W.2d 717 (S.D. 1989).
B.J.B.A. v. M.J.B., 620 P.2d 652 (Alaska 1980).
B.R.T. v. Executive Director of Social Services Bd., 391 N.W.2d 594 (N.D. 1986).
Barbry v. Dauzat, 576 So.2d 1013 (La. Ct. App. 3d Cir. 1991).
Becker County Welfare Dept. v. Bellcourt, 453 N.W.2d 543 (Minn. Ct. App. 1990).
Bird Head v. Tail, 209 Neb. 575, 308 N.W.2d 837 (1981).
Brown of Behalf of Brown v. Rice, 760 F.Supp. 1459 (D. Kan. 1991).
C.E.H. v. L.M.W., 837 S.W.2d 947 (Mo. App. W.D. 1992).
Catholic Social Services, Inc. v. C.A.A., 783 P.2d 1159 (Alaska 1989), *cert denied, sub nom Inlet Tribal Council v. Catholic Social Services*, 495 U.S. 948 (1990).
Chester County Department of Social Services v. Coleman, 372 S.E.2d 912 (S.C. App. 1988), *appeal after remand*, 399 S.E.2d 773 (S.C. 1990), *cert denied*, ___ U.S. ___, 111 S. Ct. 2017, 114 L.Ed.2d 103 (May 13, 1991).
Claymore v. Serr, 405 N.W.2d 650 (S.D. 1987).
Comanche Indian Tribe of Oklahoma v. Hovis, 847 F.Supp. 871 (W.D. Okla. 1994).
County of Inyo v. Jeff, 227 Cal. App. 3d 487, 227 Cal. Rptr. 841 (1991).
D.A.W. v. State, 699 P.2d 340 (Alaska 1985).
D.E.D. v. State, 704 P.2d 774 (Alaska 1985).

D.H. v. State, 723 P.2d 1274 (Alaska 1986).
D.W.H. v. Cabinet for Human Resources, 706 S.W.2d 840 (Ky. Ct. App. 1986).
Dement v. Oglala Sioux Tribal Court, 874 F.2d 510 (8th Cir. 1989).
Desjarlait v. Desjarlait, 379 N.W.2d 139 (Minn. Ct. App. 1985).
Doe v. Hughes' et al., 838 P.2d 804 (Alaska 1992).
Duncan v. Wiley, 657 P.2d 1212 (Okla. Ct. App. 1982).
E.A. v. State, 623 P.2d 1210 (Alaska 1981).
Fletcher v. Florida, et al., 858 F.Supp. 169 (M.D. Fla. 1994).
Gray v. Pann, 203 Mich. App. 461, 513 N.W.2d 154 (1994).
Harris v. Young, 473 N.W.2d 141 (S.D. 1991).
Harvick v. Harvick, 828 P.2d 769 (Alaska 1992).
Heart v. Ellenbecker, 689 F.Supp. 988 (D.S.D. 1988).
In Interest of Armell, 194 Ill. App.3d 31, 550 N.E.2d 1060 (1990), *cert denied,* ___ U.S. ___, 111 S. Ct. 345, 112 L.Ed.2d 310 (1990).
In Interest of B.B., 500 N.W.2d 9 (Iowa 1993).
In Interest of H.D., 11 Kan. App.2d 531, 729 P.2d 1234 (Kan. Ct. App. 1986).
In Interest of J.K.S., 356 N.W.2d 88 (N.D. 1984).
In Interest of J.R.H., 358 N.W.2d 311 (Iowa 1984).
In Interest of J.W., 498 N.W.2d 417 (Iowa Ct. App. 1993).
In Interest of R.L.F., 437 N.W.2d 599 (Iowa Ct. App. 1989).
In Interest of S.A.M., 703 S.W.2d 603 (Mo. Ct. App. 1986).
In Interest of S.M., 508 N.W.2d 732 (Iowa Ct. App. 1993).
In Matter of Custody of S.E.G., 521 N.W.2d 357 (Minn. 1994), *cert denied, sub nom Campell v. Leah Lake Band of Chippewa Indians,* 63 U.S.L.W. 3560 (1995).
In re Adoption of J.J., 511 Pa. 590, 515 A.2d 883 (1986).
In re Adoption of K.L.R.F., 336 Pa. Super. 555, 515 A.2d 33 (1986).
In re Adoption of Lindsay C., 229 Cal. App. 3d 404, 280 Cal. Rptr. 194 (1991).
In re Adoption of M.T.S., 489 N.W.2d 285 (Minn. Ct. App. 1992).
In re Adoption of S.S., 252 Ill. App. 3d 33, 622 N.E.2d 832 (1993).
In re Annette P., 589 A.2d 924 (Me. 1991).
In re Baby Girl A., 230 Cal. App. 3d 1611, 282 Cal. Rptr. 105 (1991).
In re Blake C., 177 Cal. App. 3d 15, 222 Cal. Rptr. 763 (1986).
In re Crystal K., 226 Cal. App. 3d 655, 276 Cal. Rptr. 619 (1990).
In re Custody of A.K.H., 502 N.W.2d 790 (Minn. Ct. App. 1993).
In re Custody of C.C.R.S., 872 P.2d 1337 (Colo. Ct. App. 1993).
In re Custody of S.B.R., 43 Wash. App. 622, 719 P.2d 154 (1986).
In re Custody of Sengstock, 165 Wis. 2d 86, 477 N.W.2d 310 (1991).
In re Dependency of Colnar, 52 Wash. App. 37, 757 P.2d 534 (1988).
In re Dependency of J.H., 117 Wash. 2d 460, 815 P.2d 1380 (1991).
In re Dependency of Roberts, 46 Wash. App. 748, 732 P.2d 528 (1987).
In re Interest of A.M., 235 Neb. 506, 455 N.W.2d 572 (1990).
In re Interest of Bird Head, 213 Neb. 741, 331 N.W.2d 785 (1983).
In re Interest of C.W., 239 Neb. 817, 479 N.W.2d 105 (1992).
In re Interest of D.S.P., 166 Wis. 2d 464, 480 N.W.2d 234 (1992).

In re Interest of J.L.M., 234 Neb. 381, 451 N.W.2d 377 (1990).
In re Interest of R.W., 509 N.W.2d 237 (Neb. 1993).
In re Jacobs, 433 Mich. 24, 444 N.W.2d 789 (1989).
In re John V., 5 Cal. App. 4th 1201, 7 Cal. Rptr.2d 629 (1992).
In re Junius M., 144 Cal. App. 3d 786, 193 Cal. Rptr. 40 (1983).
In re Kahlen W., 233 Cal. App. 3d 1414, 285 Cal. Rptr. 507 (1991).
In re L.N.W., 457 N.W.2d (Iowa Ct. App. 1990).
In re Larch, 872 F.2d 66 (4th Cir. 1989).
In re M.C.P., 153 Vt. 275, 571 A.2d 627 (1989).
In re M.E.M., 223 Mont. 234, 725 P.2d 212 (1986).
In re Marcus S., 638 A.2d 1158 (Me. 1994).
In re Riva M., 235 Cal. App. 3d 403, 286 Cal. Rptr. 592 (1991).
In re Robert T., 200 Cal. App. 3d 657, 246 Cal. Rptr. 168 (1988).
In re Smith, 46 Wash. App. 647, 731 P.2d 1149 (1987).
In re Wanomi P., 216 Cal. App. 3d 156, 264 Cal. Rptr. 623 (1989), *cert denied, sub nom Mic Mac Nation v. Giesler,* ___ U.S. ___, 111 S. Ct. 57, 112 L.Ed.2d 33 (1990).
In re Welfare of Fisher, 31 Wash. App. 550, 643 P.2d 887 (1982).
Johnson v. Frederick, 467 F.Supp. 956 (D.N.D. 1979).
Kickapoo Tribe of Oklahoma v. Rader, 822 F.2d 587 (10th Cir. 1987).
Kiowa Tribe of Oklahoma v. Lewis, 777 F.2d 587 (10th Cir. 1985), *cert denied,* 479 U.S. 872 (1986).
Lassiter v. Dept. of Social Services of Durham County, N.C., 452 U.S. 18, 101 S.Ct. 2153, 68 L.Ed.2d 640 (1981).
LeBeau v. Dakota, 815 F.Supp. 1074 (W.D. Mich. 1993).
Long v. State Dept. of Human Resources, 527 So.2d 133 (Ala. Civ. App. 1988).
Malaterre v. Malaterre, 293 N.W.2d 139 (N.D. 1980).
Matter of Adoption of Baade, 462 N.W.2d 485 (S.D. 1990).
Matter of Adoption of Baby Boy D., 742 P.2d 1059 (Okla. 1985), *cert denied, sub nom Harjo v. Duello,* 484 U.S. 1072 (1988).
Matter of Adoption of Baby Boy L., 231 Kan. 199, 643 P.2d 168 (1982).
Matter of Adoption of Baby Boy W., 831 P.2d 643 (Okla. 1992).
Matter of Adoption of Baby Child, 102 N.M. 735, 700 P.2d 198 (N.M. Ct. App. 1985).
Matter of Adoption of Baby Nancy, 27 Wash. App. 278, 616 P.2d 1263 (1980).
Matter of Adoption of Child of Indian Heritage, 111 N.J. 155, 543 A.2d 925 (1988).
Matter of Adoption of Crews, 118 Wash. 2d 561, 825 P.2d 305 (1992).
Matter of Adoption of D.M.J., 741 P.2d 1366 (Okla. 1985).
Matter of Adoption of F.H., 851 P.2d 1361 (Alaska 1993).
Matter of Adoption of Halloway, 732 P.2d 962 (Utah 1986).
Matter of Adoption of J.J.B., 117 N.M. 31, 868 P.2d 1256 (N.M. Ct. App. 1993).
Matter of Adoption of M., 66 Wash. App. 475, 832 P.2d 518 (1992).
Matter of Adoption of R.R.R., 763 P.2d 94 (Okla. 1988).
Matter of Adoption of Rebecca, 158 Misc.2d 644, 601 N.Y.S.2d 682 (N.Y. Surr. 1993).

Matter of Adoption of T.R.M., 525 N.E.2d 298 (Ind. 1988), *cert denied,* 490 U.S. 1069 (1989).
Matter of Appeal in Coconino County Juvenile Action No. J-10175, 153 Ariz. 346, 736 P.2d 829 (Ariz. Ct. App. 1987).
Matter of Appeal in Maricopa County Juvenile Action No. A-25525, 136 Ariz. 528, 667 P.2d 228 (Ariz Ct. App. 1983).
Matter of Appeal in Maricopa County Juvenile Action No. JS-7359, 159 Ariz. 232, 766 P.2d 105 (Ariz. Ct. App. 1988).
Matter of Appeal in Pima County Juvenile Action No. S-903, 130 Ariz. 202, 635 P.2d 187 (Ariz. Ct. App. 1981).
Matter of B.B., 511 So.2d 918 (Miss. 1987), *rev'd sub nom Miss. Band of Choctaw Indians v. Holyfield*, 490 U.S. 30 (1989).
Matter of B.J.E., 422 N.W.2d 597 (S.D. 1988).
Matter of B.R.B., 381 N.W.2d 283 (S.D. 1986).
Matter of Baby Boy Doe, 123 Idaho 464, 849 P.2d 925 (1993).
Matter of Baby Girl Doe, 262 Mont. 380, 865 P.2d 1090 (1993).
Matter of Begay, 107 N.M. 810, 765 P.2d 1178 (N.M. Ct. App. 1988).
Matter of Bluebird, 105 N.C. App. 42, 411 S.E.2d 820 (1992).
Matter of C.L.T., 597 P.2d 518 (Alaska 1980).
Matter of Custody of K.K.S., 508 N.W.2d 813 (Minn. Ct. App. 1993).
Matter of Custody of S.E.G., 521 N.W.2d 357 (Minn. 1994).
Matter of D.S., 577 N.E.2d 572 (Ind. 1991).
Matter of Dependency and Neglect of A.L., 442 N.W.2d 233 (S.D. 1989).
Matter of F.P., 843 P.2d 1214 (Alaska 1993).
Matter of G.L.O.C., 205 Mont. 352, 668 P.2d 235 (1983).
Matter of Guardianship of Ashley Elizabeth R., 116 N.M. 416, 863 P.2d 451 (N.M. Ct. App. 1993).
Matter of Guardianship of D.L.L., 291 N.W.2d 278 (S.D. 1980).
Matter of Guardianship of Q.G.M., 808 P.2d 684 (Okla. 1991).
Matter of Hanson, 188 Mich. App. 392, 470 N.W.2d 669 (1991).
Matter of J.B., 643 P.2d 306 (Okla. 1982).
Matter of J.L.H., 299 N.W.2d 812 (S.D. 1980).
Matter of J.L.H., 316 N.W.2d 650 (S.D. 1982).
Matter of J.M., 718 P.2d 150 (Alaska 1986).
Matter of J.R.B., 715 P.2d 1170 (Alaska 1986).
Matter of J.R.S., 690 P.2d 10 (Alaska 1984).
Matter of J.W., 742 P.2d 1171 (Okla. Ct. App. 1987).
Matter of Jason Y., 106 N.M. 406, 744 P.2d 181 (N.M. Ct. App. 1987).
Matter of Johanson, 156 Mich. App. 608, 402 N.W2d 13 (1986).
Matter of K.A.B.E., 325 N.W.2d 840 (S.D. 1982).
Matter of K.E., 744 P.2d 1173 (Alaska 1987).
Matter of K.L.N., 813 P.2d 276 (Alaska 1991).
Matter of Kiogma, 189 Mich. App. 6, 472 N.W.2d 13 (1991), *cert denied,* ___ U.S. ___, 112 S. Ct. 952, 117 L.Ed.2d 120 (1992).

Matter of Kreft, 148 Mich. App. 682, 384 N.W.2d 843 (1986).
Matter of L.A.M., 727 P.2d 1057 (Alaska 1986).
Matter of Laurie R., 107 N.M. 529, 757 P.2d 1259 (N.M. Ct. App. 1988).
Matter of M.E.M., 195 Mont. 329, 635 P.2d 1319 (1981).
Matter of M.E.M., 209 Mont. 192, 679 P.2d 1241 (1984).
Matter of M.R.D.B., 241 Mont. 455, 787 P.2d 1219 (1990).
Matter of Maricopa County Juvenile Action No. JD500200, 163 Ariz. 457, 788 P.2d 1208 (Ariz. Ct. App. 1989).
Matter of Maricopa County Juvenile Action No. JS 8287, 171 Ariz. 104, 828 P.2d 1245 (Ariz. Ct. App. Div. 1 1991).
Matter of Miller, 182 Mich. App. 70, 451 N.W.2d 576 (1990).
Matter of Morgan, 140 Mich. App. 594, 364 N.W.2d 754 (1985).
Matter of N.A.H., 418 N.W.2d 310 (S.D. 1988).
Matter of N.L., 754 P.2d 863 (Okla. 1988).
Matter of N.S., 474 N.W.2d 96 (S.D. 1991).
Matter of Oscar C., Jr., 147 Misc. 2d 761, 559 N.Y.S. 431 (N.Y. Fam. Ct. 1990).
Matter of R.M.B., 213 Mont. 29, 689 P.2d 281 (1984).
Matter of R.M.M., 316 N.W.2d 538 (Minn. Ct. App. 1982).
Matter of R.N., 303 N.W.2d 102 (S.D. 1981).
Matter of R.W., 108 N.M. 332, 772 P.2d 366 (N.M. Ct. App. 1989).
Matter of S.C., 833 P.2d 1249 (Okla. 1992).
Matter of S.D., 402 N.W.2d 346 (S.D. 1987).
Matter of S.L., 349 N.W.2d 428 (S.D. 1984).
Matter of S.Z., 325 N.W.2d 53 (S.D. 1982).
Matter of Shawboose, 175 Mich. App. 637, 438 N.W.2d 272 (1989).
Matter of T.I.S., 224 Ill. App. 3d 475, 586 N.E.2d 690 (1991).
Matter of T.J.D., 189 Mont. 147, 615 P.2d 212 (1980).
Matter of T.N.F., 781 P.2d 973 (Alaska 1989).
Matter of T.S., 245 Mont. 242, 801 P.2d 77 (1990), *cert denied, sub nom King Island Nations Community v. Montana Dept. of Soc. Serv.*, ___ U.S. ___, 111 S. Ct. 2013, 114 L.Ed.2d 100 (1991).
Matter of Termination of Parental Rights of T.O., 759 P.2d 1308 (Alaska 1988).
Matter of W.E.G., 710 P.2d 410 (Alaska 1985).
Matter of W.L., 260 Mont. 325, 859 P.2d 1019 (1993).
Matter of Wayne R.N., 107 N.M. 341, 757 P.2d 1333 (N.M. Ct. App. 1988).
Matter of Welfare of B.W., 454 N.W.2d 437 (Minn. Ct. App. 1990).
Matter of Welfare of Chosa, 290 N.W.2d 766 (Minn. 1980).
Matter of Welfare of D.L., 486 N.W.2d 375 (Minn. 1992).
Matter of Welfare of J.A.S., 488 N.W.2d 332 (Minn. Ct. App. 1992).
Matter of Welfare of M.S.S., 465 N.W.2d 212 (Minn. Ct. App. 1991).
Matter of Welfare of R.I., 402 N.W.2d 173 (Minn. Ct. App. 1987).
Matter of Welfare of T.J.J., 366 N.W.2d 651 (Minn. Ct. App. 1985).
Matter of Welfare of W.R., 379 N.W.2d 544 (Minn. Ct. App. 1985).

Mississippi Band of Choctaw Indians v. Holyfield, 490 U.S. 30, 109 S.Ct. 1597, 104 L.Ed.2d 29 (1989).
Native Village of Nenana v. State Dept of Health and Human Services, 722 P.2d 219 (Alaska 1986), *cert denied*, 479 U.S. 1008 (1986).
Native Village of Noatak v. Hoffman, 896 F.2d 1157 (9th Cir. 1990).
Native Village of Stevens v. Smith, 770 F.2d 1486 (9th Cir. 1985), *cert denied*, 475 U.S. 1121 (1986).
Native Village of Venetie I.R.A. Council v. State of Alaska, 944 F.2d 548 (9th Cir. 1991).
Native Village of Venetie I.R.A. Council v. State of Alaska, 918 F.2d 797 (9th Cir. 1990).
Navajo Nation v. District Court for Utah County, Fourth Judicial District, 831 F.2d 929 (9th Cir. 1987).
Navajo Nation v. Hodel, 645 F. Supp. 825 (D. Ariz. 1986).
New York City Dept. of Social Services on Behalf of Oscar C., Jr. v. Oscar C., 192 A.D.2d 280, 600 N.Y.S.2d 957 (1993).
People, Dept. of Social Services in Interest of A.E.V., 782 P.2d 858 (Colo. Ct. App. 1989).
People ex rel. South Dakota Dept. of Social Services in interest of C.H., 510 N.W.2d 119 (S.D. 1993).
People in Interest of A.E., 749 P.2d 450 (Colo. Ct. App. 1987).
People in Interest of A.R.P., 519 N.W.2d 56 (S.D. 1994).
People In Interest of C.A.J., 709 P.2d 604 (Colo. Ct. App. 1985).
People in Interest of C.R.M., 307 N.W.2d 131 (S.D. 1981).
People in Interest of E.M., 466 N.W.2d 168 (S.D. 1991).
People in Interest of J.J., 454 N.W.2d 317 (S.D. 1990).
People in Interest of J.L.G., 687 P.2d 477 (Colo. Ct. App. 1984).
People In Interest of J.L.P., 870 P.2d 1252 (Colo. Ct. App. 1994).
People in Interest of M.C., 504 N.W.2d 598 (S.D. 1993).
People in Interest of P.B., 371 N.W.2d 366 (S.D. 1985).
People In Interest of S.R., 323 N.W.2d 885 (S.D. 1982).
Quinn v. Walters, 117 Or. App. 579, 845 P.2d 206 (1993), *rev'd*, 881 P2d. 795 (Or. 1994).
Roman Nose v. New Mexico Dept of Human Resources, 967 F.2d 435 (9th Cir. 1992).
S.A. v. E.J.P., 571 So.2d 1187 (Ala. Civ. App. 1990).
Sandman v. Dakota, 816 F.Supp. 448 (W.D. Mich. 1992).
Santosky v. Kramer, 455 U.S. 745, 102 S.Ct. 1388, 71 L.Ed.2d 599 (1982).
State ex rel. Children's Services Div. v. Campbell, 122 Or. App. 371, 857 P.2d 888 (1993).
State ex rel. Children's Services Div. v. Graves, 118 Or. App. 488, 848 P.2d 133 (1993).
State ex rel. Juvenile Dept. of Clackamas County v. Charles, 106 Or. App. 637, 810 P.2d 393 (1991).
State ex rel. Juvenile Dept. of Lane County v. Shuey, 119 Or. App. 185, 850 P.2d 378 (1993).

State ex rel. Juvenile Dept. of Lane County v. Tucker, 76 Or. App. 673, 710 P.2d 793 (1985).

State ex rel. Juvenile Dept. of Multnomah County v. Charles, 299 Or. 341, 701 P.2d 1052 (1985).

State ex rel. Juvenile Dept. of Multnomah County v. Cooke, 88 Or. App. 176, 744 P.2d 596 (1987).

State ex rel. Juvenile Dept. Multnomah County v. England, 292 Or. 545, 640 P.2d 608 (1982).

State ex rel. Juvenile Dept. of Multnomah County v. Woodruff, 108 Or. App. 352, 816 P.2d 623 (1991).

State ex rel. May v. Seneca-Cayuga Tribe of Oklahoma, 711 P.2d 77 (Okla. 1985).

State In Interest of T.D.C., 748 P.2d 201 (Utah 1988).

U.S. v. Jim, 409 U.S. 80 (1972).

Ute Indian Tribe v. State of Utah, 521 F.Supp. 1072 (D.Utah 1981).

Selected Bibliography

Allbaugh, Diane, *Tribal Jurisdiction over Indian Children:* Mississippi Band of Choctaw Indians v. Holyfield, 16 AM. INDIAN L. REV. 533 (1991).

Atwood, Barbara Ann, *Fighting over Indian Children: The Uses and Abuses of Jurisdictional Ambiguity,* 36 UCLA L. REV. 1051 (Aug. 1989).

Barsh, *The Indian Child Welfare Act of 1978: A Critical Analysis,* 31 HASTINGS L.J. 1287 (1980).

Bartholet, Elizabeth, *Where Do Black Children Belong? The Politics of Race Matching in Adoption,* 139 U. PA. L. REV. 1163 (May 1991).

Bennett, Michelle K., *Native American Children: Caught in the Web of the Indian Child Welfare Act,* 16 HAMLINE L. REV. 953 (Spring 1993).

Berlin, I. N., *Anglo Adoptions of Native Americans: Repercussions in Adolescence,* Vol. 17(2), AMERICAN ACADEMY OF CHILD PSYCHIATRY 387-388 (1978).

______, *Suicide among American Indian Adolescents: An Overview,* 17(3) SUICIDE AND LIFE THREATENING BEHAVIOR 218-232 (1987).

Biggs, Gretchen G., *Is There Indian Country in Alaska? Forty-Four Million Acres in Legal Limbo,* 64 U. COLO. L. REV. 849 (1993).

Brandton, Fredric, *Tradition and Judicial Review in the American Indian Tribal Court System,* 38 UCLA L. REV. 991 (April 1991).

Bryde, John F., *Modern Indian Psychology,* Institute of Indian Studies, University of South Dakota (1971).

Caduto, Michael J., and Joseph Bruchac, *Keepers of the Animals: Native American Stories and Wildlife Activities for Children,* Fulcrum Publishing (1991).

Campbell, Sen. Ben Nighthorse, *Introduction,* in Indian Law Symposium, 24 N.M. L. REV. 171 (Spring 1994).

Clinton, Robert N., *Redressing the Legacy of Conquest: A Vision Quest for a Decolonized Federal Indian Law,* 46 ARK. L. REV. 77 (1993).

______, *The Rights of Indigenous Peoples as Collective Group Rights,* 32 ARIZ. L. REV. 739 (1990).

______, *Tribal Courts and the Federal Union,* 26 WILLAMETTE L. REV. 841 (Fall 1990).

Cohen, Felix S., *Handbook of Federal Indian Law,* 1982 Edition, Michie Bobbs-Merrill.

Connelly, Michael E., *Tribal Jurisdiction under Section 1911(b) of the Indian Child Welfare Act of 1978: Are the States Respecting Indian Sovereignty?,* 23 N.M. L. REV. 479 (Spring 1993).

Dale, Michael J., *State Court Jurisdiction under the Indian Child Welfare Act and the Unstated Best Interest of the Child Test,* 27 GONZ. L. REV. 353 (1991/92).

Davis, Toni Hahn, *The Existing Indian Family Exception to the Indian Child Welfare Act,* 69 N.D. L. REV. 465 (1993).

Deloria, Ella Cara, *Waterlilly,* University of Nebraska Press (1990).

DEPARTMENT OF HEALTH AND HUMAN SERVICES, OFFICE OF INSPECTOR GENERAL, SPECIAL REPORT, OPPORTUNITIES FOR ACF TO IMPROVE CHILD WELFARE SERVICES AND PROTECTIONS FOR NATIVE AMERICAN CHILDREN (August 1994).

Desmond, Brenda C., *Montana Tribal Courts: Influencing the Development of Contemporary Indian Law,* 52 MONT. L. REV. 211 (Summer 1991).

Di Pietro, Susanne, *Tribal Court Jurisdiction and Public Law 280: What Role for Tribal Courts in Alaska?,* 10 ALASKA L. REV. 335 (December 1993).

Dorsay, Craig J., *The Indian Child Welfare Act and Laws Affecting Indian Juveniles,* Indian Law Support Center, Native American Rights Fund (1984).

Dorsay, Craig J., Steven C. Moore and Thomas J. Van Norman, *1992 Update to the Indian Child Welfare Act and Laws Affecting Indian Juveniles Manual,* Indian Law Support Center (1992).

Dussias, Allison M., *Geographically Based and Membership-Based Views of Indian Tribal Sovereignty: The Supreme Court's Changing Vision,* 55 U. PITT. L. REV. 1 (Fall 1993).

Eubanks, JoBeth, *Transracial Adoption in Texas: Should the Best Interests Standard Be Color-Blind?,* 24 ST. MARY'S L.J. 1225 (1993).

Executive Summary of the Preliminary Report of the Ninth Circuit Task Force on Gender Bias, 45 STAN. L. REV. 2153 (July 1993).

Fallek, Susan B., *In the Child's Best Interests: Termination of Parental Rights in Minnesota: In re* J.J.B., 390 N.W.2d 274, 10 HAMLINE L. REV. 693 (Fall 1987).

Fenton, Zanita E., *In a World Not Their Own: The Adoption of Black Children,* 10 HARV. BLACKLETTER J. 39 (Spring 1993).

Forde-Mazrui, Kim, *Black Identity and Child Placement: The Best Interests of Black and Biracial Children,* 92 MICH. L. REV. 925 (February 1994).

Frickey, Phillip P., *Congressional Intent, Practical Reasoning, and the Dynamic Nature of Federal Indian Law,* 78 CAL. L. REV. 1137 (October 1990).

Gillingham, John W., Pathfinder: *Tribal, Federal, and State Court Subject Matter Jurisdictional Bounds: Suits Involving Native American Interests,* 18 AM. INDIAN L. REV. 73 (1993).

Glynn, Timothy P., *The Role of Race in Adoption Proceedings: A Constitutional Critique of the Minnesota Preference Statute,* 77 MINN. L. REV. 925 (April 1993).

Goldsmith, Donna J., *Individual vs. Collective Rights: Indian Child Welfare Act,* 13 HARV. WOMEN'S L. J. 1 (Spring 1990).

______, *"There Is Only One Child, and Her Name Is Children,"* 36 FED. B. NEWS & J. 446 (November 1989).

Goldstein, Joseph, Anna Freud and Albert J. Solnit, *Beyond the Best Interests of the Child,* New York Free Press. (1973).

Gover, Stetson, and P.C. Williams, *Tribal-State Dispute Resolution: Recent Attempts,* 36 S.D. L. REV. 277 (1991).

Hansen, Sandra, *Survey of Civil Jurisdiction in Indian Country,* 16 AM. INDIAN L. REV. 319 (1991).

Howard, Margaret, *Transracial Adoption: Analysis of the Best Interests Standard,* 59 NOTRE DAME L. REV. 503 (1984).

Indermark, Kristen Jones, *Permissive Intervention—Grandparents' Key to Entering Adoption Proceedings,* 26 GA. L. REV. 787 (Spring 1992).

Jannetta, James M., *Reciprocity between State and Tribal Legal Systems,* 71 MICH. B. J. 400 (May 1992).

Jones, B.J., *Tribal Considerations in Comity and Full Faith and Credit Issues,* 68 N.D. L. REV. 689 (1992).

Juvenile and Family Law, 16 HAMLINE L. REV. 624 (Spring 1993).

Kerbeshian, Lynn A., *Indians—Domicile: Federal Definition of Domicile Determines Jurisdiction under Indian Child Welfare Act,* 66 N.D. L. REV. 553 (1990).

Kim, Ester C., Mississippi Band of Choctaw Indians v. Holyfield: *The Contemplation of All, The Best Interests of None,* 43 RUTGERS L. REV. 761 (Spring 1991).

Koch, Rebecca L., *Transracial Adoption in Light of the Foster Care Crisis: A Horse of a Different Color,* 10 N.Y.L. SCH. J. HUM. RTS. 147 (Fall 1992).

Kunesh-Hartman, Patrice, *The Indian Child Welfare Act of 1978: Protecting Essential Tribal Interests,* 60 U. COLO. L. REV. 131 (1989).

Lehmann, Michelle L., The Indian Child Welfare Act of 1978: *Does It Apply to the Adoption of an Illegitimate Indian Child?,* 38 CATH. U. L. REV. 511 (Winter 1989).

Lewis, Wendy, *The Role of Domicile in Adopting Indian Children:* Mississippi Band of Choctaw Indians v. Holyfield, 1990 UTAH L. REV. 899 (1990).

Mahoney, Joan, *The Black Baby Doll: Transracial Adoption and Cultural Preservation,* 59 UMKC L. REV. 487 (Spring 1991).

Mails, Thomas, *Fools Crow: Wisdom and Power,* Council Oak Books (1991).

McCartney, Richard, *The American Indian Child Welfare Crisis: Cultural Genocide or First Amendment Preservation?,* 7 COLUM. HUM. RTS. L. REV. 529 (1975).

McLish, Thomas P., *Tribal Sovereign Immunity: Searching for Sensible Limits,* 88 COLUM. L. REV. 173 (January 1988).

McShane, D., *An Analysis of Mental Health Research with American Indian Youth,* 11(2) JOURNAL OF ADOLESCENCE, 87–116 (1988).

O'Brien, Sharon, *Tribes and Indians: With Whom Does the United States Maintain a Relationship?,* 66 NOTRE DAME L. REV. 1461 (1991).

Paquin, Michelle Therese, *A Minnesota Lawyer's Guide to the Indian Child Welfare Act,* 10 LAW & INEQ. 311 (June 1992).

Pearce, Elizabeth A., *Self-Determination for Native Americans: Land Rights and the Utility of Domestic and International Law,* 22 COLUM. HUM. RTS. L. REV. 361 (Spring 1991).

Perry, Twila L., *Race and Child Placement: The Best Interests Test and the Cost of Discretion,* 29 J. FAM. L. 51 (1990/1991).

Pommersheim, Frank R., *The Crucible of Sovereignty: Analyzing Issues of Tribal Jurisdiction,* 31 ARIZ. L. REV. 329 (April 1989).

______, *The Reservation as Place: A South Dakota Essay,* 34 S.D. L. REV. 246 (1989).

Ragsdale, John W., Jr., *Indian Reservations and the Preservation of Tribal Culture: Beyond Wardship to Stewardship,* 59 UMKC L. REV. 503 (Spring 1991).

Renner, John Robert, *The Indian Child Welfare Act and Equal Protection Limitations on the Federal Power over Indian Affairs,* 17 AM. INDIAN. L. REV. 129 (1992).

Rethinking the Trust Doctrine in Federal Indian Law, 98 HARV. L. REV. 422 (December 1984).

Schnuelle, Kim Laree, *When the Bough Breaks: Federal and Washington State Indian Child Welfare Law and Its Applications,* 17 U. PUGET SOUND L. REV. 101 (Fall 1993).

Schwartz, Laura J., *Religious Matching for Adoption: Unraveling the Interests behind the "Best Interests" Standard,* 25 FAM. L. Q. 171 (Summer 1991).

Silva, Darla M., *Family Law,* 21 N.M. L. REV. 677 (Summer 1991).

Skibine, Alex Tallchief, *Applicability of Federal Laws—General Application to Indian Tribes and Reservation Indians,* 25 U. C. DAVIS L. REV. 85 (Fall 1991).

______, *Deference Owed Tribal Court's Jurisdictional Determinations: Towards Co-existence, Understanding, and Respect between Different Cultural and Judicial Norms,* 24 N.M. L. REV. 191 (Spring 1994).

Slider, Patti, *Indian Tribal Law,* 63 J. KAN. B.A. 20 (May 1994).

Streissgurth, A., *A Manual on Adolescents and Adults with Fetal Alcohol Syndrome with Special Reference to American Indians,* Washington, D.C.,

Indian Health Services publication (1988).

Strickland, Rennard, *Indian Law and the Miner's Canary: The Signs of Poison Gas,* 39 CLEV. ST. L. REV. 483 (1991).

Taylor, Richard B., *Curbing the Erosion of the Rights of Native Americans: Was the Supreme Court Successful* in Mississippi Band of Choctaw Indians v. Holyfield?, 29 J. FAM. L. 171 (1990/1991).

Tellinghuisen, Roger A., *The Indian Child Welfare Act of 1978: A Practical Guide with (Limited) Commentary,* 34 S.D. L. REV. 660 (1988/1989).

Thompson, Edward L., *Protecting Abused Children: A Judge's Perspective on Public Law Deprived Child Proceedings and the Impact of the Indian Child Welfare Acts,* 15 AM. INDIAN L. REV. 1 (1990).

Ujke, David M., *Tribal Court Jurisdiction in Domestic Relations Matters Involving Indian Children: Not Just a Matter of Comity,* 66 WIS. LAW REV. 10 (August 1993).

Uthe, Lynn Klicker, *The Best Interests of Indian Children in Minnesota,* 17 AM. INDIAN L. REV. 237 (1992).

Utley, Robert M., *The Lance and the Shield: The Life and Times of Sitting Bull,* Henry Holt and Company (1993).

Valencia-Weber, Gloria, *Tribal Courts: Custom and Innovative Law,* 24 N.M. L. REV. 225 (Spring 1994).

Voss, Ivy N., *In the Best Interest: The Adoption of F. H., An Indian Child,* 8 BYU J. PUB. L. 151 (January 1993).

Wagman, Bruce A., *Advancing Tribal Sovereign Immunity as a Pathway to Power,* 27 U.S.F. L. REV. 419 (Winter 1993).

Wald, Patricia M., *"One Nation Indivisible with Liberty and Justice for All": Lessons from the American Experience for New Democracies,* 59 FORDHAM L. REV. 283 (November 1990).

Watts, Stan, *Voluntary Adoptions under the Indian Child Welfare Act of 1978: Balancing the Interests of Children, Families, and Tribes,* 63 S. CAL. L. REV. 213 (November 1989).

Westermeyer, J., *The Apple Syndrome in Minnesota: A Complication of Racial-Ethnic Discontinuity,* 10(2) JOURNAL OF OPERATIONAL PSYCHIATRY 134–140 (1979).

Williams, David, *Legitimation and Statutory Interpretation: Conquest, Consent, and Community in Federal Indian Law,* 80 VA. L. REV. 403 (March 1994).

Williams, Robert A., *Encounters on the Frontiers of International Human Rights Law: Redefining the Terms of Indigenous Peoples' Survival in the World,* 1990 DUKE L. J. 660 (September 1990).

Wright, Gorden K., *Recognition of Tribal Decisions in State Courts,* 37 STAN. L. REV. 1397 (May 1985).

Yarbrough, Marlon N., *Trans-Racial Adoption: The Genesis or Genocide of Minority Cultural Existence,* 15 S.U. L. REV. 353 (Fall 1988).

APPENDIX • A

Part III
Department of the Interior
Bureau of Indian Affairs
Guidelines for State Courts; Indian Child Custody Proceedings

This notice is published in exercise of authority delegated by the Secretary of the Interior to the Assistant Secretary —Indian Affairs by 209 DM 8.

There was published in the Federal Register, Vol. 44, No. 79/Monday, April 23, 1979 a notice entitled Recommended Guidelines for State Courts—Indian Child Custody Proceedings. This notice pertained directly to implementation of the Indian Child Welfare Act of 1978, Pub. L. 95-608. 92 Stat. 3069, 25 U.S.C. 1901 *et seq.* A subsequent Federal Register notice which invited public comment concerning the above was published on June 5, 1979. As a result of comments received, the recommended guidelines were revised and are provided below in final form.

Introduction

Although the rulemaking procedures of the Administrative Procedures Act have been followed in developing these guidelines, they are not published as regulations because they are not intended to have binding legislative effect. Many of these guidelines represent the interpretation of the Interior Department of certain provisions of the Act. Other guidelines provide procedures which, if followed, will help assure that rights guaranteed by the Act are protected when state courts decide Indian child custody matters. To the extent that the Department's interpretations of the Act are correct, contrary interpretations by the courts would be violations of the Act. If procedures different from those recommended in these guidelines are adopted by a state, their adequacy to protect rights guaranteed by the Act will have to be judged on their own.

Where Congress expressly delegates to the Secretary the primary responsibility for interpreting a statutory term, regulations interpreting that term have legislative effect. Courts are not free to set aside those regulations simply because they would have interpreted that statute in a different manner. Where, however, primary responsibility for interpreting a statutory term rests with the courts, administrative interpretations of statutory terms are given important but not controlling significance. Batterton v. Francis, 432 US. 416. 424-425 (1977).

In other words, when the Department writes rules needed to carry out responsibilities Congress has explicitly imposed on the Department, those rules are binding. A violation of those rules is a violation of the law. When, however, the Department writes rules or guidelines advising some other agency how it should carry out responsibilities explicitly assigned to it by Congress, those rules or guidelines are not, by themselves, binding. Courts will take what this Department has to say into account in such instances, but they are free to act contrary to what the Department has said if they are convinced that the Department's guidelines are not required by the statute itself.

Portions of the Indian Child Welfare Act do expressly delegate to the Secretary of the Interior responsibility for interpreting statutory language. For example, under 25 U.S.C. 1918, the Secretary is directed to determine whether a plan for reassumption of jurisdiction is "feasible" as that term is used in the statute. This and other areas where primary responsibility for implementing portions of the Act rest with this Department, are covered in regulations promulgated on July 31, 1979, at 44 FR 45092.

Primary responsibility for interpreting other language used in the Act, however, rests with the courts that decide Indian child custody cases. For example, the legislative history of the Act states explicitly that the use of the term "good cause" was designed to provide state courts with flexibility in determining the disposition of a placement proceeding involving an Indian child. S. Rep. No. 95-597, 95th Cong., 1st Sess. 17 (1977). The Department's interpretation of statutory language of this type is published in these guidelines.

Some commenters asserted that Congressional delegation to this Department of authority to promulgate regulations with binding legislative effect with respect to all provisions of the Act is found at 25 U.S.C. 1952, which states, "Within one hundred and eighty days after November 8, 1978, the Secretary shall promulgate such rules and regulations as may be necessary to carry out the provisions of this chapter." Promulgation of regulations with legislative effect with respect to most of the responsibilities of state or tribal courts under the Act, however, is not necessary to carry out the Act. State and tribal courts are fully capable of carrying out the responsibility imposed on them by Congress without being under the direct supervision of this Department.

Nothing in the legislative history indicates that Congress intended this Department to exercise supervisory control over state or tribal courts or to legislate for them with respect to Indian child custody matters. For Congress to assign to an administrative agency such supervisory control over courts would be an extraordinary step.

Nothing in the language or legislative history of 25 U.S.C. 1952 compels the conclusion that Congress intended to vest this Department with such extraordinary power. Both the language and the legislative history indicate that the purpose of that section was simply to assure that the Department moved promptly to promulgate regulations to carry out the responsibilities Congress had assigned it under the Act.

Assignment of supervisory authority over the courts to an administrative agency is a measure so at odds with concepts of both federalism and separation of powers that it should not be imputed to Congress in the absence of an express declaration of Congressional intent to that affect.

Some commenters also recommended that the guidelines be published as regulations and that the decision of whether the law permits such regulations to be binding be left to the court. That approach has not been adopted because the Department has an obligation not to assert authority that it concludes it does not have.

Each section of the revised guidelines is accompanied by commentary explaining why the Department believes states should adopt that section and to provide some guidance where the guidelines themselves may need to be interpreted in the light of specific circumstances.

The original guidelines used the word "should" instead of "shall" in most provisions. The term "should" was used to communicate the fact that the guidelines were the Department's interpretations of the Act and were not intended to have binding legislative effect. Many commenters, however, interpreted that use of "should" as an attempt by this Department to make statutory requirements themselves optional. That was not the intent. If a state adopts those guidelines, they should be stated in mandatory terms. For that reason the word "shall" has replaced "should" in the revised guidelines. The status of these guidelines as interpretative rather than legislative in nature is adequately set out in the introduction.

In some instances a state may wish to establish rules that provide even greater protection for rights guaranteed by the Act than those suggested by these guidelines. These guidelines are not intended to discourage such action. Care should be taken, however, that the provision of additional protections to some parties to a child custody proceeding does not deprive other parties of rights guaranteed to them by the Act.

In some instances the guidelines do little more than restate the statutory language. This is done in order to make the guidelines more complete so that they can be followed without the need to refer to the statute in every instance. Omission of any statutory language, of course, does not in any way affect the applicability of the statute.

A number of commenters recommended that special definitions of residence and domicile be included in the guidelines. Such definitions were not included because these terms are well defined under existing state law. There is no indication that these state law definitions tend to undermine in any way the purposes of the Act. Recommending special definitions for the purpose of this Act alone would simply provide unnecessary complications in the law.

A number of commenters recommended that the guidelines include recommendations for tribal-state agreements under 25 U.S.C. 1919. A number of other commenters, however, criticized the one provision in the original guidelines addressing that subject as tending to impose on such agreements restrictions that Congress did not intend should be imposed. Because of the wide variation in the situations and attitudes of states and tribes, it is difficult to deal with that issue in the context of guidelines. The Department is currently developing materials to aid states and tribes with such agreements. The Department hopes to have those materials available later this year. For these reasons, the provision in the original guidelines concerning tribal-state agreements has been deleted from the guidelines.

The Department has also received many requests for assistance from tribal courts in carrying out the new responsibilities resulting from the passage of this Act. The Department intends to provide additional guidance and assistance in that area also in the future. Providing guidance to state courts was given a higher priority because the Act imposes many more procedures on state courts than it does on tribal courts.

Many commenters have urged the Department to discuss the effect of the Act on the financial responsibilities of states and tribes to provide services to Indian children. Many such services are funded in large part by the Department of Health, Education, and Welfare. The policies and regulations of that Department will have a significant impact on the issue of financial responsibility. Officials of Interior and HEW will be discussing this issue with each other. It is anticipated that more detailed guidance on questions of financial responsibility will be provided as a result of those consultations.

One commenter recommended that the Department establish a monitoring procedure to exercise its right under 25 U.S.C. 1915(e) to review state court placement records. HEW currently reviews state placement records on a systematic basis as part of its responsibilities with respect to statutes it administers. Interior Department officials are discussing with HEW officials the establishment of a procedure for collecting data to review compliance with the Indian Child Welfare Act.

Inquiries concerning these recommended guidelines may be directed to the nearest of the following regional and field offices of the Solicitor for the Interior Department:

Office of the Regional Solicitor, Department of the Interior, 510 L Street, Suite 408, Anchorage, Alaska 99501, (907) 265-5301.

Office of the Regional Solicitor, Department of the Interior, Richard B. Russell Federal Building, 75 Spring St. SW., Suite 1328, Atlanta, Georgia 30303, (404) 221-4447.

Office of the Regional Solicitor, Department of the Interior, c/o U.S. Fish & Wildlife Service, Suite 306, 1 Gateway Center. Newton Corner, Massachusetts 02158, (617) 829-9258.

Office of the Field Solicitor, Department of the Interior, 686 Federal Building, Fort Snelling, Twin Cities, Minnesota 55111, (612) 725-3540.

Office of the Regional Solicitor, Department of the Interior, P.O. Box 25007, Denver Federal Center, Denver, Colorado 80225, (303) 234-3175.

Office of the Field Solicitor, Department of the Interior, P.O. Box 549, Aberdeen, South Dakota 57401, (605) 225-7254.

Office of the Field Solicitor, Department of the Interior, P. O. Box 1538, Billings, Montana 59103 (406) 245-6711.

Office of the Regional Solicitor, Department of the Interior, Room E-2753, 2800 Cottage Way, Sacramento, California 95825, (916) 484-4331.

Office of the Field Solicitor, Department of the Interior, Valley Bank Center, Suite 280, 201 North Central Avenue, Phoenix, Arizona 85073, (602) 261-4756.

Office of the Field Solicitor, Department of the Interior, 3610 Central Avenue, Suite 104, Riverside, California 92506, (714) 787-1560.

Office of the Field Solicitor, Department of the Interior, Window Rock, Arizona 86515, (602) 871-5151.

Office of the Regional Solicitor, Department of the Interior, Room 3068, Page Belcher Federal Building, Tulsa, Oklahoma 74103, (918) 581-7501.

Office of the Field Solicitor, Department of the Interior, Room 7102, Federal Building & Courthouse, 500 Gold Avenue, S.W., Albuquerque, New Mexico 87101, (505) 766-2547.

Office of the Field Solicitor, Department of the Interior, P.O. Box 397, W.C.D. Office Building, Route 1, Anadarko, Oklahoma 73005, (405) 247-6673.

Office of the Field Solicitor, Department of the Interior, P.O. Box 1508, Room 319, Federal Building, 5th and Broadway, Muskogee, Oklahoma 74401, (918) 683-3111.

Office of the Field Solicitor, Department of the Interior, c/o Osage Agency, Grandview Avenue, Pawhuska, Oklahoma 74058, (918) 287-2431.

Office of the Regional Solicitor, Department of the Interior, Suite 6201, Federal Building, 125 South State Street, Salt Lake City, Utah 84138, (801) 524-5877.

Office of the Regional Solicitor, Department of the Interior, Lloyd 500 Building, Suite 607, 500 N.E. Multnomab Street, Portland, Oregon 97232, (503) 231-2125.

Guidelines for State Courts

A. Policy
B. Pre-trial requirements
   1. Determination that child is an Indian
   2. Determination of Indian child's tribe
   3. Determination that placement is covered by the Act
   4. Determination of jurisdiction
   5. Notice requirements
   6. Time limits and extensions
   7. Emergency removal of an Indian child
   8. Improper removal from custody
C. Requests for transfer to tribal court
   1. Petitions under 25 U.S.C. § 1911(b) for transfer of proceed ing
   2. Criteria and procedures for ruling on 25 U.S.C. § 1911(b) transfer petitions
   3. Determination of good cause to the contrary
   4. Tribal court declination of transfer
D. Adjudication of involuntary placements, adoption or termination's of parental rights
   1. Access to reports
   2. Efforts to alleviate need to remove child from parents or Indian custodians
   3. Standards of evidence
   4. Qualified expert witnesses
E. Voluntary proceedings
   1. Execution of consent

2. Content of consent document
3. Withdrawal of consent to placement
4. Withdrawal of consent to adoption

F. Dispositions
1. Adoptive placements
2. Foster care or pre-adoptive placements
3. Good cause to modify preferences

G. Post-trial rights
1. Petition to vacate adoption
2. Adult adoptee rights
3. Notice of change in child's status
4. Maintenance of records

A. Policy

(1) Congress through the Indian Child Welfare Act has expressed its clear preference for keeping Indian children with their families, deferring to tribal judgment on matters concerning the custody of tribal children, and placing Indian children who must be removed from their homes within their own families or Indian tribes. Proceedings in state courts involving the custody of Indian children shall follow strict procedures and meet stringent requirements to justify any results in an individual case contrary to these preferences. The Indian Child Welfare Act, the federal regulations implementing the Act, the recommended guidelines and any state statutes, regulations or rules promulgated to implement the Act shall be liberally construed in favor of a result that is consistent with these preferences. Any ambiguities in any of such statutes, regulations, rules or guidelines shall be resolved in favor of the result that is most consistent with these preferences.

(2) In any child custody proceeding where applicable state or other federal law provides a higher standard of protection to the rights of the parent or Indian custodian than the protection accorded under the Indian Child Welfare Act, the state court shall apply the state or other federal law, provided that application of that law does not infringe any right accorded by the Indian Child Welfare Act to an Indian tribe or child.

A. *Commentary*

The purpose of this section is to apply to the Indian Child Welfare Act the canon of construction that remedial statutes are to be liberally construed to achieve their purpose. The three major purposes are derived from a reading to the Act itself. In order to fully implement the Congressional intent the rule shall be applied to all implementing rules and state legislation as well.

Subsection A. (2) applies to canon of statutory construction that specific language shall be given precedence over general language. Congress has given certain specific rights to tribes and Indian children. For example, the tribe has a right to intervene in involuntary custody proceedings. The child has a right to learn of tribal affiliation upon becoming 18 years old. Congress did not intend 25 U.S.C. 1921 to have the effect of eliminating those rights where a court concludes they are in derogation of a parental right provided under a state statute. Congress intended for this section to apply primarily in those instances where a state provides greater protection for a right accorded to parents under the Act. Examples of this include State laws which: impose a higher burden of proof than the Act for removing a child from a home, give the parents more time to prepare after receiving notice, require more effective notice, impose stricter emergency removal procedure requirements on these removing a child, give parents greater access to documents, or contain additional safeguard to assure the voluntariness of consent.

B. Pretrial requirements

B.1. Determination That Child Is an Indian

(a) When a state court has reason to believe a child involved in a child custody proceeding is an Indian, the court shall seek verification of the child's status from either the Bureau of Indian Affairs or the child's tribe. In a voluntary placement proceeding where a consenting parent evidences a desire for anonymity, the court shall make its inquiry in a manner that will not cause the parent's identity to become publicly known.

(b) (i) The determination by the tribe that a child is not a member of that tribe, is or is not eligible for membership in that tribe, or that the biological parent is or is not a member of that tribe is conclusive.

(ii) Absent a contrary determination by the tribe that is alleged to be the Indian child's tribe, a determination by the Bureau of Indian Affairs that a child is or is not an Indian child is conclusive.

(c) Circumstances under which a state court has reason to believe a child involved in a child custody proceeding is an Indian include but are not limited to the following:

(i) Any party to the case, Indian tribe, Indian organization or public or private agency informs the court that the child is an Indian child.

(ii) Any public or state-licensed agency involved in child protection services or family support has discovered information which suggests that the child is an Indian child.

(iii) The child who is the subject of the proceeding gives the court reason to believe he or she is an Indian child.

(iv) The residence or the domicile of the child, his or her biological parents, or the Indian custodian is known by the court to be or is shown to be a predominantly Indian community.

(v) An officer of the court involved in the proceeding has knowledge that the child may be an Indian child.

B.1. Commentary

This guideline makes clear that the best source of information on whether a particular child is Indian is the tribe itself. It is the tribe's perogative to determine membership criteria and to decide who meets those criteria. Cohen, Handbook of Federal Indian Law 133 (1942). Because of the Bureau of Indian Affairs' long experience in determining who is an Indian for a variety of purposes, its determinations are also entitled to great deference. See, e.g., United States v. Sandoval, 231, U.S. 28, 27 (1913).

Although tribal verification is preferred, a court may want to seek verification from the BIA in those voluntary placement cases where the parent has requested anonymity and the tribe does not have a system for keeping child custody matters confidential.

Under the Act confidentially is given a much higher priority in voluntary proceedings than in involuntary ones. The Act mandates a tribal right of notice and intervention in involuntary proceedings but not in voluntary ones. Cf. 25 U.S.C. § 1912 with 25 U.S.C. § 1913. For voluntary placements, however, the Act specifically directs state courts to respect parental requests for confidentiality. 25 U.S.C. § 1915(c) The most common voluntary placement involves a newborn infant. Confidentiality has traditionally been a high priority in such placements. The Act reflects that traditional approach by requiring deference to request for anonymity in voluntary placements but not in involuntary ones. This guideline specifically provides that anonymity not be compromised in seeking verification of Indian status. If anonymity were compromised at that point, the statutory requirement that requests for anonymity be respected in applying the preferences would be meaningless.

Enrollment is not always required in order to be a member of a tribe. Some tribes do not have written rolls. Others have rolls that list only persons that were members as of a certain date. Enrollment is the common evidentiary means of establishing Indian status, but it is not the only means nor is it necessarily determinative. United States v. Broncheau, 597 F. 2nd 1260, 1263 (9th Cir. 1979).

The guidelines also list several circumstances which shall trigger an inquiry by the court and petitioners to determine whether a child is an Indian for purposes of this Act. This listing is not intended to be complete, but it does list the most common circumstances giving rise to a reasonable belief that a child may be an Indian.

B.2. Determination of Indian Child's Tribe

(a) Where an Indian child is a member of more than one tribe or is eligible for membership in more than one tribe but is not a member of any of them, the court is called upon to determine with which tribe the child has more significant contacts.

(b) The court shall send the notice specified in recommended guideline B.4. to each such tribe. The notice shall specify the other tribe or tribes that are being considered as the child's tribe and invite each tribe's views on which tribe shall be so designated.

(c) In determining which tribe shall be designated the Indian child's tribe, the court shall consider, among other things, the following factors:

(i) length of residence on or near the reservation of each tribe and frequency of contacts with each tribe;

(ii) child's participation in activities of each tribe;

(iii) child's fluency in the language of each tribe;

(iv) whether there has been a previous adjudication with respect to the child by a court of one of the tribes;

(v) residence on or near one of the tribes' reservation by the child's relatives;

(vi) tribal membership of custodial parent or Indian custodian;

(vii) interest asserted by each tribe in response to the notice specified in subsection B.2. (b) of these guidelines; and

(viii) the child's self identification.

(d) The court's determination together with the reasons for it shall be set out in a written document and made a part of the record of the proceeding. A copy of that document shall be sent to each party to the proceeding and to each person or government agency that received notice of the proceeding.

(e) If the child is a member of only one tribe, that tribe shall be designated the Indian child's tribe even though the child is eligible for membership in another tribe. If a child becomes a member of one tribe during or after the proceeding, that tribe shall be designated as the Indian child's tribe with respect to all subsequent actions related to the proceeding. If the child becomes a member of a tribe other than the one designated by the court as the Indian child's tribe, actions taken based on the court's determination prior to the child's becoming a tribal member continue to be valid.

B.2. Commentary

This guideline requires the court to notify all tribes that are potentially the Indian child's tribe so that each tribe may assert its claim to that status and the court may have the benefit of the views of each tribe. Notification of all the tribes is also necessary so the court can consider the comparative interest of each tribe in the child's welfare in making its decision. That factor has long been regarded an important consideration in making child custody decisions.

The significant factors listed in this section are based on recommendations by tribal officials involved in child welfare matters. The Act itself and the legislative history make it clear that tribal rights are to be based on the existence of a political relationship between the family and the tribe. For that reason, the guidelines make actual tribal membership of the child conclusive on this issue.

The guidelines do provide, however, that previous decisions of a court made on its own determination of the Indian child's tribe are not invalidated simply because the child becomes a member of a different tribe. This provision is included because of the importance of stability and continuity to a child who has been placed outside the home by a court. If a child becomes a member before a placement is made or before a change of placement becomes necessary for other reasons, however, then that membership decision can be taken into account without harm to the child's need for stable relationships.

We have received several recommendations that "Indian child's tribe" status be accorded to all tribes in which a child is eligible for membership. The fact that Congress, in the definition of "Indian child's tribe," provided a criterion for determining which is *the* Indian child's tribe, is a clear indication of legislative intent that there be only one such tribe for each child. For purposes of transfer of jurisdiction, there obviously can be only one tribe to adjudicate the case. To give more than one tribe "Indian child's tribe" status for purposes of the placement preferences would dilute the preference accorded by Congress to the tribe with which the child has the more significant contacts.

A right of intervention could be accorded a tribe with which a child has less significant contacts without undermining the right of the other tribe. A state court can, if it wishes and state law permits, permit intervention by more than one tribe. It could also give a second tribe preference in placement after attempts to place a child with a member of the first tribe or in a home or institution designated by the first tribe had proved unsuccessful. So long as the special rights of *the* Indian child's tribe are respected, giving special status to the tribe with the less significant contacts is not prohibited by the Act and may, in many instances, be a good way to comply with the spirit of the Act.

Determinations of the Indian child's tribe for purposes of this Act shall not serve as any precedent for other situations. The standards in this statute and these guidelines are designed with child custody matters in mind. A different determination may be entirely appropriate in other legal contexts.

B.3. Determination That Placement Is Covered by the Act

(a) Although most juvenile delinquency proceedings are not covered by the Act, the Act does apply to status offenses, such as truancy and incorrigibility, which can only be committed by children, and to any juvenile delinquency proceeding that results in the termination of a parental relationship.

(b) Child custody disputes arising in the context of divorce or separation proceedings or similar domestic relations proceedings are not covered by the Act so long as custody is awarded to one of the parents.

(c) Voluntary placements which do not operate to prohibit the child's parent or Indian custodian from regaining custody of the child at any time are not covered by the Act. Where such placements are made pursuant to a written agreement, that agreement shall state explicitly the right of the parent or custodian to regain custody of the child upon demand.

B.3. Commentary

The purpose of this section is to deal with some of the questions the Department has been receiving concerning the coverage of the Act.

The entire legislative history makes it clear that the Act is directed primarily at attempts to place someone other than the parent or Indian custodian in charge of raising an Indian child—whether on a permanent or temporary basis. Although there is some overlap, juvenile delinquency proceedings are primarily designed for other purposes. Where the child is taken out of the home for committing a crime it is usually to protect society from further offenses by the child and to punish the child in order to persuade that child and others not to commit other offenses.

Placements based on status offenses (actions that are not a crime when committed by an adult), however, are usually premised on the conclusion that the present custodian of the child is not providing adequate care or supervision. To the extent that a status offense poses any immediate danger to society, it is usually also punishable as an offense which would be a crime if committed by an adult. For that reason status offenses are treated the same as dependency proceedings and are covered by the Act and these guidelines, while other juvenile delinquency placements are excluded.

While the Act excludes placements based on an act which would be a crime if committed by an adult, it does cover terminations of parental rights even where they are based on an act which would be a crime if committed by an adult. Such terminations are not intended as punishment and do not prevent the child from committing further offenses. They are based on the conclusion that someone other than the present custodian of the child should be raising the child. Congress has concluded that courts shall make such judgments only on the basis of evidence that serious physical or emotional harm to the child is likely to result unless the child is removed.

The Act excludes from coverage an award of custody to one of the parents "in a divorce proceeding." If construed narrowly, this provision would leave custody awards resulting from proceedings between husband and wife for separate maintenance, but not for dissolution of the marriage bond within the coverage of the Act. Such a narrow interpretation would not be in accord with the intent of Congress. The legislative history indicates that the exemption for divorce proceedings, in part, was included in response to the views of this Department that the protections provided by this Act are not needed in proceedings between parents. In terms of the purposes of this Act, there is no reason to treat separate maintenance or similar domestic relations proceedings. For that reason the statutory term "divorce proceeding" is construed to include other domestic relations proceedings between spouses.

The Act also excludes from its coverage any placements that do not deprive the parents or Indian custodians of the right to regain custody of the child upon demand. Without this exception a court appearance would be required every time an Indian child left home to go to school. Court appearances would also be required for many informal caretaking arrangements that Indian parents and custodians sometimes make for their children. This statutory exemption is restated here in the hope that it will reduce the instances in which Indian parents are unnecessarily inconvenienced by being required to give consent in court to such informal arrangements.

Some private groups and some states enter into formal written agreements with parents for temporary custody (See e.g. Alaska Statutes § 47.10.230). The guidelines recommend that the parties to such agreements explicitly provide for return of the child upon demand if they do not wish the Act to apply to such placements. Inclusion of such a provision is advisable because courts frequently assume that when an agreement is reduced to writing, the parties have only those rights specifically written into the agreement.

B.4. Determination of Jurisdiction

(a) In any Indian child custody proceeding in state court, the court shall determine the residence and domicile of the child. Except as provided in Section B.7. of these guidelines, if either the residence or domicile is on a reservation where the tribe exercises exclusive jurisdiction over child custody proceedings, the proceedings in state court shall be dismissed.

(b) If the Indian child has previously resided or been domiciled on the reservation, the state court shall contact the tribal court to determine whether the child is a ward of the tribal court. Except as provided in Section B.7. of these guidelines, if the child is a ward of a tribal court, the state court proceedings shall be dismissed.

B.4. Commentary

The purpose of this section is to remind the state court of the need to determine whether it has jurisdiction under the Act. The action is dismissed as soon as it is determined that the court lacks jurisdiction except in emergency situations. The procedures for emergency situations are set out in Section B.7.

B.5. Notice Requirements

(a) In any involuntary child custody proceeding, the state court shall make inquiries to determine if the child involved is a member of an Indian tribe or if a parent of the child is a member of an Indian tribe and the child is eligible for membership in an Indian tribe.

(b) In any involuntary Indian child custody proceeding, notice of the proceeding shall be sent to the parents and Indian custodians, if any, and to any tribes that may be the Indian child's tribe by registered mail with return receipt requested. The notice shall be written in clear and understandable language and include the following information:

(i) The name of the Indian child.

(ii) His or her tribal affiliation.

(iii) A copy of the petition, complaint or other document by which the proceeding was initiated.

(iv) The name of the petitioner and the name and address of the petitioner's attorney.

(v) A statement of the right of the biological parents or Indian custodians and the Indian child's tribe to intervene in the proceeding.

(vi) A statement that if the parents or Indian custodians are unable to afford counsel, counsel will be appointed to represent them.

(vii) A statement of the right of the natural parents or Indian custodians and the Indian child's tribe to have, on request, twenty days (or such additional item as may be permitted under state law) to prepare for the proceedings.

(viii) The location, mailing address and telephone number of the court.

(ix) A statement of the right of the parents or Indian custodians or the Indian child's tribe to petition the court to transfer the proceeding to the Indian child's tribal court.

(x) The potential legal consequences of an adjudication on future custodial rights of the parents of Indian custodians.

(xi) A statement in the notice to the tribe that since child custody proceedings are usually conducted on a confidential basis, tribal officials should keep confidential the information contained in the notice concerning the particular proceeding and not reveal it to anyone who does not need the information in order to exercise the tribe's right under the Act.

(c) The tribe, parents or Indian custodians receiving notice from the petitioner of the tendency of a child custody proceeding has the right, upon request, to be granted twenty days (or such additional time as may be permitted under state law) from the date upon which the notice was received to prepare for the proceeding.

(d) The original or a copy of each notice sent pursuant to this section shall be filed with the court together with any return receipt or other proof of service.

(e) Notice may be personally served on any person entitled to receive notice in lieu of mail service.

(f) If a parent or Indian custodian appears in court without an attorney, the court shall inform him or her of the right to appointed counsel, the right to request that the proceeding be transferred to tribal court or to object to such transfer, the right to request additional time to prepare for the proceeding and the right (if the parent or Indian custodian is not already a party) to intervene in the proceedings.

(g) If the court or a petitioning party has reason to believe that a parent or Indian custodian is not likely to understand the contents of the notice because of lack of adequate comprehension of written English, a copy of the notice shall be sent to the Bureau of Indian Affairs agency nearest to the residence of that person requesting that Bureau of Indian Affairs personnel arrange to have the notice explained to that person in the language that he or she best understands.

B.5. Commentary

This section recommends that state courts routinely inquire of participants in child custody proceedings whether the child is an Indian. If anyone asserts that the child is an Indian or that there is reason to believe the child may be an Indian, then the court shall contact the tribe or the Bureau of Indian Affairs for verification. Refer to sections B.1 and B.2 of these guidelines.

This section specifies the information to be contained in the notice. This information is necessary so the persons who receive notice will be able to exercise their rights in a timely manner. Subparagraph (xi) provides that tribes shall be requested to assist in maintaining the confidentiality of the proceeding. Confidentiality may be difficult to maintain—especially where small tribes are involved and the likelihood that the family involved is well known by tribal officials is great. Although Congress was concerned with confidentiality, it concluded that the interest of tribes in the welfare of their children justified taking some risks with confidentiality—especially in involuntary proceedings. It is reasonable, however, to ask tribal officials to maintain as much confidentiality as possible consistent with the exercise of tribal rights under the Act.

The time limits are minimum ones required by the Act. In many instances, more time may be available under state court procedures or because of the circumstances of the particular case.

In such instances, the notice shall state that additional time is available.

The Act requires notice to the parent or Indian custodian. At a minimum, parents must be notified if termination of parental rights is a potential outcome since it is their relationship to the child that is at stake. Similarly, the Indian custodians must be notified of any action that could lead to the custodians' losing custody of the child. Even where only custody is an issue, noncustodial parents clearly have a legitimate interest in the matter. Although notice to both parents and Indian custodians may not be required in all instances by the Act or the Fourteenth Amendment to the U.S. Constitution, providing notice to both is in keeping with the spirit of the Act. For that reason, these guidelines recommend notice be sent to both.

Subsection (d) requires filing the notice with the court so there will be a complete record of efforts to comply with the Act.

Subsection (e) authorizes personal services since it is superior to mail services and provides greater protection of rights as authorized by 25 U.S.C. 1921. Since serving the notice does not involve any assertion of jurisdiction over the person served, personal notice may be served without regard to state or reservation boundaries.

Subsections (f) and (g) provide procedures to increase the likelihood that rights are understood by parents and Indian custodians.

B.6. Time Limits and Extensions

(a) A tribe, parent or Indian custodian entitled to notice of the pendency of a child custody proceeding has a right, upon request, to be granted an additional twenty days from the date upon which notice was received to prepare for participation in the proceeding.

(b) The proceeding may not begin until all of the following dates have passed:

(i) Ten days after the parent or Indian custodian (or Secretary where the parent or Indian custodian is unknown to the petitioner) has received notice;

(ii) Ten days after the Indian child's tribe (or the Secretary if the Indian child's tribe is unknown to the petitioner) has received notice;

(iii) Thirty days after the parent or Indian custodian has received notice if the parent or Indian custodian has requested an additional twenty days to prepare for the proceeding; and

(iv) Thirty days after the Indian child's tribe has received notice if the Indian child's tribe requested an additional twenty days to prepare for the proceeding.

(c) The time limits listed in this section are the minimum time periods required by the Act. The court may grant more time to prepare where state law permits.

B.6. Commentary

This section attempts to clarify the waiting periods required by the Act after notice has been received of an involuntary Indian child custody proceeding. Two independent rights are involved—the right of the parents or Indian custodians and the right of the Indian child's tribe. The proceeding may not begin until the waiting periods to which both are entitled have passed.

This section also makes clear that additional extensions of time may be granted beyond the minimum required by the Act.

B.7. Emergency Removal of an Indian Child

(a) Whenever an Indian child is removed from the physical custody of the child's parents or Indian custodians pursuant to the emergency removal or custody provisions of state law, the agency responsible for the removal action shall immediately cause an inquiry to be made as to the residence and domicile of the child.

(b) When a court order authorizing continued emergency physical custody is sought, the petition for that order shall be accompanied by an affidavit containing the following information:

(i) The name, age and last known address of the Indian child.

(ii) The name and address of the child's parents and Indian custodians, if any. If such persons are unknown, a detailed explanation of what efforts have been made to locate them shall be included.

(iii) Facts necessary to determine the residence and the domicile of the Indian child and whether either the residence or domicile is on an Indian reservation. If either the residence or domicile is believed to be on an Indian reservation, the name of the reservation shall be stated.

(iv) The tribal affiliation of the child and of the parents and/or Indian custodians.

(v) A specific and detailed account of the circumstances that lead the agency responsible for the emergency removal of the child to take that action.

(vi) If the child is believed to reside or be domiciled on a reservation where the tribe exercises exclusive jurisdiction over child custody matters, a statement of efforts that have been made and are being made to transfer the child to the tribe's jurisdiction.

(vii) A statement of the specific actions that have been taken to assist the parents or Indian custodians so the child may safely be returned to their custody.

(c) If the Indian child is not restored to the parents or Indian custodians or jurisdiction is not transferred to the tribe, the agency responsible for the child's removal must promptly commence a state court proceeding for foster care placement. If the child resides or is domiciled on a reservation where the tribe exercises exclusive jurisdiction over child custody matters, such placement must terminate as soon as the imminent physical damage or harm to the child which resulted in the emergency removal no longer exists or as soon as the tribe exercises jurisdiction over the case—whichever is earlier.

(d) Absent extraordinary circumstances, temporary emergency custody shall not be continued for more than 90 days without a determination by the court, supported by clear and convincing evidence and the testimony of at least one qualified expert witness, the custody of the child by the parent or Indian custodian is likely to result in serious emotional or physical damage to the child.

B.7. Commentary

Since jurisdiction under the Act is based on domicile and residence rather than simple physical presence, there may be instances in which action must be taken with respect to a child who is physically located off a reservation but is subject to exclusive tribal jurisdiction. In such instances the tribe will usually not be able to take swift action to exercise its jurisdiction. For that reason Congress authorized states to take temporary emergency action.

Since emergency action must be taken without the careful advance deliberation normally required, procedures must be established to assure that the emergency actions are quickly subjected to review. This section provides procedures for prompt review of such emergency actions. It presumes the state already has such review procedures and only prescribes additional procedures that shall be followed in cases involving Indian children.

The legislative history clearly states that placements under such emergency procedures are to be as short as possible. If the emergency ends, the placement shall end. State action shall also end as soon as the tribe is ready to take over the case.

Subsection (d) refers primarily to the period between when the petition is filed and when the trial court renders its decision. The Act requires that, except for emergencies, Indian children are not to be removed from their parents unless a court finds clear and convincing evidence that the child would be in serious danger unless removed from the home. Unless there is some kind of time limit on the length of an "emergency removal" (that is, any removal not made pursuant to a finding by the court that there is clear and convincing evidence that continued parental custody would make serious physical or emotional harm likely), the safeguards of the Act could be evaded by use of long-term emergency removals.

Subsection (d) recommends what is, in effect, a speedy trial requirement. The court shall be required to comply with the requirements of the Act and reach a decision within 90 days unless there are "extraordinary circumstances" that make additional delay unavoidable.

B.8. Improper Removal From Custody

(a) If, in the course of any Indian child custody proceeding, the court has reason to believe that the child who is the subject of the proceeding may have been improperly removed from the custody of his or her parent or Indian custodian or that the child has been improperly retained after a visit or other temporary relinquishment of custody, and that the child has been improperly retained after a visit or other temporary relinquishment of custody, and that the petitioner is responsible for such removal or retention, the court shall immediately stay the proceedings until a determination can be made on the question of improper removal or retention.

(b) If the court finds that the petitioner is responsible for an improper removal or retention, the child shall be immediately returned to his or her parents or Indian custodian.

B.8. Commentary

This section is designed to implement 25 U.S.C. § 1920. Since a finding of improper removal goes to the jurisdiction of the court to hear the case at all, this section provides that the court will decide the issue as soon as it arises before proceeding further on the merits.

C. Requests for Transfer to Tribal Court

C.1. Petitions under 25 U.S.C. § 1911(b) for transfer of proceeding

Either parent, the Indian custodian or the Indian child's tribe may, orally or in writing, request the court to transfer the Indian child custody proceeding to the tribal court of the child's tribe. The request shall be made promptly after receiving notice of the proceeding. If the request is made orally it shall be reduced to writing by the court and made a part of the record.

C.1. Commentary

Reference is made to 25 U.S.C. 1911(b) in the title of this section in order to clarify that this section deals only with transfers where the child is not domiciled or residing on an Indian reservation.

So that transfers can occur as quickly and simply as possible, requests can be made orally.

This section specifies that requests are to be made promptly after receiving notice of the proceeding. This is a modification of the timeliness requirement that appears in the earlier version of the guidelines. Although the statute permits proceedings to be commenced even before actual notice is received by parties entitled to notice, those parties do not lose their right to request a transfer simply because neither the petitioner nor the Secretary was able to locate them earlier.

Permitting late transfer requests by persons and tribes who were notified late may cause some disruption. It will also, however, provide an incentive to the petitioners to make a diligent effort to give notice promptly in order to avoid such disruptions.

The Department received a number of comments objecting to any timeliness requirement at all. Commenters pointed out that the statue does not explicitly require transfer requests to be timely. Some commenters argued that imposing such a requirement violated tribal and parental rights to intervene at any point in the proceedings under 25 U.S.C. § 1911(c) of the Act.

While the Act permits intervention at any point in the proceeding, it does not explicitly authorize transfer requests at any time. Late interventions do not have nearly the disruptive effect on the proceeding that last minute transfers do. A case that is almost completed does not need to be retried when intervention is permitted. The problems resulting from late intervention are primarily those of the intervenor, who has lost the opportunity to influence the portion of the proceedings that was completed prior to intervention.

Although the Act does not explicitly require transfer petitions to be timely, it does authorize the court to refuse to transfer a case for good cause. When a party who could have petitioned earlier waits until the case is almost complete to ask that it be transferred to another court and retried, good cause exists to deny the request.

Timeliness is a proven weapon of the courts against disruption caused by negligence or obstructionist tactics on the part of counsel. If a transfer petition must be honored at any point before judgment, a party could wait to see how the trial is going in state court and then obtain another trial if it appears the other side will win. Delaying a transfer request could be used as a tactic to wear down the other side by requiring the case to be tried twice. The Act was not intended to authorize such tactics and the "good cause" provision is ample authority for the court to prevent them.

C.2. Criteria and Procedures for Ruling on 25 U.S.C. § 1911(b) Transfer Petitions

(a) Upon receipt of a petition to transfer by a parent, Indian custodian or the Indian child's tribe, the court must transfer unless either parent objects to such transfer, the tribal court declines jurisdiction, or the court determines that good cause to the contrary exists for denying the transfer.

(b) If the court believes or any party asserts that good cause to the contrary exists, the reasons for such belief or assertion shall be stated in writing and made available to the parties who are petitioning for transfer. The petitioners shall have the opportunity to provide the court with their views on whether or not good cause to deny transfer exists.

C.2. Commentary

Subsection (a) simply states the rule provided in 25 U.S.C. § 1911(b).

Since the Act gives the parents and the tribal court of the Indian child's tribe an absolute veto over transfers, there is no need for any adversary proceedings if the parents or the tribal court opposes transfer. Where it is proposed to deny transfer on the grounds of "good cause," however, all parties need an opportunity to present their views to the court.

C.3. Determination of Good Cause to the Contrary

(a) Good cause not to transfer the proceeding exists if the Indian child's tribe does not have a tribal court as defined by the Act to which the case can be transferred.

(b) Good cause not to transfer the proceeding may exist if any of the following circumstances exists:

(i) The proceeding was at an advanced stage when the petition to transfer was received and the petitioner did not file the petition promptly after receiving notice of the hearing.

(ii) The Indian child is over twelve years of age and objects to the transfer.

(iii) The evidence necessary to decide the case could not be adequately presented in the tribal court without undue hardship to the parties or the witnesses.

(iv) The parents of a child over five years of age are not available and the child has had little or no contact with the child's tribe or members of the child's tribe.

(c) Socio-economic conditions and the perceived adequacy of tribal or Bureau of Indian Affairs social services or judicial systems may not be considered in a determination that good cause exists.

(d) The burden of establishing good cause to the contrary shall be on the party opposing the transfer.

C.3. Commentary

All five criteria that were listed in the earlier version of the guidelines were highly controversial. Comments on the first two criteria were almost unanimously negative. The first criterion was whether the parents were still living. The second was whether an Indian custodian or guardian for the child had been appointed. These criteria were criticized as irrelevant and arbitrary. It was argued that children who are orphans or have no appointed Indian custodian or guardian are no more nor less in need of the Act's protections than other children. It was also pointed out that these criteria are contrary to the decision in Wisconsin Potawatomies of the Hannahville Indian Community v. Houston, 397 F. Supp. 719 (W.D. Mich 1973), which was explicitly endorsed by the committee that drafted that Act. The court in that case found that tribal jurisdiction existed even through the children involved were orphans for whom no guardian had been appointed.

Although there was some support for the third and fourth criteria, the preponderance of the comment concerning them was critical. The third criteria was whether the child had little or no contact with his or her Indian tribe for a significant period of time. The fourth was whether the child had ever resided on the reservation for a significant period of time. These criteria were criticized, in part, because they would virtually exclude from transfers infants who were born off the reservation. Many argued that the tribe has a legitimate interest in the welfare of members who have not had significant previous contact with the tribe or the reservation. Some also argued that these criteria invited the state courts to be making the kind of cultural decisions that the Act contemplated should be made by tribes. Some argued that the use of vague words in these criteria accorded state courts too much discretion.

The fifth criteria was whether a child over the age of twelve objected to the transfer. Comment on this criteria was much more evenly divided and many of the critics were ambivalent. They worried that young teenagers could be too easily influenced by the judge or by social workers. They also argued that fear of the unknown would cause many teenagers to make an ill-considered decision against transfer.

The first four criteria in the earlier version were all directed toward the question of whether the child's connections with the reservation were so tenuous that transfer back to the tribe is not advised. The circumstance under which it may be proper for the state court to take such considerations into account are set out in the revised subsection (iv).

It is recommended that in most cases state court judges not be called upon to determine whether or not a child's contacts with a reservation are so limited that a case should not be transferred. This may be a valid consideration since the shock of changing cultures may, in some cases, be harmful to the child. This termination, however, can be made by the parent, who has a veto over transfer to tribal court.

This reasoning does not apply, however, where there is no parent available to make that decision. The guidelines recommend that state courts be authorized to make such determinations only in those cases where there is no parent available to make it.

State court authority to make such decisions is limited to those cases where the child is over five years of age. Most children younger than five years can be expected to adjust more readily to a change in cultural environment.

The fifth criterion has been retained. It is true that teenagers may make some unwise decisions, but it is also true that their judgment has developed to the extent that their views ought to be taken into account in making decisions about their lives.

The existence of a tribal court is made an absolute requirement for transfer of a case. Clearly, the absence of a tribal court is good cause not to ask the tribe to try the case.

Consideration of whether or not the case can be properly tried in tribal court without hardship to the parties or witnesses was included on the strength of the section-by-section analysis in the House Report on the Act, which stated with respect to the § 1911(b), "The subsection is intended to permit a State court to apply a modified doctrine of *forum non conveniens,* in appropriate cases, to insure that the rights of the child as an Indian, the Indian parents or custodian, and the tribe are fully protected." Where a child is in fact living in a dangerous situation, he or she should not be forced to remain there simply because the witnesses cannot afford to travel long distances to court.

Application of this criterion will tend to limit transfers to cases involving Indian children who do not live very far from the reservation. This problem may be alleviated in some instances by having the court come to the witnesses. The Department is aware of one case under that Act where transfer was conditioned on having the tribal court meet in the city where the family lived. Some cities have substantial populations of members of tribes from distant reservations. In such situations some tribes may wish to appoint members who live in those cities as tribal judges.

The timeliness of the petition for transfer, discussed at length in the commentary to section C.1, is listed as a factor to be considered. Inclusion of this criterion is designed to encourage the prompt exercise of the right to petition for transfer in order to avoid unnecessary delays. Long periods of uncertainty concerning the future are generally regarded as harmful to the well-being of children. For that reason, it is especially important to avoid unnecessary delays in child custody proceedings.

Almost all commenters favored retention of the paragraph stating that reservation socio-economic conditions and the perceived adequacy of tribal institutions are not to be taken into account in making good cause determinations. Some commenters did suggest, however, that a case not be transferred if it is clear that a particular disposition of the case that could only be made by the state court held especially great promise of benefiting the child.

Such considerations are important but they have not been listed because the Department believes such judgments are best made by trial courts. Parties who believe that state court adjudication would be better for such reasons can present their reasons to the tribal court and urge it to decline jurisdiction. The Department is aware of one case under the Act where this approach is being used and believes it is more in keeping with the confidence Congress has expressed in tribal courts.

Since Congress has established a policy of preferring tribal control over custody decisions affecting tribal members, the burden of proving that an exception to that policy ought to be made in a particular case rests on the party urging that an exception be made. This rule is reflected in subsection(d).

C.4. Tribal Court Declination of Transfer

(a) A tribal court to which transfer is requested may decline to accept such transfer.

(b) Upon receipt of a transfer petition the state court shall notify the tribal court in writing of the proposed transfer. The notice shall state how long the tribal court has to make its decision. The tribal court shall have at least twenty days from the receipt of notice of a proposed transfer to decide whether to decline the transfer. The tribal court may inform the state court of its decision to decline either orally or in writing.

(c) Parties shall file with the tribal court any arguments they wish to make either for or against tribal declination of transfer. Such arguments shall be made orally in open court or in written pleadings that are served on all other parties.

(d) If the case is transferred the state court shall provide the tribal court with all available information on the case.

C.4. Commentary

The previous version of this section provided that the state court should presume the tribal court has declined to accept jurisdiction unless it hears otherwise. The comments on this issue were divided. This section has been revised to require the tribal court to decline the transfer affirmatively if it does not wish to take the case. This approach is in keeping with the apparent intent of Congress. The language in the Act providing that transfers are "subject to declination by the tribal court" indicates that affirmative action by the tribal court is required to decline a transfer.

The recommended time limit for a decision has been extended from ten to twenty days. The additional time is needed for the court to become apprised of factors it may want to consider in determining whether or not to decline the transfer.

A new paragraph has been added recommending that the parties assist the tribal court in making its decision on declination by giving the tribal court their views on the matter.

Transfers ought to be arranged as simply as possible consistent with due process. Transfer procedures are a good subject for tribal-state agreements under 25 U.S.C. § 1919.

D. Adjudication of Involuntary Placements, Adoptions, or Terminations or Terminations of Parental Rights.

D.1. Access to Reports

Each party to a foster care placement or termination of parental rights proceeding under State law involving an Indian child has the right to examine all reports or other documents filed with the court upon which any decision with respect to such action may be based. No decision of the court shall be based on any report or other document not filed with the court.

D.1. Commentary

The first sentence merely restates the statutory language verbatim. The second sentence makes explicit the implicit assumption of Congress—that the court will limit its considerations to those documents and reports that have been filed with the court.

D.2. Efforts To Alleviate Need To Remove Child From Parents or Indian Custodians

Any party petitioning a state court for foster care placement or termination of parental rights to an Indian child must demonstrate to the court that prior to the commencement of the proceeding active efforts have been made to alleviate the need to remove the Indian child from his or her parents or Indian custodians These efforts shall take into account the prevailing social and cultural conditions and way of life of the Indian child's tribe. They shall also involve and use the available resources of the extended family, the tribe, Indian social service agencies and individual Indian care givers.

D.2. Commentary

This section elaborates on the meaning of "breakup of the Indian family" as used in the Act. "Family breakup" is sometimes used as a synonym for divorce. In the context of this statute, however, it is clear that Congress meant a situation in which the family is unable or unwilling to raise the child in a manner that is not likely to endanger the child's emotional or physical health.

This section also recommends that the petitioner take into account the culture of the Indian child's tribe and use the resources of the child's extended family and tribe in attempting to help the family function successfully as a home for the child. The term "individual Indian care givers" refers to medicine men and other individual tribal members who may have developed special skills that can be used to help the child's family succeed.

One commenter recommended that detailed procedures and criteria be established in order to determine whether family support efforts had been adequate. Establishing such procedures and requirements would involve the court in second-guessing the professional judgment of social service agencies. The Act does not contemplate such a role for the courts and they generally lack the expertise to make such judgments.

D.3. Standards of Evidence

(a) The court may not issue an order affecting a foster care placement of an Indian child unless clear and convincing evidence is presented, including the testimony of one or more qualified expert witnesses, demonstrating that the child's parents continued custody with the child's Indian custodian is likely to result in serious emotional or physical damage to the child.

(b) The court may not order a termination of parental rights unless the court's order is supported by evidence beyond a reasonable doubt, including the testimony of one or more qualified expert witnesses, that continued custody of the child by the parent or

Indian custodian is likely to result in serious emotional or physical damage to the child.

(c) Evidence that only shows the existence of community or family poverty, crowded or inadequate housing, alcohol abuse, or non-conforming social behavior does not constitute clear and convincing evidence that continued custody is likely to result in serious emotional or physical damage to the child. To be clear and convincing, the evidence must show the existence of particular conditions in the home that are likely to result in serious emotional or physical damage to the particular child who is the subject of the proceeding. The evidence must show the causal relationship between the conditions that exist and the damage that is likely to result.

D.3. Commentary

The first two paragraphs are essentially restatement of the statutory language. By imposing these standards, Congress has changed the rules of law of many states with respect to the placement of Indian children. A child may not be removed simply because there is someone else willing to raise the child who is likely to do a better job or that it would be "in the best interests of the child" for him or her to live with someone else. Neither can a placement or termination of parental rights be ordered simply based on a determination that the parents or custodians are "unfit parents." It must be shown that it is shown that it is dangerous for the child to remain with his or her present custodians. Evidence of that must be "clear and convincing" for placements and "beyond a reasonable doubt" for terminations.

The legislative history of the Act makes it pervasively clear that Congress attributes many unwarranted removals of Indian children to cultural bias on the part of the courts and social workers making the decisions. In many cases children were removed merely because the family did not conform to the decision-maker's stereotype of what a proper family should be—without any testing of the implicit assumption that only a family that conformed to that stereotype could successfully raise children. Subsection (c) makes it clear that mere non-conformance with such stereotypes or the existence of other behavior or conditions that are considered bad does not justify a placement or termination under the standards imposed by Congress. The focus must be on whether the particular conditions are likely to cause serious damage.

D.4. Qualified Expert Witnesses

(a) Removal of an Indian child from his or her family must be based on competent testimony from one or more experts qualified to speak specifically to the issue of whether continued custody by the parents or Indian custodians is likely to result in serious physical or emotional damage to the child.

(b) Persons with the following characteristics are most likely to meet the requirements for qualified expert witness for purposes of Indian child custody proceedings:

(i) A member of the Indian child's tribe who is recognized by the tribal community as knowledgeable in tribal customs as they pertain to the family organization and childrearing practices.

(ii) A lay expert witness having substantial experience in the delivery of child and family services to Indians, and extensive knowledge of prevailing social and cultural standards and childrearing practices within the Indian child's tribe.

(iii) A professional person having substantial education and experience in the area of his or her specialty.

(c) The court or any party may request the assistance of the Indian child's tribe or the Bureau of Indian Affairs agency serving the Indian child's tribe in locating persons qualified to serve as expert witnesses.

D.4. Commentary

The first subsection is intended to point out that the issue on which qualified expert testimony is required is the question of whether or not serious damage to the child is likely to occur if the child is not removed. Basically two questions are involved. First, is it likely that the conduct of the parents will result in serious physical or emotional harm to the child? Second, if such conduct will likely cause such harm, can the parents be persuaded to modify their conduct?

The party presenting an expert witness must demonstrate that the witness is qualified by reason of educational background and prior experience to make judgments on those questions that are substantially more reliable than judgments that would be made by nonexperts.

The second subsection makes clear that knowledge of tribal culture and childrearing practices will frequently be very valuable to the court. Determining the likelihood of future harm frequently involves predicting future behavior—which is influenced to a large degree by culture. Specific behavior patterns will often need to be placed in the context of the total culture to determine whether they are likely to cause serious emotional harm.

Indian tribes and Bureau of Indian Affairs personnel frequently know persons who are knowledgeable concerning the customs and cultures of the tribes they serve. Their assistance is available in helping to locate such witnesses.

E. Voluntary Proceedings

E.1. Execution of Consent

To be valid, consent to a voluntary termination of parental rights or adoption must be executed in writing and recorded before a judge or magistrate of a court of competent jurisdiction. A certificate of the court must accompany any consent and must certify that the terms and consequences of the consent were explained in detail and in the language of the parent or Indian custodian, if English is to the primary language, and were fully understood by the parent or Indian custodian. Execution of consent need not be in open court where confidentiality is requested or indicated.

E.1. Commentary

This section provides that consent may be executed before either a judge or magistrate. The addition of magistrates was made in response to a suggestion from Alaska where magistrates are found in most small communities but "judges" are more widely scattered. The term "judge" as used in the statute is not a term of art and can certainly be construed to include judicial officers who are called magistrates in some states. The statement that consent need not be in open court where confidentiality is desired or indicated was taken directly from the House Report on the Act. A recommendation that the guideline list the consequences of consent that must be described to the parent or custodian has not been adopted because the consequences can vary widely depending on the nature of the proceeding, state law and the particular facts of individual cases.

E.2. Content of Consent Document

(a) The consent document shall contain the name and birthdate of the Indian child, the name of the Indian child's tribe, any identifying number or other indication of the child's membership in the tribe, if any, and the name and address of the consenting parent or Indian custodian.

(b) A consent to foster care placement shall contain, in addition to the information specified in (a), the name and address of the person or entity by or through whom the placement was arranged, if any, or the name and address of the prospective foster parents, if known at the time.

(c) A consent to termination of parental rights or adoption shall contain in addition to the information specified in (a), the name and address of the person or entity by or through whom any preadoptive or adoptive placement has been or is to be arranged.

E.2. Commentary

This section specifies the basic information about the placement or termination to which the parent or Indian custodian is consenting to assure that consent is knowing and also to document what took place.

E.3. Withdrawal of Consent to Placement

Where a parent or Indian custodian has consented to a foster care placement under state law, such consent may be withdrawn at any time by filing, in the court where consent was executed and filed, an instrument executed by the parent or Indian custodian. When a parent or Indian custodian withdraws consent to foster care placement, the child shall as soon as is practicable be returned to that parent or Indian custodian.

E.3. Commentary

This section specifies that withdrawal of consent shall be filed in the same court where the consent document itself was executed.

E.4. Withdrawal of Consent to Adoption

A consent to termination of parental rights or adoption may be withdrawn by the parent at any time prior to entry of a *final decree of voluntary termination or adoption* by filing in the court where the consent is filed an instrument executed under oath by the parent stipulating his or her intention to withdraw such consent. The clerk of the court where the withdrawal of consent is filed shall promptly notify the party by or through whom any preadoptive or adoptive placement has been arranged of such filing and that party shall insure the return of the child to the parent as soon as practicable.

E.4. Commentary

This provision recommends that the clerk of the court be responsible for notifying the family with whom the child has been placed that consent has been withdrawn. The court's involvement frequently may be necessary since the biological parents are often not told who the adoptive parents are.

F. Dispositions

F.1. Adoptive Placements

(a) In any adoptive placement of an Indian child under state law preference must be given (in the order listed below) absent good cause to the contrary, to placement of the child with:

(i) A member of the child's extended family;

(ii) Other members of the Indian child's tribe; or

(iii) Other Indian families, including families of single parents.

(b) The Indian child's tribe may establish a different order of preference by resolution. That order of preference must be followed so long as placement is the least restrictive setting appropriate to the child's needs.

(c) Unless a consenting parent evidences a desire for anonymity, the court or agency shall notify the child's extended family and the Indian child's tribe that their members will be given preference in the adoption decision.

F.1. Commentary

This section makes clear that preference shall be given in the order listed in the Act. The Act clearly recognizes the role of the child's extended family in helping to raise children. The extended family should be looked to first when it becomes necessary to remove the child from the custody of his or her parents. Because of differences in cultures among tribes, placement within the same tribe is preferable.

This section also provides that single parent families shall be considered for placements. The legislative history of the Act makes it clear that Congress intended custody decisions to be made based on a consideration of the present or potential custodian's ability to provide the necessary care, supervision and support for the child rather than on preconceived notions of proper family composition.

The third subsection recommends that the court or agent make an active effort to find out if there are families entitled to preference who would be willing to adopt the child. This provision recognizes, however, that the consenting parent's request for anonymity takes precedence over efforts to find a home consistent with the Act's priorities.

F.2. Foster Care or Preadoptive Placements

In any foster care or preadoptive placement of an Indian child:

(a) The child must be placed in the least restrictive setting which

(i) Most approximates a family;

(ii) In which his or her special needs may be met; and

(iii) Which is in reasonable proximity to his or her home.

(b) Preference must be given in the following order, absent good cause to the contrary, to placement with:

(i) A member of the Indian child's extended family;

(ii) A foster home, licensed, approved or specified by the Indian child's tribe, whether on or off the reservation;

(iii) An Indian foster home licensed or approved by an authorized non-Indian licensing authority, or

(iv) An institution for children approved by an Indian tribe or operated by an Indian organization which has a program suitable to meet the child's needs.

(c) The Indian child's tribe may establish a different order of preference by resolution, and that order of preference shall be followed so long as the criteria enumerated in subsection (a) are met.

F.2. Commentary

This guideline simply restates the provisions of the Act.

F.3. Good Cause To Modify Preferences

(a) For purposes of foster care, preadoptive or adoptive placement, a determination of good cause not to follow the order of preference set out above shall be based on one or more of the following considerations:

(i) The request of the biological parents or the child when the child is of sufficient age.

(ii) The extraordinary physical or emotional needs of the child as established by testimony of a qualified expert witness.

(iii) The unavailability of suitable families for placement after a diligent search has been completed for families meeting the preference criteria.

(b) The burden of establishing the existence of good cause not to follow the order of preferences established in subsection (b) shall be on the party urging that the preferences not be followed.

F.3. Commentary

The Act indicates that the court is to give preference to confidentiality requests by parents in making placements. Paragraph (i) is intended to permit parents to ask that the order of preference not be followed because it would prejudice confidentiality or for other reasons. The wishes of an older child are important in making an effective placement.

In a few cases a child may need highly specialized treatment services that are unavailable in the community where the families who meet the preference criteria live. Paragraph (ii) recommends that such considerations be considered as good cause to the contrary.

Paragraph (iii) recommends that a diligent attempt to find a suitable family meeting the preference criteria be made before consideration of a non-preference placement be considered. A diligent attempt to find a suitable family includes at minimum, contact with the child's tribal social service program, a search of all county or state listings of available Indian homes and contact with nationally known Indian programs with available placement resources.

Since Congress has established a clear preference for placements within the tribal culture, it is recommended in subsection (b) that the party urging an exception be made be required to bear the burden of proving an exception is necessary.

G. Post-Trial Rights

G.1. Petition To Vacate Adoption

(a) Within two years after a final decree adoption of any Indian child by a state court, or within any longer period of time permitted by the law of the state, a parent who executed a consent to termination of paternal rights or adoption of that child may petition the court in which the final adoption decree was entered to vacate the decree and revoke the consent on the grounds that such consent was obtained by fraud or duress.

(b) Upon the filing of such petition, the court shall give notice to all parties to the adoption proceedings and shall proceed to hold a hearing on the petition. Where the court finds that the parent's consent was obtained through fraud or duress, it must vacate the decree of adoption and order the consent revoked and order the child returned to the parent.

G.1. Commentary

The section recommends that the petition to vacate an adoption be brought in the same court in which the decree was entered, since that court clearly has jurisdiction, and witnesses on the issue of fraud or duress are most likely to be within its jurisdiction.

G.2. Adult Adoptee Rights

(a) Upon application by an Indian individual who has reached age 18 who was the subject of an adoptive placement, the court which entered the final decree must inform such individual of the tribal affiliations, if any, of the individual's biological parents and provide such other information necessary to protect any rights flowing from the individual's tribal relationship.

(b) This section applies regardless of whether or not the original adoption was subject to the provisions of the Act.

(c) Where state law prohibits revelation of the identity of the biological parent, assistance of the Bureau of Indian Affairs shall be sought where necessary to help an adoptee who is eligible for membership in a tribe establish that right without breaching the confidentiality of the record.

G.2. Commentary

Subsection (b) makes clear that adoptions completed prior to May 7, 1979, are covered by this provision. The Act states that most portions of Title I do not "affect a proceeding under State law" initiated or completed prior to May 7, 1979. Providing information to an adult adoptee, however, cannot be said to affect the proceeding by which the adoption was ordered.

The legislative history of the Act makes is clear that this Act was not intended to supersede the decision of state legislatures on whether adult adoptees may be told the names of their biological parents. The intent is simply to assure the protection of rights deriving from tribal membership. Where a state law prohibits disclosure of the identity of the biological parents, tribal rights can be protected by asking the BIA to check confidentially whether the adult adoptee meets the requirements for membership in an Indian Tribe. If the adoptee does meet those requirements, the BIA can certify that fact to the appropriate tribe.

G.3. Notice of Change in Child's Status

(a) Whenever a final decree of adoption of an Indian child has been vacated or set aside, or the adoptive parent has voluntarily consented to the termination of his or her parental rights to the child, or whenever an Indian child is removed from a foster care home or institution for the purpose of further foster care, preadoptive placement, or adoptive placement, notice by the court or an agency authorized by the court shall be given to the child's biological parents or prior Indian custodians. Such notice shall inform the recipient of his or her right to petition for return of custody of the child.

(b) A parent or Indian custodian may waive his or her right to such notice by executing a written waiver of notice filed with the court. Such waiver may be revoked at any time by filing with the court a written notice of revocation, but such revocation would not affect any proceeding which occurred before the filing of the notice of revocation.

G.3. Commentary

This section provides guidelines to aid courts in applying the provisions of Section 106 of the Act. Section 106 gives legal standing to a biological parent or prior Indian custodian to petition for return of a child in cases of failed adoptions or changes in placement in situations where there has been a termination of parental rights. Section 106(b) provides that whenever an Indian child is removed from a foster care home or institution for the purpose of further foster care, preadoptive placement, or adoptive placement, such placement is to be in accordance with the provisions of the Act—which requires notice to the biological parents.

The Act is silent on the question of whether a parent or Indian custodian can waive the right to further notice. Obviously, there will be cases in which the biological parents will prefer not to receive notice one their parental rights have been relinquished or terminated. This section provides for such waivers but, because the Act establishes an absolute right to participate in any future proceedings and to petition the court for return of the child, the waiver is revocable.

G.4. Maintenance of Records

The state shall establish a single location where all records of every adoptive placement of Indian children by courts of that state will be available within seven days of a request by an Indian child's tribe or the Secretary. The records shall contain, at a minimum, the petition or complaint, all substantive orders entered in the proceeding, and the complete record of the placement determination.

G.4. Commentary

This section of the guidelines provides a procedure for implementing the provisions of 25 U.S.C. § 1915(e). This section has been modified from the previous version which required that all records be maintained in a single location within the state. As revised, this section provides only that the records be retrievable by a single office that would make them available to the requester within seven days of a request. For some states (especially Alaska) centralization of the records themselves would create major administrative burdens. So long as the records can be promptly made available at a single location. The intent of this section that the records be readily available will be satisfied.

Forrest J. Gerard,
Assistant Secretary, Indian Affairs.
November 18, 1979.

APPENDIX • B

Tribal Entities Recognized and Eligible to Receive Services from the United States Bureau of Indian Affairs (58 Fed. Reg. 54366-54369)

Absentee-Shawnee Tribe of Indians of Oklahoma
Agua Caliente Band of Cahuilla Indians of the Agua Caliente Indian Reservation, California
Ak Chin Indian Community of Papago Indians of the Maricopa, Ak Chin Reservation, Arizona
Alabama and Coushatta Tribes of Texas
Alabama-Quassarte Tribal Town of the Creek Nation of Oklahoma
Alturas Rancheria of Pit River Indians of California
Apache Tribe of Oklahoma
Arapahoe Tribe of the Wind River Reservation, Wyoming
Aroostook Band of Micmac Indians of Maine
Assiniboine and Sioux Tribes of the Fort Peck Indian Reservation, Montana
Augustine Band of Cahuilla Mission Indians of the Augustine Reservation, California
Bad River Band of the Lake Superior Tribe of Chippewa Indians of the Bad River Reservation, Wisconsin
Bay Mills Indian Community of the Sault Ste. Marie Band of Chippewa Indians, Bay Mills Reservation, Michigan
Berry Creek Rancheria of Maidu Indians of California
Big Lagoon Rancheria of Smith River Indians of California
Big Pine Band of Owens Valley Paiute Shoshone Indians of the Big Pine Reservation, California
Big Sandy Rancheria of Mono Indians of California
Big Valley Rancheria of Pomo & Pit River Indians of California
Blackfeet Tribe of the Blackfeet Indian Reservation of Montana
Blue Lake Rancheria of California
Bridgeport Paiute Indian Colony of California
Buena Vista Rancheria of Me-Wuk Indians of California
Burns Paiute Tribe of the Burns Paiute Indian Colony of Oregon
Cabazon Band of Cahuilla Mission Indians of the Cabazon Reservation, California
Cachil DeHe Band of Wintun Indians of the Colusa Indian Community of the Colusa Rancheria, California

Caddo Indian Tribe of Oklahoma
Cahto Indian Tribe of the Laytonville Rancheria, California
Cahuilla Band of Mission Indians of the Cahuilla Reservation, California
Campo Band of Diegueno Mission Indians of the Campo Indian Reservation, California
Capitan Grande Band of Diegueno Mission Indians of California: Barona Group of Capitan Grande Band of Mission Indians of the Barona Reservation, California
Viejas (Baron Long) Group of Capitan Grande Band of Mission Indians of the Viejas Reservation, California
Cayuga Nation of New York
Cedarville Rancheria of Northern Paiute Indians of California
Chemehuevi Indian Tribe of the Chemehuevi Reservation, California
Cher-Ae Heights Indian Community of the Trinidad Rancheria, California
Cherokee Nation of Oklahoma
Cheyenne-Arapaho Tribes of Oklahoma
Cheyenne River Sioux Tribe of the Cheyenne River Reservation, South Dakota
Chickasaw Nation of Oklahoma
Chicken Ranch Rancheria of Me-Wuk Indians of California
Chippewa-Cree Indians of the Rocky Boy's Reservation, Montana
Chitimacha Tribe of Louisiana
Choctaw Nation of Oklahoma
Citizen Band Potawatomi Indian Tribe of Oklahoma
Cloverdale Rancheria of Pomo Indians of California
Coast Indian Community of Yurok Indians of the Resighini Rancheria, California
Cocopah Tribe of Arizona
Coeur D'Alene Tribe of the Coeur D'Alene Reservation, Idaho
Cold Springs Rancheria of Mono Indians of California
Colorado River Indian Tribes of the Colorado River Indian Reservation, Arizona and California
Comanche Indian Tribe of Oklahoma
Confederated Salish & Kootenai Tribes of the Flathead Reservation, Montana
Confederated Tribes of the Chehalis Reservation, Washington
Confederated Tribes of the Colville Reservation, Washington
Confederated Tribes of the Coos, Lower Umpqua and Siuslaw Indians of Oregon
Confederated Tribes of the Goshute Reservation, Nevada and Utah
Confederated Tribes of the Grand Ronde Community of Oregon
Confederated Tribes of the Siletz Reservation, Oregon
Confederated Tribes of the Umatilla Reservation, Oregon
Confederated Tribes of the Warm Springs Reservation of Oregon
Confederated Tribes and Bands of the Yakima Indian Nation of the Yakima Reservation, Washington
Coquille Tribe of Oregon
Cortina Indian Rancheria of Wintun Indians of California
Coushatta Tribe of Louisiana
Covelo Indian Community of the Round Valley Reservation, California
Cow Creek Band of Umpqua Indians of Oregon
Coyote Valley Band of Pomo Indians of California
Creek Nation of Oklahoma
Crow Tribe of Montana
Crow Creek Sioux Tribe of the Crow Creek Reservation, South Dakota

Cuyapaipe Community of Diegueno Mission Indians of the Cuyapaipe Reservation, California
Death Valley Timbi-Sha Shoshone Band of California
Delaware Tribe of Western Oklahoma
Devils Lake Sioux Tribe of the Devils Lake Sioux Reservation, North Dakota
Dry Creek Rancheria of Pomo Indians of California
Duckwater Shoshone Tribe of the Duckwater Reservation, Nevada
Eastern Band of Cherokee Indians of North Carolina
Eastern Shawnee Tribe of Oklahoma
Elem Indian Colony of Pomo Indians of the Sulphur Bank Rancheria, California
Elk Valley Rancheria of Smith River Tolowa Indians of California
Ely Shoshone Tribe of Nevada
Enterprise Rancheria of Maidu Indians of California
Flandreau Santee Sioux Tribe of South Dakota
Forest County Potawatomi Community of Wisconsin Potawatomie Indians, Wisconsin
Fort Belknap Indian Community of the Fort Belknap Reservation of Montana
Fort Bidwell Indian Community of Paiute Indians of the Fort Bidwell Reservation, California
Fort Independence Indian Community of Paiute Indians of the Fort Independence Reservation, California
Fort McDermitt Paiute and Shoshone Tribes of the Fort McDermitt Indian Reservation, Nevada
Fort McDowell Mohave-Apache Indian Community of the Fort McDowell Indian Reservation, Arizona
Fort Mojave Indian Tribe of Arizona
Fort Sill Apache Tribe of Oklahoma
Gila River Pima-Maricopa Indian Community of the Gila River Indian Reservation of Arizona
Grand Traverse Band of Ottawa & Chippewa Indians of Michigan
Greenville Rancheria of Maidu Indians of California
Grindstone Indian Rancheria of Wintun-Wailaki Indians of California
Guidiville Rancheria of California
Hannahville Indian Community of Wisconsin Potawatomie Indians of Michigan
Havasupai Tribe of the Havasupai Reservation, Arizona
Hoh Indian Tribe of the Hoh Indian Reservation, Washington
Hoopa Valley Tribe of the Hoopa Valley Reservation, California
Hopi Tribe of Arizona
Hopland Band of Pomo Indians of the Hopland Rancheria, California
Houlton Band of Maliseet Indians of Maine
Hualapai Tribe of the Hualapai Indian Reservation, Arizona
Inaja Band of Diegueno Mission Indians of the Inaja and Cosmit Reservation, California
Iowa Tribe of Kansas and Nebraska
Iowa Tribe of Oklahoma
Jackson Rancheria of Me-Wuk Indians of California
Jamestown Klallam Tribe of Washington
Jamul Indian Village of California
Jicarilla Apache Tribe of the Jicarilla Apache Indian Reservation, New Mexico
Kaibab Band of Paiute Indians of the Kaibab Indian Reservation, Arizona
Kalispel Indian Community of the Kalispel Reservation, Washington
Karuk Tribe of California

Kashia Band of Pomo Indians of the Stewarts Point Rancheria, California
Kaw Indian Tribe of Oklahoma
Keweenaw Bay Indian Community of L'Anse and Ontonagon Bands of Chippewa Indians of the L'Anse Reservation, Michigan
Kialegee Tribal Town of the Creek Indian Nation of Oklahoma
Kickapoo Tribe of Indians of the Kickapoo Reservation in Kansas
Kickapoo Tribe of Oklahoma
Kickapoo Traditional Tribe of Texas
Kiowa Indian Tribe of Oklahoma
Klamath Indian Tribe of Oregon
Kootenai Tribe of Idaho
La Courte Oreilles Band of Lake Superior Chippewa Indians of the Lac Courte Oreilles Reservation of Wisconsin
La Jolla Band of Luiseno Mission Indians of the La Jolla Reservation, California
La Posta Band of Diegueno Mission Indians of the La Posta Indian Reservation, California
Lac du Flambeau Band of Lake Superior Chippewa Indians of the Lac du Flambeau Reservation of Wisconsin
Lac Vieux Desert Band of Lake Superior Chippewa Indians of Michigan
Las Vegas Tribe of Paiute Indians of the Las Vegas Indian Colony, Nevada
Los Coyotes Band of Cahuilla Mission Indians of the Los Coyotes Reservation, California
Lovelock Paiute Tribe of the Lovelock Indian Colony, Nevada
Lower Brule Sioux Tribe of the Lower Brule Reservation, South Dakota
Lower Elwha Tribal Community of the Lower Elwha Reservation, Washington
Lower Sioux Indian Community of Minnesota Mdewakanton Sioux Indians of the Lower Sioux Reservation in Minnesota
Lummi Tribe of the Lummi Reservation, Washington
Lytton Rancheria of California
Makah Indian Tribe of the Makah Indian Reservation, Washington
Manchester Band of Pomo Indians of the Manchester-Point Arena Rancheria, California
Manzanita Band of Diegueno Mission Indians of the Manzanita Reservation, California
Mashantucket Pequot Tribe of Connecticut
Mechoopda Indian Tribe of Chico Rancheria, California
Menominee Indian Tribe of Wisconsin
Mesa Grande Band of Diegueno Mission Indians of the Mesa Grande Reservation, California
Mescalero Apache Tribe of the Mescalero Reservation, New Mexico
Miami Tribe of Oklahoma
Miccosukee Tribe of Indians of Florida
Middletown Rancheria of Pomo Indians of California
Minnesota Chippewa Tribe, Minnesota (Six component reservations: Bois Forte Band (Nett Lake); Fond du Lac Band; Grand Portage Band; Leech Lake Band; Mille Lac Band; White Earth Band)
Mississippi Band of Choctaw Indians, Mississippi
Moapa Band of Paiute Indians of the Moapa River Indian Reservation, Nevada
Modoc Tribe of Oklahoma
Mooretown Rancheria of Maidu Indians of California

Morongo Band of Cahuilla Mission Indians of the Morongo Reservation, California
Muckleshoot Indian Tribe of the Muckleshoot Reservation, Washington
Narragansett Indian Tribe of Rhode Island
Navajo Tribe of Arizona, New Mexico & Utah
Nez Perce Tribe of Idaho
Nisqually Indian Community of the Nisqually Reservation, Washington
Nooksack Indian Tribe of Washington
Northern Cheyenne Tribe of the Northern Cheyenne Indian Reservation, Montana
Northfork Rancheria of Mono Indians of California
Northwestern Band of Shoshoni Indians of Utah (Washakie)
Oglala Sioux Tribe of the Pine Ridge Reservation, South Dakota
Omaha Tribe of Nebraska
Oneida Nation of New York
Oneida Tribe of Wisconsin
Onondaga Nation of New York
Osage Tribe of Oklahoma
Ottawa Tribe of Oklahoma
Otoe-Missouria Tribe of Oklahoma
Paiute Indian Tribe of Utah
Paiute-Shoshone Indians of the Bishop Community of the Bishop Colony, California
Paiute-Shoshone Tribe of the Fallon Reservation and Colony, Nevada
Paiute-Shoshone Indians of the Lone Pine Community of the Lone Pine Reservation, California
Pala Band of Luiseno Mission Indians of the Pala Reservation, California
Pascua Yaqui Tribe of Arizona
Passamaquoddy Tribe of Maine
Pauma Band of Luiseno Mission Indians of the Pauma & Yuima Reservation, California
Pawnee Indian Tribe of Oklahoma
Pechanga Band of Luiseno Mission Indians of the Pechanga Reservation, California
Penobscot Tribe of Maine
Peoria Tribe of Oklahoma
Picayune Rancheria of Chukchansi Indians of California
Pinoleville Rancheria of Pomo Indians of California
Pit River Tribe of California (includes Big Bend, Lookout, Montgomery Creek & Roaring Creek Rancherias & XL Ranch)
Poarch Band of Creek Indians of Alabama
Ponca Tribe of Indians of Oklahoma
Ponca Tribe of Nebraska
Port Gamble Indian Community of the Port Gamble Reservation, Washington
Potter Valley Rancheria of Pomo Indians of California
Prairie Band of Potawatomi Indians of Kansas
Prairie Island Indian Community of Minnesota Mdewakanton Sioux Indians of the Prairie Island Reservation, Minnesota
Pueblo of Acoma, New Mexico
Pueblo of Cochiti, New Mexico
Pueblo of Jemez, New Mexico
Pueblo of Isleta, New Mexico
Pueblo of Laguna, New Mexico
Pueblo of Nambe, New Mexico
Pueblo of Picuris, New Mexico
Pueblo of Pojoaque, New Mexico
Pueblo of San Felipe, New Mexico
Pueblo of San Juan, New Mexico
Pueblo of San Ildefonso, New Mexico
Pueblo of Sandia, New Mexico
Pueblo of Santa Ana, New Mexico
Pueblo of Santa Clara, New Mexico
Pueblo of Santo Domingo, New Mexico
Pueblo of Taos, New Mexico
Pueblo of Tesuque, New Mexico
Pueblo of Zia, New Mexico

Puyallup Tribe of the Puyallup Reservation, Washington
Pyramid Lake Paiute Tribe of the Pyramid Lake Reservation, Washington
Quapaw Tribe of Oklahoma
Quartz Valley Rancheria of Karok, Shasta & Upper Klamath Indians of California
Quechan Tribe of the Fort Yuma Indian Reservation, California
Quileute Tribe of the Quileute Reservation, Washington
Quinault Tribe of the Quinault Reservation, Washington
Ramona Band or Village of Cahuilla Mission Indians of California
Red Cliff Band of Lake Superior Chippewa Indians of Wisconsin
Red Lake Band of Chippewa Indians of the Red Lake Reservation, Minnesota
Redding Rancheria of Pomo Indians of California
Redwood Valley Rancheria of Pomo Indians of California
Reno-Sparks Indian Colony, Nevada
Rincon Band of Luiseno Mission Indians of the Rincon Reservation, California
Robinson Rancheria of Pomo Indians of California
Rohnerville Rancheria of Bear River or Mattole Indians of California
Rosebud Sioux Tribe of the Rosebud Indian Reservation, South Dakota
Rumsey Indian Rancheria of Wintun Indians of California
Sac & Fox Tribe of Mississippi in Iowa
Sac & Fox Tribe of Missouri in Kansas and Nebraska
Sac & Fox Tribe of Oklahoma
Saginaw Chippewa Indian Tribe of Michigan, Isabella Reservation
Salt River Pima-Maricopa Indian Community of the Salt River Reservation, Arizona
San Carlos Apache Tribe of the San Carlos Reservation, Arizona
San Juan Southern Paiute Tribe of Arizona
San Manual Band of Serrano Mission Indians of the San Manual Reservation, California
San Pasqual Band of Diegueno Mission Indians of California
Santa Rosa Indian Community of the Santa Rosa Rancheria, California
Santa Rosa Band of Cahuilla Mission Indians of the Santa Rosa Reservation, California
Santa Ynez Band of Chumash Mission Indians of the Santa Ysabel Reservation, California
Santa Ysabel Band of Diegueno Mission Indians of the Santa Ysabel Reservation, California
Santee Sioux Tribe of the Santee Reservation of Nebraska
Sauk-Suiattle Indian Tribe of Washington
Sault Ste. Marie Tribe of Chippewa Indians of Michigan
Scotts Valley Band of Pomo Indians of California
Seminole Nation of Oklahoma
Seminole Tribe of Florida, Dania, Big Cypress & Brighton Reservations
Seneca Nation of New York
Seneca-Cayuga Tribe of Oklahoma
Shakopee Mdewakanton Sioux Community of Minnesota (Prior Lake)
Sheep Ranch Rancheria of Me-Wuk Indians of California
Sherwood Valley Rancheria of Pomo Indians of California
Shingle Springs Band of Miwok Indians, Shingle Springs Rancheria (Verona Tract), California
Shoalwater Bay Tribe of the Shoalwater Bay Indian Reservation, Washington

Shoshone Tribe of the Wind River Reservation, Wyoming
Shoshone-Bannock Tribes of the Fort Hall Reservation of Idaho
Shoshone-Paiute Tribes of the Duck Valley Reservation, Nevada
Sisseton-Wahpeton Sioux Tribe of the Lake Traverse Reservation, South Dakota
Skokomish Indian Tribe of the Skokomish Reservation, Washington
Skull Valley Band of Goshute Indians of Utah
Smith River Rancheria of California
Soboba Band of Luiseno Mission Indians of the Soboba Reservation, California
Sokoagon Chippewa Community of the Mole Lake Band of Chippewa Indians, Wisconsin
Southern Ute Indian Tribe of the Southern Ute Reservation, Colorado
Spokane Tribe of the Spokane Reservation, Washington
Squaxin Island Tribe of the Squaxin Island Reservation, Washington
St. Croix Chippewa Indians of Wisconsin, St. Croix Reservation
St. Regis Band of Mohawk Indians of New York
Standing Rock Sioux Tribe of North & South Dakota
Stillaguamish Tribe of Washington
Stockbridge-Munsee Community of Mohican Indians of Wisconsin
Summit Lake Paiute Tribe of Nevada
Suquamish Indian Tribe of the Port Madison Reservation, Washington
Susanville Indian Rancheria of Paiute, Maidu, Pit River & Washoe Indians of California
Swinomish Indians of the Swinomish Reservation, Washington
Sycuan Band of Diegueno Mission Indians of California
Table Bluff Rancheria of Wiyot Indians of California
Table Mountain Rancheria of California
Te-Moak Tribes of Western Shoshone Indians of Nevada
Thlopthlocco Tribal Town of the Creek Nation of Oklahoma
Three Affiliated Tribes of the Fort Berthold Reservation, North Dakota
Tohono O'odham Nation of Arizona (formerly known as the Papago Tribe of the Sells, Gila Bend & San Xavier Reservation, Arizona)
Tonawanda Band of Seneca Indians of New York
Tonkawa Tribe of Indians of Oklahoma
Tonto Apache Tribe of Arizona
Torres-Martinez Band of Cahuilla Mission Indians of California
Tule River Indian Tribe of the Tule River Reservation, California
Tulalip Tribes of the Tulalip Reservation, Washington
Tunica-Biloxi Indian Tribe of Louisiana
Tuolumne Band of Me-Wuk Indians of the Tuolumne Rancheria of California
Turtle Mountain Band of Chippewa Indians of North Dakota
Tuscarora Nation of New York
Twenty-Nine Palms Band of Luiseno Mission Indians of California
United Keetoowah Band of Cherokee Indians of Oklahoma
Upper Lake Band of Pomo Indians of Upper Lake Rancheria of California
Upper Sioux Indian Community of the Upper Sioux Reservation, Minnesota
Upper Skagit Indian Tribe of Washington
Ute Indian Tribe of the Uintah & Ouray Reservation, Utah

Ute Mountain Tribe of the Ute Mountain Reservation, Colorado, New Mexico & Utah
Utu Utu Gwaitu Paiute Tribe of the Benton Paiute Reservation, California
Walker River Paiute Tribe of the Walker River Reservation, California
Wampanoag Tribe of Gay Head (Aquinnah) of Massachusetts
Washoe Tribe of Nevada & California (Carson Colony, Dresslerville & Washoe Ranches)
White Mountain Apache Tribe of the Fort Apache Reservation, Arizona
Wichita and Affiliated Tribes (Wichita, Keechi, Waco & Tawakonie) of Oklahoma
Winnebago Tribe of Nebraska
Winnemucca Indian Colony of Nevada
Wisconsin Winnebago Indian Tribe of Wisconsin
Wyandotte Tribe of Oklahoma
Yankton Sioux Tribe of South Dakota
Yavapai-Apache Indian Community of the Camp Verde Reservation, Arizona
Yavapai-Prescott Tribe of the Yavapai Reservation, Arizona
Yerington Paiute Tribe of the Yerington Colony & Campbell Ranch, Nevada
Yomba Shoshone Tribe of the Yomba Reservation, Nevada
Ysleta Del Sur Pueblo of Texas
Yurok Tribe of the Hoopa Valley Reservation, California
Zuni Tribe of the Zuni Reservation, New Mexico

Native Entities within the State of Alaska Recognized and Eligible to Receive Services from the United States Bureau of Indian Affairs

Village of Afognak
Native Village of Akhiok
Akiachak Native Community
Akiak Native Community
Native Village of Akutan
Village of Alakanuk
Alatna Village
Native Village of Aleknagik
Algaaciq Native Village (St. Mary's)
Allakaket Village
Native Village of Ambler
Village of Anaktuvuk Pass
Yupiit of Andreafski
Angoon Community Association
Village of Aniak
Anvik Village
Arctic Village (See Native Village of Venetie Tribal Government)
Native Village of Atka
Atqasuk Village (Atkasook)
Village of Atmautluak
Native Village of Barrow
Beaver Village
Native Village of Belkofski
Village of Bill Moore's Slough
Birch Creek Village
Native Village of Brevig Mission
Native Village of Buckland
Native Village of Cantwell
Native Village of Chanega (aka Chenega)
Chalkyitsik Village
Village of Chefornak
Chevak Native Village
Chickaloon Native Village
Native Village of Chignik
Native Village of Chignik Lagoon
Chignik Lake Village
Chilkat Indian Village (Kluckwan)
Chilkoot Indian Association (Haines)
Chinik Eskimo Community (Golovin)
Native Village of Chistochina
Native Village of Chitina
Native Village of Chuatbaluk (Russion Mission, Kuskokwim)
Chuloonawick Native Village
Circle Native Community
Village of Clarks's Point
Native Village of Council
Craig Community Association

Village of Crooked Creek
Native Village of Deering
Native Village of Dillingham
Native Village of Diomede (aka Inalik)
Village of Dot Lake
Douglas Indian Association
Native Village of Eagle
Native Village of Eek
Egegik Village
Eklutna Native Village
Native Village of Ekuk
Ekwok Village
Native Village of Elim
Emmonak Village
Evansville Village (aka Bettles Field)
Native Village of Eyak (Cordova)
Native Village of False Pass
Native Village of Fort Yukon
Native Village of Gakona
Galena Village (aka Louden Village)
Native Village of Gambell
Native Village of Georgetown
Native Village of Goodnews Bay
Organized Village of Grayling (aka Holikachuk)
Gulkana Village
Native Village of Hamilton
Healy Lake Village
Holy Cross Village
Hoonah Indian Association
Native Village of Hooper Bay
Hughes Village
Huslia Village
Hydaburg Cooperative Association
Igiugig Village
Village of Iliamna
Inupiat Community of the Arctic Slope
Ivanoff Bay Village
Kaguyak Village
Organized Village of Kake
Kaktovik Village (aka Barter Island)
Village of Kalskag
Village of Kaltag
Native Village of Kanatak
Native Village of Karluk
Organized Village of Kasaan
Native Village of Kasigluk
Kenaitze Indian Tribe
Ketchikan Indian Corporation
Native Village of Kiana
Agdaagux Tribe of King Cove
King Island Native Community
Native Village of Kipnuk
Native Village of Kivalina
Klawock Cooperative Association
Native Village of Kluti Kaah (aka Copper Center)
Knik Village
Native Village of Kobuk
Kokhanok Village
Koliganek Village
Native Village of Kongiganak
Village of Kotlik
Native Village of Kotzebue
Native Village of Koyuk
Koyukuk Native Village
Organized Village of Kwethluk
Native Village of Kwigillingok
Native Village of Kwinhagak (aka Quinhagak)
Native Village of Larsen Bay
Levelock Village
Lesnoi Village (aka Woody Island)
Lime Village
Village of Lower Kalskag
Manley Hot Springs Village
Manokotak Village
Native Village of Marshall (aka Fortuna Ledge)
Native Village of Mary's Igloo
McGrath Native Village
Native Village of Mekoryuk
Mentasta Lake Village
Metlakatla Indian Community, Annette Island Reserve
Native Village of Minto
Native Village of Mountain Village
Naknek Native Village
Native Village of Nanwalek (aka English Bay)
Native Village of Napaimute
Native Village of Napakiak
Native Village of Napaskiak

Native Village of Nelson Lagoon
Nenana Native Association
New Stuyahok Village
Newhalen Village
Newtok Village
Native Village of Nightmute
Nikolai Village
Native Village of Nikolski
Ninilchik Village
Native Village of Noatak
Nome Eskimo Community
Nondalton Village
Noorvik Native Community
Northway Village
Native Village of Nuiqsut (aka Nooiksut)
Nulato Village
Native Village of Nunapitchuk
Village of Ohogamiut
Village of Old Harbor
Orutsararmuit Native Village (aka Bethel)
Oscarville Traditional Village
Native Village of Ouzinkie
Native Village of Paimiut
Pauloff Harbor Village
Pedro Bay Village
Native Village of Perryville
Petersburg Indian Association
Native Village of Pilot Point
Pilot Station Traditional Village
Native Village of Pitka's Point
Platinum Traditional Village
Native Village of Point Hope
Native Village of Point Lay
Native Village of Port Graham
Native Village of Port Heiden
Native Village of Port Lions
Portage Creek Village (aka Ohgsenakale)
Pribilof Islands Aleut Communities of St. Paul & St. George Islands
Qagan Toyagungin Tribe of Sand Point Village
Rampart Village
Village of Red Devil
Native Village of Ruby
Native Village of Russion Mission (Yukon)
Village of Salamatoff
Organized Village of Saxman
Native Village of Savoonga
Saint George (See Pribilof Islands Aleut Communities of St. Paul & St. George Islands)
Native Village of Saint Michael
Saint Paul (See Pribilof Islands Aleut Communities of St. Paul & St. George Islands)
Native Village of Scammon Bay
Native Village of Selawik
Seldovia Village Tribe
Shageluk Native Village
Native Village of Shaktoolik
Native Village of Sheldon's Point
Native Village of Shishmaref
Native Village of Shungnak
Sitka Tribe of Alaska
Skagway Village
Village of Sleetmute
Village of Solomon
South Naknek Village
Stebbins Community Association
Native Village of Stevens
Village of Stony River
Takotna Village
Native Village of Tanacross
Native Village of Tanana
Native Village of Tatitlek
Native Village of Tazlina
Telida Village
Native Village of Teller
Native Village of Tetlin
Traditional Village of Togiak
Native Village of Toksook Bay
Tuluksak Native Community
Native Village of Tuntutuliak
Native Village of Tununak
Twin Hills Village
Native Village of Tyonek
Ugashik Village
Umkumiute Native Village
Native Village of Unalakleet
Qawalingin Tribe of Unalaska

Native Village of Unga
Village of Venetie (See Native Village of Venetie Tribal Government)
Native Village of Venetie Tribal Government (Arctic Village and Village of Venetie)
Village of Wainwright
Native Village of Wales
Native Village of White Mountain
Wrangell Cooperative Association
Yakutat Tlingit Tribe

APPENDIX • C

Tribal Addresses of Federally Recognized Tribes

Alabama

Poarch Band of Creek Indians
Route 3, Box 243-A
Atmore, AL 36502
Phone: 205-368-9136
Fax: 205-368-4502

Arizona

Ak-Chin Indian Community Council
Route 2
PO Box 27
Maricopa, AZ 85239
Phone: 602-568-2227
Fax: 602-254-6133

Cocapah Tribal Council
Box Bin G
Somerton, AZ 85350
Phone: 602-627-2102
Fax: 602-627-3173

Colorado River Tribal Council
Route 1, Box 23-B
Parker, AZ 85344
Phone: 602-669-9211
Fax: 602-669-5675

Gila River Indian Community Council
PO Box 97
Sacaton, AZ 85247
Phone: 602-562-3311/963-4323
Fax: 602-562-3422

Havasupai Tribal Council
PO Box 10
Supai, AZ 86435
Phone: 602-448-2961
Fax: 602-448-2551

Hualapai Tribal Council
PO Box 168
Peach Springs, AZ 86434
Phone: 602-769-2216
Fax: 602-769-2326

Kaibab Paiute Tribe
HC 65, Box 2
Fredonia, AZ 86022
Phone: 602-643-7245
Fax: 602-643-7260

Mohave Apache Community Council
PO Box 17779
Fountain Hills, AZ 85268
Phone: 602-990-0995
Fax: 602-837-1630

Navajo Tribal Council
PO Box 308
Window Rock, AZ 86515
Phone: 602-871-4941
Fax: 602-871-4025

Pascua Yaqui Tribal Council
7474 S. Camino De Oeste
Tucson, AZ 85746
Phone: 602-883-2838
Fax: 602-883-7770

Quechan Tribal Council
PO Box 1352
Yuma, AZ 85364
Phone: 619-572-0213
Fax: 619-572-2102

Salt River Pima-Maricopa Indian Community Council
Route 1, Box 216
Scottsdale, AZ 85256
Phone: 602-941-7277
Fax: 602-949-2909

San Carlos Tribal Council
PO Box O
San Carlos, AZ 85550
Phone: 602-475-2361
Fax: 602-475-2566

San Juan Southern Paiute Tribe
PO Box 2656
Tuba City, AZ 86045
Phone: 602-283-4583/4587
Fax: 602-283-5761

The Hopi Tribe
PO Box 123
Kykotsmovi, AZ 86039
Phone: 602-734-2441 x100
Fax: 602-724-6665

Tohono O'odham Council
PO Box 837
Sells, AZ 85634
Phone: 602-383-2221
Fax: 602-383-2479

Tonto Apache Tribal Council
Tonto Reservation #30
Payson, AZ 85541
Phone: 602-474-5000
Fax: 602-474-9125

White Mountain Apache Tribal Council
PO Box 700
Whiteriver, AZ 85941
Phone: 602-338-4346
Fax: 602-338-4778

Yavapai-Apache Community Council
PO Box 1188
Camp Verde, AZ 86322
Phone: 602-567-3649
Fax: 602-778-9445

Yavapai-Prescott Board of Directors
530 E. Merritt St.
Prescott, AZ 86301-2038
Phone: 602-445-8790
Fax: 602-778-9445

California

Agua Caliente Tribal Council
960 E. Tahquitz Way, #106
Palm Springs, CA 92262
Phone: 619-325-5673/7685
Fax: 619-325-0593

Alturas Rancheria
PO Box 1035
Alturas, CA 96101
Phone: 916-233-5571

Barona Band of Mission Indians
1095 Barona Road
Lakeside, CA 92040
Phone: 619-443-6612/6613

Benton Paiute Reservation
Star Route 4, Box 56-A
Benton, CA 93512
Phone: 619-933-2321

Berry Creek Rancheria
1779 Mitchell Avenue
Oroville, CA 95965
Phone: 916-534-3859

Big Lagoon Rancheria
PO Box 3060
Trinidad, CA 95570
Phone: 707-826-2079

Big Pine Reservation
PO Box 700
Big Pine, CA 93513
Phone: 619-938-2121
Fax: 619-938-2942

Big Sandy Rancheria
PO Box 337
Auberry, CA 93602
Phone: 209-855-4003

Big Valley Rancheria
PO Box 153
Finley, CA 95453

Bishop Indian Tribal Council
PO Box 548
Bishop, CA 93514
Phone: 619-873-3584

Blue Lake Rancheria
PO Box 428
Blue Lake, CA 95525
Phone: 707-668-5101

Bridgeport Indian Colony
PO Box 37
Bridgeport, CA 93517
Phone: 619-932-7083

Buena Vista Rancheria
4650 Coalmine Road
Ione, CA 95640

Cabazon Indians of California
84-245 Indio Spring Drive
Indio, CA 92201
Phone: 619-342-2593
Fax: 619-347-7880

Cahuilla Band of Mission Indians
PO Box 860
Anza, CA 92306
Phone: 714-763-5549/619-926-3319

Campo Band of Mission Indians
1779 Campo Truck Trail
Campo, CA 92006
Phone: 619-478-9046
Fax: 619-478-5818

Cedarville Rancheria
PO Box 126
Cedarville, CA 96104
Phone: 916-279-2270

Chemehuevi Indian Tribe
PO Box 1976
Chemehuevi Valley, CA 92363
Phone: 619-858-4531
Fax: 619-858-4818

Chicken Ranch Rancheria
PO Box 1699
Jamestown, CA 95327
Phone: 209-984-3057

Cloverdale Rancheria
285 Santana Drive
Cloverdale, CA 95424
Phone: 707-894-5773

Coast Indian Community of the
Resighini Rancheria
PO Box 529
Klamath, CA 95548
Phone: 707-482-2431

Cold Springs Rancheria
PO Box 209
Tollhouse, CA 93667
Phone: 209-855-2326

Colusa Rancheria
PO Box 8
Colusa, CA 95932
Phone: 916-458-8231

Cortina Rancheria
PO Box 7470
Citrus Heights, CA 95621-7470
Phone: 916-726-7118

Coyote Valley Reservation
PO Box 39
Redwood Valley, CA 95470-0039
Phone: 707-485-8723
Fax: 707-485-1247

Cuyapaipe Band of Mission Indians
4390 La Posta Trucktrail
Pine Valley, CA 92062
Phone: 619-478-5289

Dry Creek Rancheria
PO Box 607
Geyserville, CA 95441
Phone: 707-431-8232

Elem Indian Colony of Pomo Indians
Sulphur Bank Rancheria
PO Box 618
Clearlake Oaks, CA 95423
Phone: 707-998-3315

Elk Valley Rancheria
PO Box 1042
Crescent City, CA 95531
Phone: 707-464-4680

Fort Bidwell Community Council
PO Box 127
Fort Bidwell, CA 96112
Phone: 916-279-6310
Fax: 916-279-2233

Fort Independence Reservation
PO Box 67
Independence, CA 93526
Phone: 619-878-2126

Fort Mojave Tribal Council
500 Merriman Avenue
Needles, CA 92363
Phone: 619-326-4591
Fax: 619-326-2468

Greennile Rancheria
1304 East Street #106
Redding, CA 96001-0837
Phone: 916-284-6446

Grindstone Rancheria
PO Box 63
Elk Creek, CA 95939
Phone: 916-968-5116

Hoopa Valley Indian Rancheria
Hoopa Valley Business Council
PO Box 1348
Hoopa, CA 95546
Phone: 916-625-4211
Fax: 916-625-4594

Hopland Reservation
PO Box 610
Hopland, CA 95449
Phone: 707-744-1647
Fax: 707-744-1560

Inaja & Cosmit Band of Mission Indians
715 B Street #5
Ramona, CA 92065

Jackson Rancheria
1600 Bingo Way
Jackson, CA 95642
Phone: 209-223-3931

Jamul Indian Village
461 Las Brisas
Escondido, CA 92027
Phone: 619-669-0301

Karuk Tribe of California
PO Box 1016
Happy Camp, CA 96039
Phone: 916-493-5305

La Jolla Band of Mission Indians
Star Route, Box 158
Valley Center, CA 92082
Phone: 619-742-3771/3772
Fax: 619-742-1704

La Posta Band of Mission Indians
1064 Barona Road
Lakeside, CA 92040
Phone: 619-561-2924

Laytonville Rancheria
PO Box 48
Laytonville, CA 95454
Phone: 707-984-6197

Lone Pine Tribal Council
Star Route 1
1101 South Main Street
Lone Pine, CA 93545
Phone: 619-876-5414

Los Coyotes General Council
PO Box 86
Warner Springs, CA 92086
Phone: 619-782-3269

Manchester/Point Arena Rancheria
PO Box 623
Point Arena, CA 95468
Phone: 707-882-2788

Manzanita General Council
PO Box 1302
Boulevard, CA 92005
Phone: 619-478-5028

Mesa Grande Band of Mission Indians
PO Box 270
Santa Ysabel, CA 92070
Phone: 619-782-3835

Middletown Rancheria
PO Box 292
Middeltown, CA 95461

Mooretown Rancheria
1900 Oro Dam Blvd., #8
PO Box 1842
Oroville, CA 95965
Phone: 916-533-3625
Fax: 916-533-1531

Morongo Band of Mission Indians
11581 Potrero Road
Banning, CA 92220
Phone: 714-849-4697/4698
Fax: 714-849-4425

North Fork Rancheria
PO Box 120
North Fork, CA 93643

Pala Band of Mission Indians
PO Box 43
Pala, CA 92059
Phone: 619-742-3784
Fax: 619-742-1411

Pauma Band of Mission Indians
PO Box 86
Pauma Valley, CA 92061
Phone: 619-742-1289

Pechanga Band of Mission Indians
PO Box 1477
Temecula, CA 92390
Phone: 714-676-2768
Fax: 714-699-6983

Picayune Rancheria
PO Box 708
Coarsegold, CA 93614
Phone: 209-683-6633
Fax: 209-683-0599

Pinoleville Rancheria
367 N. State Street
Suite 204
Ukiah, CA 95482
Phone: 707-463-1454

Pit River Tribal Council
PO Drawer 1570
Burney, CA 96013
Phone: 916-335-5421

Potter Valley Rancheria
PO Box 2273
West Sacramento, CA 95619
Phone: 916-372-3428

Quartz Valley Indian Reservation
PO Box 737
Etna, CA 96027
Phone: 916-467-3307/5407

Ramona Band of Cahuilla Indians
PO Box 26
Anza, CA 92306

Redding Rancheria
1786 California Street
Redding, CA 96001
Phone: 916-241-1871
Fax: 916-241-1879

Redwood Valley Rancheria
PO Box 499
Redwood Valley, CA 95470
Phone: 707-485-0361

Rincon Band of Mission Indians
PO Box 68
Valley Center, CA 92082
Phone: 619-749-1051
Fax: 619-749-8901

Robinson Rancheria
PO Box 1119
Nice, CA 95464
Phone: 707-275-0527

Rohnerville Rancheria
PO Box 108
Eureka, CA 95502
Phone: 707-443-6150

Round Valley Reservation
PO Box 448
Covelo, CA 95428
Phone: 707-983-6126

Rumsey Rancheria
PO Box 18
Brooks, CA 95606
Phone: 916-796-3400

San Manuel Band of Mission Indians
5438 North Victoria Avenue
Highland, CA 92346
Phone: 714-862-8509

San Pasqual Band of Mission Indians
PO Box 365
Valley Center, CA 92082
Phone: 619-749-3200

Santa Rosa Rancheria
16835 Alkali Drive
Lemoore, CA 93245
Phone: 209-924-1278

Santa Rosa Reservation
325 North Western Avenue
Hemet, CA 92343
Phone: 619-741-5211

Santa Ynez Band of Mission Indians
PO Box 517
Santa Ynex, CA 93460
Phone: 805-688-7997

Santa Ysabel Band of Mission Indians
PO Box 130
Santa Ysabel, CA 92070
Phone: 619-765-0845

Sherwood Valley Rancheria
2141 S. State Street
Ukiah, CA 95482
Phone: 707-468-1337

Shingle Springs Rancheria
PO Box 1340
Shingle Springs, CA 95682
Phone: 916-676-8010

Smith River Rancheria
PO Box 239
Smith River, CA 95567
Phone: 707-487-9255

Soboba Band of Mission Indians
PO Box 487
San Jacinto, CA 92383
Phone: 714-654-2765

Stewarts Point Rancheria
PO Box 54
Stewarts Point, CA 95480
Phone: 707-785-2594

Susanville Rancheria
PO Drawer U
Susanville, CA 96130
Phone: 916-257-6264

Sycuan Business Committee
5459 Dehesa Road
El Cajon, CA 92021
Phone: 619-445-2613
Fax: 619-445-1927

Table Bluff Rancheria
PO Box 519
Loleta, CA 95551
Phone: 707-733-5055
Fax: 707-733-5601

Table Mountain Rancheria
PO Box 243
Friant, CA 93626
Phone: 209-822-2125

Timbi-sha Shoshone Tribe
PO Box 206
Death Valley, CA 92328
Phone: 619-786-2374
Fax: 619-786-2344

Torres-Martinez Band of Mission Indians
66-725 Martinez Road
Thermal, CA 92274
Phone: 619-387-0300

Trinidad Rancheria
PO Box 630
Trinidad, CA 95570
Phone: 707-677-0211
Fax: 707-677-3921

Tule River Tribal Council
PO Box 589
Porterville, CA 93258
Phone: 209-781-4271
Fax: 209-781-4610

Tuolumne Me-wuk Rancheria
PO Box 699
19595 Miwuk Street
Tuolumne, CA 95379
Phone: 209-928-3475
Fax: 209-928-1677

Twenty Nine Palms Band of Mission Indians
c/o Glen Calac
1150 E. Palm Canyon Drive #75
Palm Springs, CA 92262
Phone: 619-322-7481

Upper Lake Rancheria
PO Box 245272
Sacramento, CA 95820
Phone: 916-371-5637

Viejas Tribal Council
PO Box 908
Alpine, CA 92001
Phone: 619-445-3810
Fax: 619-445-5337

Winnemucca Colony Council
2700 Sunkist
Susanville, CA 96130
Phone: 916-257-7093

Woodfords Community Council
96 Washoe Blvd.
Markleeville, CA 96120
Phone: 916-694-2170

Yurok Tribe
Yurok Transition Team
517 Third St., Suite 21
Eureka, CA 95501
Phone: 800-848-8765/707-444-0433

Colorado

Southern Ute Indian Tribal Council
Tribal Affairs Building
PO Box 737
Ignacio, CO 81137
Phone: 303-563-4525
Fax: 303-563-4229

Ute Mountain Ute Tribe
Tribal Office Building
Towaoc, CO 81334
Phone: 303-565-3751
Fax: 303-565-7412

Connecticut

Mashantucket Pequot Council
PO Box 160
Ledyard, CT 06339
Phone: 203-536-2681
Fax: 203-572-0421

Florida

Miccosukee Business Committee
PO Box 440021
Tamiami Station
Miami, Fl 33144
Phone: 305-223-8380/8383
Fax: 305-223-1011

Seminole Tribe of Florida
6073 Sterling Road
Hollywood, FL 33024
Phone: 305-321-1000
Fax: 305-581-8917

Iowa

Sac & Fox Tribal Council
Route 2, Box 56C
Tama, IA 52339
Phone: 515-484-4678/5358
Fax: 515-484-5218

Idaho

Coeur D' Alene Tribal Council
Plummer, ID 83851
Phone: 208-274-3101
Fax: 208-274-2824

Fort Hall Business Council
Shoshone-Bannock Tribes
PO Box 306
Fort Hall, ID 83203
Phone: 208-238-3700
Fax: 208-237-0797

Kootenai Tribal Council
PO Box 1269
Bonners Ferry, ID 83805
Phone: 208-267-3519
Fax: 208-267-2960

Nez Perce Tribe of Idaho
Box 305
Lapwai, ID 83540
Phone: 208-843-2253
Fax: 208-843-2036

Northwestern Band of Shoshoni Nation
PO Box 145
Fort Hall, ID 83203-0145
Phone: 208-238-0916
Fax: 208-237-0797

Kansas

Iowa of Kansas Executive Committee
Route 1, Box 58A
White Cloud, KS 66094
Phone: 913-595-3258
Fax: 913-595-6610

Kickapoo of Kansas Tribal Council
Route 1, Box 157A
Horton, KS 66349
Phone: 913-486-2131
Fax: 913-486-2801

Prairie Band Potawatomi Tribal Council
Route 2, Box 50A
Mayetta, KS 66509
Phone: 913-966-2255/2771
Fax: 913-966-2144

Sac & Fox of Missouri Tribal Council
Rural Route 1, Box 60
Reserve, KS 66434-9723
Phone: 913-742-7471
Fax: 913-742-3785

Louisiana

Chitimacha Tribal Council
PO Box 661
Charenton, LA 70523
Phone: 318-923-4973
Fax: 318-923-7791

Coushatta Tribal Council
PO Box 818
Elton, LA 70532
Phone: 318-584-2261
Fax: 318-584-2998

Tunica-Biloxi Indian Tribe
PO Box 311
Mansura, LA 71351
Phone: 318-253-9767
Fax: 318-253-9791

Massachusetts

Wampanoag Tribal Council of Gay Head, Inc.
State Road
RFD Box 137
Gay Head, MA 02535
Phone: 508-645-9265
Fax: 508-645-3790

Maine

Houlton Band of Maliseet Indians
PO Box 748
Bell Road
Houlton, ME 04730
Phone: 207-532-4273
Fax: 207-532-2660

Indian Township Passamaquoddy Reservation
PO Box 301
Princeton, ME 04668
Phone: 207-796-2301
Fax: 207-796-5256

*Penobscot Nation
6 River Road-Indian Island
Old Town, ME 04468
Phone: 207-827-7776
Fax: 207-827-6042

*Pleasant Point Passamaquoddy Reservation
PO Box 343
Perry, ME 04667
Phone: 207-853-2551
Fax: 207-853-6039

Michigan

Bay Mills Executive Council
Route 1
Brimley, MI 49715
Phone: 906-248-3241
Fax: 906-248-3283

Grand Traverse Band
Route 1, Box 135
Suttons Bay, MI 49682
Phone: 616-271-3538
Fax: 616-271-4230

Hannahville Indian Community Council
Hannahville Route 1, Road N14911
Wilson, MI 49896-9728
Phone: 906-466-2342
Fax: 906-466-2418

Keweenaw Bay Tribal Council
Center Building
Route 1, Box 45
Baraga, MI 49908
Phone: 906-353-6623
Fax: 906-353-7540

*Lac Courte Oreilles Governing Board
Tribal Office, Route 2
PO Box 2700
Hayward, MI 54843
Phone: 715-634-8934
Fax: 715-634-4797

Lac Vieux Desert Band of Chippewa Indians
PO Box 446
Watersmeet, MI 49969
Phone: 906-358-4577

** Tribes have exclusive jurisdiction over child welfare matters.*

Saginaw Chippewa Indian Tribe
7070 East Broadway
Mt. Pleasant, MI 48858
Phone: 517-772-5700
Fax: 517-773-3735

Sault Ste. Marie Chippewa
Tribal Council
206 Geenough Street
Sault Ste. Marie, MI 49783
Phone: 906-635-6050
Fax: 906-635-0741

Minnesota

Fond du Lac Reservation
Business Committee
105 University Road
Cloquet, MN 55720
Phone: 218-879-4593
Fax: 218-879-4146

Grand Portage Reservation
Business Committee
PO Box 428
Grand Portage, MN 55605
Phone: 218-475-2279/2277
Fax: 218-475-2309

Leech Lake Reservation
Business Committee
Route 3, Box 100
Cass Lake, MN 56633
Phone: 218-335-8200
Fax: 218-325-8309

Lower Sioux Indian Community
Council
Rural Route 1, Box 308
Morton, MN 56270
Phone: 507-697-6185
Fax: 507-697-6110

Mille Lacs Reservation Business
Committee
Star Route
Onamia, MN 56359
Phone: 612-532-4181
Fax: 612-532-4209

Minnesota Chippewa Tribal
Executive Committee
Box 217 C
Cass Lake, MN 56633
Phone: 218-335-2252
Fax: 218-335-6562

Minnesota Chippewa Tribe
White Earth Reservation Business
Committee
PO Box 418
White Earth, MN 56591
Phone: 218-983-3285
Fax: 218-983-3641

Nett Lake Reservation Business
Committee
(Bois Forte)
PO Box 16
Nett Lake, MN 55772
Phone: 218-757-3261
Fax: 218-757-3636

Prairie Island Community Council
(Minnesota Mdewakanton Sioux)
5750 Sturgeon Lake Road
Route 2, Box 1000
Welch, MN 55089
Phone: 612-388-8889
Fax: 612-388-1576

*Red Lake Tribal Council
PO Box 550
Red Lake, MN 56671
Phone: 218-679-3341
Fax: 218-679-3378

Shakopee Sioux Community Council
2330 Sioux Trail, NW
Prior Lake, MN 55372
Phone: 612-445-8900
Fax: 612-445-0446

Upper Sioux Board of Trustees
PO Box 147
Granite Falls, MN 56241
Phone: 612-564-2360/2550
Fax: 612-564-3264

** Tribes have exclusive jurisdiction over child welfare matters.*

Missouri

Eastern Shawnee Tribe of Oklahoma
PO Box 350
Seneca, MO 64865

Mississippi

Mississippi Band of Choctaw Indians
Choctaw Branch
PO Box 6010
Philadelphia, MS 39350
Phone: 601-656-5251
Fax: 601-656-1992

Montana

Assiniboine and Sioux Tribes
Fort Peck Indian Reservation
PO Box 1027
Poplar, MT 59255
Phone: 406-768-5155
Fax: 406-768-5478

Blackfeet Tribe
PO Box 850
Browning, MT 59417
Phone: 406-338-7521/7276
Fax: 406-338-7530

Chippewa Cree Business Committee
Rocky Boy Route
Box Elder, MT 59521
Phone: 406-395-4282/4285
Fax: 406-395-4497

Confederated Salish and Kootenai Tribes of the Flathead Reservation
PO Box 278
Pablo, MT 59855
Phone: 406-675-2700, X 422
Fax: 406-675-2806

Crow Tribe of Indians
PO Box 159
Crow Agency, MT 59022
Phone: 406-638-2601
Fax: 406-638-7283

Fort Belknap Community Council
Gros Ventre & Assiniboine Tribes
Rural Route 1, Box 66
Harlem, MT 59526
Phone: 406-353-2205
Fax: 406-353-2797

Northern Cheyenne Tribe
PO Box 128
Lame Deer, MT 59043
Phone: 406-477-6284
Fax: 406-477-6210

North Carolina

Eastern Band of Cherokee Indians
PO Box 455
Cherokee, NC 28719
Phone: 704-497-2771
Fax: 704-497-3220

North Dakota

Devils Lake Sioux Tribal Council
Sioux Community Center
Fort Totten, ND 58335
Phone: 701-766-4221
Fax: 701-766-4126

Standing Rock Sioux Tribe
Fort Yates, ND 58538
Phone: 701-854-7201
Fax: 701-854-7299

Three Affiliated Tribes Business Council
Fort Berthold Reservation
PO Box 220
New Town, ND 58763
Phone: 701-627-4781
Fax: 701-627-3805

Turtle Mountain Band of Chippewa Indians
PO Box 900
Belcourt, ND 58316
Phone: 701-477-6451
Fax: 701-477-6836

Nebraska

*Omaha Tribal Council
PO Box 368
Macy, NE 68039
Phone: 402-837-5391
Fax: 402-837-5308

Santee Sioux Tribal Council
Route 2
Niobrara, NE 68760
Phone: 402-857-3302
Fax: 402-857-3307

* Winnebago Tribal Council
Box 687
Winnebago, NE 68071
Phone: 402-878-2272
Fax: 402-878-2963

New Mexico

Acoma Pueblo
PO Box 309
Acomita, NM 87034
Phone: 505-552-6604
Fax: 505-552-6600

Jemez Pueblo
PO Box 100
Jemez Pueblo, NM 87024
Phone: 505-834-7359
Fax: 505-834-7678

Jicarilla Apache Tribe
PO Box 507
Dulce, NM 87528
Phone: 505-759-3242, X201
Fax: 505-759-3005

Mescalero Apache Tribal Council
PO Box 176
Mescalero, NM 87340
Phone: 505-671-4495
Fax: 505-671-4495 (Call first)

Nambe Pueblo
Route 1, Box 117-BB
Santa Fe, NM 87501
Phone: 505-455-7752

Pueblo of Cochiti
PO Box 70
Cochiti, NM 87041
Phone: 505-465-2244
Fax: 505-465-2245

Pueblo of Isleta
PO Box 317
Isleta, NM 87022
Phone: 505-869-3111/6333/3994
Fax: 505-869-4236

Pueblo of Laguna
PO Box 194
Laguna, NM 87026
Phone: 505-243-7616
Fax: 505-552-6007

Pueblo of Picuris
PO Box 127
Penasco, NM 87553
Phone: 505-587-2519
Fax: 505-587-1071

Pueblo of Pojoaque
Route 11, Box 71
Santa Fe, NM 87501
Phone: 505-455-2278
Fax: 505-455-2950

Ramah Navajo Chapter
PO Box 267
Ramah, NM 81137
Phone: 505-775-3383
Fax: 505-775-3554

San Felipe Pueblo
PO Box A
San Felipe Pueblo, NM 87001
Phone: 505-867-3381
Fax: 505-867-3383

San Ildefonso Pueblo
Route 5, Box 315-A
Santa Fe, NM 87501
Phone: 505-455-2273
Fax: 505-455-7351

* *Tribes have exclusive jurisdiction over child welfare matters.*

San Juan Pueblo
PO Box 1099
San Juan Pueblo, NM 87566
Phone: 505-852-4400/6210
Fax: 505-852-4820

Sandia Pueblo
PO Box 6008
Bernalillo, NM 87004
Phone: 505-867-3317
Fax: 505-867-9235

Santa Ana Pueblo
Star Route Box 37
Bernalillo, NM 87004
Phone: 505-867-3301
Fax: 505-867-3395

Santa Clara Pueblo
PO Box 580
Espanola, NM 87532
Phone: 505-753-7316/7326/7330
Fax: 505-753-8988

Santo Domingo Pueblo
PO Box 99
Santo Domingo Pueblo, NM 87052
Phone: 505-465-2214
Fax: 505-465-2688

Taos Pueblo
PO Box 1846
Taos, NM 87571
Phone: 505-758-9593
Fax: 505-758-4604

Tesuque Pueblo
Route 11, Box 1
Santa Fe, NM 87501
Phone: 505-983-2667
Fax: 505-455-3815

Zia Pueblo
General Delivery
San Ysidro, NM 87053
Phone: 505-867-3304
Fax: 505-867-3308

Zuni Pueblo
PO Box 339
Zuni, NM 87327
Phone: 505-782-4481
Fax: 505-782-2700

Nevada

Battle Mountain Band Council
35 Mtn. View Drive, #138-13
PO Box 578
Battle Mountain, NV 89820
Phone: 702-635-2004
Fax: 702-635-8016

Carson Colony Community Council
652 Oneida Street
Carson City, NV 89703
Phone: 702-883-6431/702-265-4191

Dresslerville Community Council
1585 Watasheamu Road
Gardnerville, NV 89410
Phone: 702-838-6431/702-265-4191

Duckwater Shoshone Tribal Council
PO Box 68
Duckwater, NV 89314
Phone: 702-863-0227
Fax: 702-863-0301

Elko Band Council
PO Box 748
Elko, NV 89801
Phone: 702-738-8889

Ely Colony Council
16 Shoshone Circle
Ely, NV 89301
Phone: 702-289-3013

Fallon Business Council
8955 Mission Road
Fallon, NV 89406
Phone: 702-423-6075
Fax: 702-423-5202

Fort McDermitt Tribal Council
PO Box 457
McDermitt, NV 89421
Phone: 702-532-8259

Las Vegas Colony Council
No. 1, Paiute Drive
Las Vegas, NV 89106
Phone: 702-386-3926
Fax: 702-383-4019

Lovelock Tribal Council
Box 878
Lovelock, NV 89419
Phone: 702-273-7861
Fax: 702-273-7030

Moapa Business Council
PO Box 56
Moapa, NV 89025
Phone: 702-865-2787
Fax: 702-865-2875

Pyramid Lake Paiute Tribe
PO Box 256
Nixon, NV 89424
Phone: 702-574-0140
Fax: 702-786-8232

Reno-Sparks Indian Council
98 Colony Road
Reno, NV 89502
Phone: 702-329-2936
Fax: 702-329-8710

Shoshone Paiute Business Council
PO Box 219
Owyhee, NV 89832
Phone: 702-757-3161
Fax: 702-757-2219

South Fork Band Council
Box B-13
Lee, NV 89829
Phone: 702-744-4273
Fax: 702-738-2345

Stewart Community Council
5258 Snyder Avenue
Carson City, NV 89701
Phone: 702-883-7767

Summit Lake Paiute Council
PO Box 1958
Winnemucca, NV 89445
Phone: 702-623-5151
Fax: 702-623-0558

Tribal Council of the Te-Moak
Western Shoshone Indians of Nevada
525 Sunset Street
Elko, NV 89801
Phone: 702-738-9251
Fax: 702-738-2345

Walker River Paiute Tribe
PO Box 220
Schurz, NV 89427
Phone: 702-773-2306
Fax: 702-773-2585

Washoe Tribal Council
Route 2, 919 Highway 395 South
Gardnerville, NV 89410
Phone: 702-265-4191/702-883-1446
Fax: 702-265-6240

Wells Indian Colony Band Council
PO Box 809
Wells, NV 89835
Phone: 702-752-3045

Yerington Paiute Tribal Council
171 Campbell Lane
Yerington, NV 89447
Phone: 702-463-3301/702-883-3895
Fax: 702-463-2416

Yomba Tribal Council
Route 1, Box 24
Austin, NV 98310
Phone: 702-964-2463/702-423-6919
Fax: 702-964-2443

New York

Cayuga Nation
PO Box 11
Versailles, NY 14168
Phone: 716-532-4847
Fax: 716-532-5417

Oneida Nation of New York
PO Box 1 - West Road
Oneida, NY 13421
Phone: 315-697-8251
Fax: 315-697-8259

Onondaga Nation
RR1, Box 270
Nedrow, NY 13120
Phone: 315-469-8507

Seneca Nation
PO Box 231
Salamanca, NY 14081
Phone: 716-945-1790
Fax: 716-945-3917

St. Regis Mohawk Council Chiefs
St. Regis Reservation
Akwesasne Community Building
Hogansburg, NY 13655
Phone: 518-358-2272
Fax: 518-358-3203

Tonawanda Band of Senecas
Council of Chiefs
7283 Parker Road
Basom, NY 14013
Phone: 716-542-9942
Fax: 716-542-9692

Tuscarora Nation
5615 Walmore Road
Lewiston, NY 14092
Phone: 716-297-4990

Oklahoma

Absentee-Shawnee Executive
Committee
2025 S Gordon Cooper Dr.
Shawnee, OK 74801-9381
Phone: 405-275-4030
Fax: 405-273-4534

Alabama-Quassarte Tribal Town
PO Box 404
Eufaula, OK 74432
Phone: 918-689-7160

Apache Business Committee
PO Box 1220
Anadarko, OK 73005
Phone: 405-247-9493

Caddo Tribal Council
PO Box 487
Binger, OK 73009
Phone: 405-656-2344
Fax: 405-656-2468

Cherokee Nation of Oklahoma
PO Box 948
Tahlequah, OK 74465
Phone: 918-456-0671
Fax: 918-456-6485

Cheyenne-Arapaho Tribes of
Oklahoma
PO Box 38
Concho, OK 73022
Phone: 405-262-0345
Fax: 405-262-0745

Chickasaw Nation of Oklahoma
PO Box 1548
Ada, OK 74820
Phone: 405-436-2603
Fax: 405-436-4287

Choctaw Nation of Oklahoma
PO Drawer 1210
16th & Locust Street
Durant, OK 74701
Phone: 405-924-8280
Fax: 405-924-1150

Citizen Band Potawatomi
Business Committee
1901 S Gordon Cooper Dr.
Shawnee, OK 74801
Phone: 405-275-3121
Fax: 405-275-0198

Comanche Tribe
HC 32
PO Box 1720
Lawton, OK 73501
Phone: 405-492-4988
Fax: 405-492-4981

Creek Nation of Oklahoma
PO Box 580
Okmulgee, OK 74447
Phone: 918-756-8700
Fax: 918-756-3340

Delaware Executive Committee
PO Box 825
Anadarko, OK 73005
Phone: 405-247-2448
Fax: 405-247-9393

Fort Sill Apache Business Committee
Route 2, Box 121
Apache, OK 73006
Phone: 405-588-2298
Fax: 405-588-3133

Iowa of Oklahoma Business Committee
Iowa Veterans Hall
PO Box 190
Perkins, OK 74059
Phone: 405-547-2403
Fax: 405-547-5294

Kaw Business Committee
Drawer 50
Kaw City, OK 74641
Phone:405-269-2552
Fax: 405-269-2301

Kialegee Tribal Town
Route 3, Box 18-C
Okemah, OK 74859
Phone: 918-656-3686

Kickapoo of Oklahoma
PO Box 70
McLoud, OK 74851
Phone: 405-964-2075
Fax: 405-964-2745

Kiowa Business Committee
PO Box 369
Carnegie, OK 73015
Phone: 405-654-2300
Fax: 405-654-2188

Miami Tribe of Oklahoma
PO Box 636
Miami, OK 74355
Phone: 918-542-1445
Fax: 918-542-7260

Modoc Tribe of Oklahoma
PO Box 939
Miami, OK 74354
Phone: 918-542-1190
Fax: 918-540-2500

Osage Tribe of Indians
Tribal Administration Building
Pawhuska, OK 74056
Phone: 918-287-4622
Fax: 918-287-1229

Otoe-Missouria Tribal Council
PO Box 68
Red Rock, OK 74058
Phone: 405-723-4434
Fax: 405-723-4273

Ottawa Tribe of Oklahoma
PO Box 110
Miami, OK 74355
Phone: 918-540-1536

Pawnee Tribal Business Council
PO Box 470
Pawnee, OK 74058
Phone: 918-762-3621
Fax: 918-762-2389

Peoria Indian Tribe of Oklahoma
PO Box 1527
Miami, OK 74355
Phone: 918-540-2535

Ponca Tribe of Oklahoma
Box 2, White Eagle
Ponca City, OK 74601
Phone: 405-762-8104
Fax: 405-762-7436

Quapaw Tribal Business Committee
PO Box 765
Quapaw, OK 74363
Phone: 918-542-1853
Fax: 918-542-1559

Sac and Fox Nation
Route 2, Box 246
Stroud, OK 74079
Phone: 918-968-3526
Fax: 918-968-3887

Seminole Nation of Oklahoma
PO Box 1498
Wewoka, OK 74884
Phone: 405-257-6287
Fax: 405-257-5017

Seneca-Cayuga Tribe of Oklahoma
PO Box 1283
Miami, OK 74355
Phone: 918-542-6609
Fax: 918-542-3684

Thlopthlocco Tribal Town
PO Box 706
Okemah, OK 74859
Phone: 918-623-2620
Fax: 918-623-2404

United Keetoowah Band of
Cherokee Indians
2450 South Muskogee Avenue
Tahlequah, OK 74464
Phone: 918-456-5491
Fax: 918-456-9601

Wichita Executive Committee
PO Box 729
Anadarko, OK 73005
Phone: 405-247-2425
Fax: 405-247-2005

Wyandotte Tribe of Oklahoma
PO Box 250
Wyandotte, OK 74370
Phone: 918-678-2297/2298
Fax: 918-678-2944

Oregon

Burns-Paiute General Council
H.C. 71, 100 Pasigo Street
Burns, OR 97720
Phone: 503-573-2088
Fax: 503-573-2323

Confederated Tribes of Coos
Lower Umpqua & Siuslaw Indians
455 South 4th Street
Coos Bay, OR 97420
Phone: 503-267-5454
Fax: 503-269-1647

Confederated Tribes of the Grande
Ronde Tribal Council
PO Box 38
Grande Ronde, OR 97347
Phone: 503-879-5215
Fax: 503-879-5964

Confederated Tribes of the Umatilla
Indian Reservation
PO Box 638
Pendleton, OR 97801
Phone: 503-276-3165
Fax: 503-276-3095

Coquille Indian Tribe
250 Hull Street
Coos Bay, OR 97420
Phone: 503-888-4274
Fax: 503-269-2573

Cow Creek Band of Umpqua Indians
2400 Stewart Parkway #300
Roseburg, OR 97470
Phone: 503-672-9405
Fax: 503-673-0432

Klamath General Council
Box 436
Chiloquin, OR 97624
Phone: 503-783-2219
Fax: 503-783-2029

Siletz Tribal Council
PO Box 549
Siletz, OR 97380
Phone: 503-444-2532/2513
Fax: 503-444-2307

Warm Springs Tribal Council
PO Box C
Warm Springs, OR 97761
Phone: 503-553-1161
Fax: 503-553-1924

Rhode Island

Narragansett Indian Tribe
PO Box 268
Charleston, RI 02813
Phone: 401-364-1100
Fax: 401-364-1104

South Dakota

Cheyenne River Sioux Tribe
PO Box 590
Eagle Butte, SD 57625
Phone: 605-964-4155
Fax: 605-964-4151

Crow Creek Sioux Tribal Council
PO Box 658
Fort Thompson, SD 57339
Phone: 605-245-2221/605-245-2222
Fax: 605-245-2470

Flandreau Santee Sioux Executive Committee
Flandreau Field Office
Box 283
Flandreau, SD 57028
Phone: 605-997-3891
Fax: 605-997-3878

Lower Brule Sioux Tribal Council
Lower Brule, SD 57548
Phone: 605-473-5561
Fax: 605-473-5606

Oglala Sioux Tribe
PO Box 468
Pine Ridge, SD 57770
Phone: 605-867-5821
Fax: 605-867-1138

Ponca Tribe of Nebraska
Ponca Tribal Council
Lake Andes, SD 57356
Phone: 605-384-3651 (BIA)
Fax: 402-342-0609

Rosebud Sioux Tribe
PO Box 38
Rosebud, SD 57570
Phone: 605-747-2381
Fax: 605-747-2243

Sisseton-Wahpeton Sioux Tribal Committee
Route 2
Agency Village
Sisseton, SD 57262
Phone: 605-698-3911
Fax: 605-698-3708

Yankton Sioux Tribal Business & Claims Committee
Box 248
Marty, SD 57361
Phone: 605-384-3641
Fax: 605-384-5687

Texas

Alabama-Coushatta Tribe of Texas
Route 3, Box 659
Livingston, TX 77351
Phone: 409-563-4391
Fax: 409-563-4397

Kickapoo Traditional Tribe of Texas
PO Box 972
Eagle Pass, TX 78853
Phone: 512-773-2105

Ysleta del Sur Pueblo
119 S. Old Pueblo Road
PO Box 17579
El Paso, TX 79917
Phone: 915-859-7913/14/18
Fax: 915-859-2988

Utah

Goshute Business Council
PO Box 6104
Ibapah, UT 84034
Phone: 801-234-1138
Fax: 801-234-1162

Northern Ute Indian Tribe
PO Box 190
Fort Duchesne, UT 84026
Phone: 801-722-5141
Fax: 801-722-2374

Skull Valley Executive Committee
c/o Unitah & Ouray Agency
PO Box 130
Fort Duchesne, UT 84026
Phone: 801-722-2406

Tribal Council of Paiute Indian Tribe of Utah
600 North 100 East Paiute Drive
Cedar City, UT 84720
Phone: 801-586-1111
Fax: 801-586-0896

Washington

Chehalis Community Council
PO Box 536
Oakville, WA 98568
Phone: 206-273-5911
Fax: 206-273-5914

*Colville Business Committee
PO Box 150
Nespelem, WA 99155
Phone: 509-634-4711
Fax: 509-634-4116

Hoh Tribal Business Committee
HC 80, Box 917
Forks, WA 98331
Phone: 206-374-6582
Fax: 206-374-6549

Jamestown Klallam Tribe
305 Old Blyn Highway
Sequim, WA 98382
Phone: 206-683-1109
Fax: 206-683-4366

Kalispel Tribal Council
PO Box 38
Usk, WA 99180
Phone: 509-445-1147
Fax: 509-445-1705

Lower Elwha Community Council
1666 Lower Elwha Road
Port Angeles, WA 98362
Phone: 206-452-8471
Fax: 206-452-3428

Lummi Business Council
2616 Kwina Road
Bellingham, WA 98226-9298
Phone: 206-734-8180
Fax: 206-384-4737

Makah Tribal Council
PO Box 115
Neah Bay, WA 98357
Phone: 206-645-2201
Fax: 206-645-2033

*Muckleshoot Indian Tribe
39015 172nd Avenue, SE
Auburn, WA 98002
Phone: 206-931-4999
Fax: 206-939-5311

Nisqually Indian Community Council
4820 She-Nah-Num Drive, SE
Olympia, WA 98503
Phone: 206-456-5221
Fax: 206-456-5280

** Tribes have exclusive jurisdiction over child welfare matters.*

Nooksack Tribal Council
PO Box 157
Deming, WA 98244
Phone: 206-592-5176
Fax: 206-592-5753

Port Gamble Community Council
PO Box 280
Kingston, WA 98346
Phone: 206-297-2646
Fax: 206-297-7097

Puyallup Tribal Council
2002 East 28th Street
Tacoma, WA 98404
Phone: 206-597-6200
Fax: 206-272-9514

Quileute Tribal Council
PO Box 279
LaPush, WA 98350
Phone: 206-374-6163
Fax: 206-374-6311

Quinault Business Committee
PO Box 189
Taholah, WA 98587
Phone: 206-276-8211
Fax: 206-276-4191

Sauk-Suiattle Tribal Council
5318 Chief Brown Lane
Darrington, WA 98241
Phone: 206-435-8366
Fax: 206-436-1511

Shoalwater Bay Tribal Council
PO Box 130
Tokeland, WA 98590
Phone: 206-267-6766
Fax: 206-267-6778

Skokomish Tribal Council
No. 80 Tribal Center Road
Shelton, WA 98584
Phone: 206-426-4232
Fax: 206-877-5943

*Spokane Tribe of Indians
PO Box 100
Wellpinit, WA 99040
Phone: 509-258-4581
Fax: 509-258-4582

Squaxin Island Tribal Council
SE 70, Squaxin Lane
Shelton, WA 98584
Phone: 206-426-9781
Fax: 206-426-3971

Stillaquamish Board of Directors
3439 Stoluckquamish Lane
Arlington, WA 98223
Phone: 206-652-7362
Fax: 206-435-2204

Suquamish Tribal Council
PO Box 498
Suquamish, WA 98392
Phone: 206-598-3311
Fax: 206-598-4666

Swinomish Indian Tribal Community
PO Box 817
LaConner, WA 98257
Phone: 206-466-3163
Fax: 206-466-5309

Tulalip Board of Directors
6700 Totem Beach Road
Marysville, WA 98270
Phone: 206-653-4585
Fax: 206-653-0278

Upper Skagit Tribal Council
2284 Community Plaza
Sedro Wooley, WA 98284
Phone: 206-856-5501
Fax: 206-856-2712

*Yakima Indian Nation
PO Box 151
Toppenish, WA 98948
Phone: 509-865-2255
Fax: 509-865-5528

** Tribes have exclusive jurisdiction over child welfare matters.*

Wisconsin

Bad River Tribal Council
Route 39
Odanah, WI 54861
Phone: 715-682-7111
Fax: 715-682-7118

Forest County Potawatomi General Council
PO Box 346
Crandon, WI 54520
Phone: 715-478-2903
Fax: 715-478-5280

Lac du Flambeau Tribal Council
PO Box 67
Lac du Flambeau, WI 54538
Phone: 715-588-3303
Fax: 715-588-7930

Menominee Indian Tribe of Wisconsin
PO Box 397
Keshena, WI 54135
Phone: 715-799-3341
Fax: 715-799-4525

Oneida Tribal Business Committee
PO Box 365
Oneida, WI 54155-0365
Phone: 414-869-2272/2214
Fax: 414-869-2194

Red Cliff Tribal Council
PO Box 529
Bayfield, WI 54814
Phone: 715-779-3701
Fax: 715-779-3704

Sokaogon Chippewa Tribal Council
Route 1, Box 625
Crandon, WI 54520
Phone: 715-478-2604
Fax: 715-478-5275

St. Croix Council
St. Croix Tribal Center
PO Box 287
Hertel, WI 54845
Phone: 715-349-2195
Fax: 715-349-5768

Stockbridge-Munsee Tribal Council
Route 1
Bowler, WI 54416
Phone: 715-793-4111
Fax: 715-793-4299

Wisconsin Winnebago Business Committee
PO Box 311
Tomah, WI 54660
Phone: 608-374-2210

Wyoming

Arapahoe Business Council
PO Box 217
Fort Washakie, WY 82514
Phone: 307-332-6120
Fax: 307-332-3055

Shoshone Business Council
PO Box 217
Fort Washakie, WY 82514
Phone: 307-332-3532
Fax: 307-332-3055

Alaska

In Alaska, each of the 460 native villages or towns is considered to be an individual tribe even though the villages may be close together and the people in the villages are of the same linguistic stock. Overlaying the village system are the twelve regional profit and non-profit corporations. The regional Profit corporations are for the purpose of administering funds from the Alaska native Claims Settlement Act. The regional Non-Profit corporations cover social and cultural matters.

Notice to an Alaskan village should proceed as below:

1. If a client (relative, collateral) states the family/child is Alaskan, ask which village they're from. Do

not ask if the family/child is enrolled in the village, since many Alaskan villages do not keep formal rolls like their tribal counterparts in the 48 contiguous states.

2. If the village name is not known, ask the client (relative, collateral) if the family/child is a member of one of the twelve regional corporations. If so, use the list of Alaskan Corporations and addresses to look up the appropriate non-profit corporation to write for assistance in locating/contacting the tribal village.

Alaska Native Regional Non-Profit Corporation Addresses

Artic Slope Native Association
Box 566
Barrow, Alaska 99723
Phone: 907-852-8633

Mauneluk (Maniilaq) Association
Box 256
Kotzebue, Alaska 99752
Phone: 907-442-3314

Tanana Chiefs Conference
First and Hall Streets
Fairbanks, Alaska 99701
Phone: 907-456-1275

Bristol Bay Native Association
Box 237
Dillingham, Alaska 99576
Phone: 907-842-5257/5258

Tlingit-Haida Central Council
One Sealaska Plaza
Juneau, Alaska 99801
Phone: 907-586-1432

Aleutian/Pribilof Islands
Associations, Inc.
1689 C Street
Anchorage, Alaska 99501
Phone: 907-276-2700

Kodiak Area Native Association
Box 172
Kodiak, Alaska 99615
Phone: 907-486-5725

North Pacific Rim Native Association
903 West Northern Lights, Suite 203
Anchorage, Alaska 99503
Phone: 907-276-2121

Cook Inlet Native Association
670 West Fireweek Lane
Anchorage, Alaska 99503
Phone: 907-278-4641

Cooper River Native Association, Inc.
Drawer G
Copper Center, Alaska 99573
Phone: 907-822-5241

Kawerak, Inc.
Box 505
Nome, Alaska 99762
Phone: 907-443-5231

Association of Village Council
Presidents
Box 219
Bethel, Alaska 99559
Phone: 907-543-3521

APPENDIX • D

Bureau of Indian Affairs Division of Social Services Areas

ABERDEEN AREA:
115 4th Avenue SE, Aberdeen, SD 57401-4382; Phone: 605-226-7343; Fax: 605-782-7446

Aberdeen Area Tribes:
Cheyenne River Sioux
Crow Creek Sioux
Devils Lake Sioux
Flandreau Santee Sioux
Fort Berthold (Mandan, Hidatsa, Arickara)
Lower Brule Sioux
Lake Traverse Sioux (Sisseton-Wahpeton)
Omaha
Pine Ridge (Oglala) Sioux
Ponca Tribe of Nebraska
Rosebud Sioux
Santee Sioux of Nebraska
Standing Rock Sioux
Turtle Mountain (Chippewa)
Winnebago
Yankton Sioux

ALBUQUERQUE AREA:
P.O. Box 26567, 615 1st Street NW, Albuquerque, NM 87125-6567; Phone: 505-766-3170; Fax: 505-474-2666

Albuquerque Area Tribes:
Acoma Pueblo
Cochiti Pueblo
Isleta Pueblo
Jemez Pueblo
Jicarilla Apache
Laguna Pueblo
Mescalero Apache
Nambe Pueblo
Picuris Pueblo
Pojoaque Pueblo
Ramah Navajo
San Felipe Pueblo
San Ildefonso Pueblo
San Juan Pueblo
Sandia Pueblo
Santa Ana Pueblo
Santa Clara Pueblo
Santo Domingo Pueblo
Southern Ute
Taos Pueblo
Tesuque Pueblo

Ute Mountain Ute
Ysleta Del Sur Pueblo
Zia Pueblo
Zuni Pueblo

ANADARKO AREA:

WCD Office Complex, Box 368, Anadarko, OK 73005-0368; Phone: 405-247-6673; Fax: 405-743-7233

Anadarko Area Tribes:
Absentee-Shawnee
Alabama-Coushatta
Apache
Caddo
Cheyenne-Arapaho
Citizens Band of Potawatomi
Comanche
Delaware
Fort Sill Apache
Iowa of Kansas
Iowa of Oklahoma
Kaw
Kickapoo of Kansas
Kickapoo of Oklahoma
Kiowa
Otoe-Missouria
Pawnee
Ponca
Prairie Band Potawatomi
Sac & Fox of Missouri
Sac & Fox of Oklahoma
Texas Kickapoo
Wichita

BILLINGS AREA:

316 North 26th Street, Billings, MT 58101-1397, Phone: 406-657-6315; Fax: 406-585-6559

Billings Area Tribes:
Blackfeet
Crow
Fort Belknap (Assiniboine, Gros Ventre)
Fort Peck (Assiniboine, Sioux)
Northern Cheyenne
Rocky Boy's (Chippewa, Cree)
Wind River Arapahoe
Wind River Shoshone

EASTERN AREA:

1951 Constitution Avenue, NW, MS-260 Virginia Square, Washington, DC 20245-0001; Phone: 703-235-2571; Fax: 703-235-8610

Eastern Area Tribes:
Big Cypress (Seminole)
Brighton (Seminole)
Cattaraugus (Seneca)
Cayuga
Chitimacha
Coushatta
Dania (Hollywood) (Seminole)
Eastern Band of Cherokee
Houlton Maliseet Band
Mashantucket Pequot
Miccosukee
Mississippi Choctaw
Narragansett
Oneida
Onondaga
Passamaquoddy-Indian Township
Passamaquoddy-Pleasant Point
Penobscot
Poarch Band of Creek
Saint Regis Mohawk
Tonawanda Band of Senecas

Tunica-Biloxi
Tuscarora
Wampanoag
Winnemucca

MINNEAPOLIS AREA:
15 South 5th Street -10th Floor, Minneapolis, MN 55401-1020; Phone: 612-349-3631; Fax: 612-349-3365

Minneapolis Area Tribes:
Bad River (Chippewa - Ojibwa)
Bay Mills (Chippewa - Ojibwa)
Fond Du Lac Chippewa
Forest County Potawatomi
Grand Portage Chippewa
Grand Traverse Band (Chippewa)
Hannahville
Keweenaw Bay
Lac Courte Orielles
Lac Du Flambeau (Chippewa)
Lac Vieux Desert Chippewa
Leech Lake Chippewa
Lower Sioux
Menominee
Mille Lacs Chippewa
Minnesota Chippewa
Nett Lake Chippewa
Oneida
Prairie Island Sioux
Red Cliff
Red Lake (Chippewa)
Sac & Fox
Saginaw Chippewa-Sagining
Saint Croix
Sault Ste Marie Chippewa
Shakopee Sioux
Sokaogon Chippewa
Stockbridge-Munsee
Upper Sioux
White Earth Chippewa
Wisconsin Winnebago

MUSKOGEE AREA:
5th & West Okmulgee, Muskogee, OK 74401-4898; Phone: 918-687-2296; Fax: 918-736-2571

Muskogee Area Tribes:
Alabama-Quassarte
Cherokee
Chickasaw
Chocktaw
Creek
Eastern Shawnee
Kialegee
Miami
Modoc
Osage
Ottawa
Peoria
Quapaw
Seminole
Seneca-Cayuga
Thlopthlocco Creek
United Keetoowah Cherokee
Wyandotte

NAVAJO AREA:
P.O. Box M, Window Rock, AZ 86515-0714; Phone: 602-871-5151; Fax: 602-479-5122

Navajo Area Tribes:
Alamo Navajo
Canoncito Pueblo
Chinle Navajo
Fort Defiance Navajo
Navajo
Shiprock Navajo
Western Navajo

PHOENIX AREA:

1 North First Street, P.O. Box 10, Phoenix, AZ 85001-0010; Phone: 602-379-6600; Fax: 602-261-4413

Phoenix Area Tribes:

Ak Chin
Camp Verde (Yavapai-Apache)
Carson Colony (Washoe)
Chemehuevi
Cocopah
Colorado River
Dresslerville Colony (Washoe)
Duck Valley (Shoshone-Paiute)
Duckwater Shoshone
Ely
Fallon
Fort Apache (White Mountain)
Fort McDermitt
Fort McDowell (Mohave Apache)
Fort Mojave
Fort Yuma (Quechan)
Gila River
Goshute
Havasupai
Hopi
Hualapai
Kaibab
Las Vegas
Lovelock
Moapa
Papago (Tohono O'Odham)
Pascua Yaqui
Pyramid Lake Paiute
Reno-Sparks
Salt River (Maricopa, Pima Maricopa)
San Carlos (Apache)
San Juan Southern Paiute
Skull Valley (Goshute)
Summit Lake Paiute
Tonto Apache (Payson)
Uintah & Ouray
Utah Paiute
Walker River Paiute
Washoe
Woodfords Colony (Washoe)
Yerington Paiute
Yomba
Te-Moak Battle Mtn (4 Bands of Western Te-Moak Shoshone)
Te-Moak Elko (4 Banks of Western Te-Moak Shoshone)
Te-Moak South Fork (4 Bands of Western Te-Moak Shoshone)
Te-Moak Wells Indian (4 Bands of Western Te-Moak Shoshone)
Te-Moak Western Shoshone

PORTLAND AREA:

The Holladay Federal Bldg, 911 N.E., 11th Avenue, Portland, OR 97232-4169; Phone: 503-231-6702; Fax: 503-429-6731

Portland Area Tribes:

Burns-Paiute
Chehalis
Coeur D'alene
Colville
Coos Lower Umpqua & Siuslaw
Coquille
Flathead (Salish, Kootenai)
Fort Hall (Shoshone, Bannock)
Grande Ronde
Hoh River
Jamestown Klallam
Kalispel
Klamath
Kootenai
Lower Elwha
Lummi
Makah
Muckelshoot
Nez Perce
Nisqually
Nooksack
Northwestern Band Shoshoni
Port Gamble
Puyallup
Quileute

Quinault
Sauk-Suiattle
Shoalwater Bay
Siletz
Skokomish
Spokane
Squaxin Island
Stillaquamish
Suquamish
Swinomish
Tulalip
Umatilla
Umpqua Cow Creek Band
Upper Skagit
Warm Springs
Yakima

SACRAMENTO AREA:
2800 Cottage Way, Sacramento, CA 95825-1884; Phone: 916-978-4691; Fax: 906-460-4695

Sacramento Area Tribes:
Agua Caliente
Alturas Rancheria
Barona Rancheria
Benton Paiute
Berry Creek Rancheria
Big Bend Rancheria
Big Lagoon Rancheria
Big Pine
Big Sandy Rancheria
Big Valley Rancheria
Bishop Rancheria
Blue Lake Rancheria
Bridgeport Rancheria
Buena Vista Rancheria
Cabazon
Cahuilla
Campo
Cedarville Rancheria
Chicken Ranch Rancheria
Cloverdale Rancheria
Cold Springs Rancheria
Colusa Rancheria
Cortina Rancheria
Coyote Valley Rancheria
Cuyapaipe
Dry Creek Rancheria
Elk Valley Rancheria
Fort Bidwell
Fort Independence
Greenville Rancheria
Grindstone Creek Rancheria
Hoopa Valley
Hopland Rancheria
Inaja & Cosmit
Jackson Rancheria
Jamul Village
Karuk
La Jolla
La Posta
Laytonville Rancheria
Lone Pine
Los Coyotes
Manchester/Point Arena Rancheria
Manzanita
Mesa Grande
Middeltown Rancheria
Montgomery Creek Rancheria
Mooretown Rancheria
Morongo
North Fork Rancheria
Pala
Pauma
Pechanga
Picayune Rancheria
Pinoleville Rancheria
Pit River
Potter Valley Rancheria
Quartz Valley Rancheria
Ramona Band of Cahuilla
Redding Rancheria
Redwood Valley Rancheria
Resighini Rancheria/Coast Indian
Rincon
Roaring Creek Rancheria
Robinson Rancheria
Rohnerville Rancheria
Round Valley

Rumsey Rancheria
San Manuel
San Pasqual
Santa Rosa Rancheria
Santa Ynez
Santa Ysabel
Sherwood Valley Rancheria
Shingle Springs Rancheria
Smith River Rancheria
Soboba Band of Mission Indians
Stewarts Point Rancheria
Sulphur Bank Rancheria
Susanville Rancheria
Sycuan
Table Bluff Rancheria
Table Mountain Rancheria
Timbi-Sha Shoshone
Torres Martinez
Trinidad Rancheria
Tule River
Tuolumne Me-Wuk Rancheria
Twenty Nine Palms
Upper Lake Rancheria
Viejas
XI Rancheria
Yurok

JUNEAU AREA:
Federal Building, P.O. Box 3-8000, Juneau, AK 99802-1219; Phone: 907-586-7177; Fax: 907-871-7169

Native villages in Alaska have been organized into regional Profit and Non-Profit Corporations.

APPENDIX • E

Listing of Tribal Courts and/or ICWA Contacts

Absenee Shawnee Tribal Court
P.O. Box 1747
Shawnee, OK 74801
Phone: (405) 275-4030
FAX: (405) 275-5637
ICWA Director
Phone: (405) 275-2281

Acoma Pueblo Court
P.O. Box 347
Pueblo of Acoma, NM 87034
Phone: (505) 552-6604
Fax: (505) 552-6600

Ak-Chin Indian Community Court
Route 1, Box 12
Maricopa, AZ 85239
Phone: (602) 568-2221
Fax: (602) 254-6133
ICWA Social Worker
Phone: (602) 568-2227

Alabama-Coushatta Tribe of Texas
Route 3, Box 640
Livingston, TX 77351
Phone: (409) 563-4391
Fax: (409) 563-4397
(In regard to ICWA matters, ask to speak to the Tribal Administrator)

Apache Tribe of Oklahoma Tribal Court
P.O. Box 1220
Apache, OK 73005
Phone: (405) 588-2219
Fax: (405) 247-9232

CFR Court
P.O. Box 309
Anadarko, OK 73005
Phone: (405) 247-6673
Fax: (405) 247-6673 x233 *(must call first)*

Bad River Tribal Court
Route 2
Ashland, WI 54806
Phone: (715) 682-7102
Fax: (715) 682-7118

Battle Mountain Tribal Court
P.O. Box 1528
Battle Mountain, NV 89820
Phone: (702) 635-2004
Fax: (702) 635-8016
ICWA Director
Phone: (702) 635-2004

Blackfeet Tribal Court
P.O. Box 1200
Browning, MT 59417
Phone: (406) 338-5061
Fax: (406-338-7530
ICWA Director
Phone: (406) 338-7806

Burns Paiute Tribal Court
HC 71-100 Pasigu Street
Burns, OR 97720
Phone: (503) 573-2793
Fax: (503) 573-2323

Caddo Indian Tribe CFR COURT
P.O. Box 487
Binger, OK 73009
Phone: (405) 656-2344
Fax: (405) 656-2468
ICWA Director
Phone: (405) 247-9603

Camp Verdi Yavapai Apache Tribal Court
P.O. Box 1188
Camp Verdi, AZ 86332
Phone: (602) 567-3649
Fax: (602) 567-9455
ICWA Social Worker
Phone: (602) 567-3246

Central Illinois Chippewa
505 South Main
Tuscola, IL 61953
Phone: (217) 253-2279
Fax: (271) 253-2015

Chickasaw Nation Tribal Court
P.O. Box 1548
Ada, OK 74820
Phone: (405) 436-3557
Fax: (405) 436-4287

Chippewa Cree Tribal Court
Box 544, Rocky Boy
Box Elder, MT 59521
Phone: (406) 395-4735
Fax: (406) 395-4497
ICWA Director
Phone: (406) 395-4733

Chippewa-Ottowa Conservation Court
Route 1
Brimley, MI 49715
Phone: (906) 248-3243
Fax: (906) 248-3283

Chitimacha Tribe of Louisiana
P.O. Box 610
Charenton, LA 70523-0610
Phone: (318) 923-7806
Fax: (318) 923-4965
ICWA
Phone: (318) 923-7000

Choctaw Nation Tribal Court
P.O. Drawer 1210
Durant, OK 74701
Phone: (405) 924-8280
Fax: (405) 924-1150
ICWA Director
Phone: (405) 924-8280

Choctaw Court on Indian Offenses
421 Powell Street
Philadelphia, MS 39350
Phone: (601) 656-5352
Fax: (601) 656-1992
ICWA Social Worker

Chehalis Tribal Court
(NORTHWEST INTERNATIONAL COURT SYSTEM)
P.O. Box 536
Oakville, WA 98568
Phone: (206) 273-5911
Fax: (206) 273-5914

Chemehuevi Tribal Council
P.O. Box 1976
Chemehuevi Valley, CA 92363
Phone: (619) 858-4531
Fax: (619) 858-4818
(In regard to ICWA matters, ask to speak to the Judicial Administrator)

Cherokee Nation Tribal Court
P.O. Box 948
Talequah, OK 74465
Phone: (918) 456-0671
Fax: (918) 456-6485

Cheyenne & Arapaho Supreme Court
P.O. Box 38
Concho, OK 73022
Phone: (405) 262-7330
Fax: (405) 262 7901

Cheyenne & Arapaho Tribes Tribal Court
P.O. Box 38
Concho, OK 73022
Phone: (405) 262-7330
Fax: (405) 262 7901

Cheyenne River Sioux Appeals Court
P.O. Box 590
Eagle Butte, SD 57625
Phone: (605) 964-6602
Fax: (605) 964-4151
ICWA Director
Phone: (605) 964-6460

Cheyenne River Sioux Tribal Court
P.O. Box 590
Eagle Butte, SD 57625
Phone: (605) 964-6602
Fax: (605) 964-4151

Citizen Band Potowatomi Tribe Supreme Court
1901 South Gordon Copper Drive
Shawnee, OK 74801
Phone: (405) 275-3121
Fax: (405) 275-0198
ICWA Director
Phone: (405) 273-5068

Citizen Band Potowatomi Tribe Tribal Court
1901 South Gordon Copper Drive
Shawnee, OK 74801
Phone: (405) 275-3121
Fax: (405) 275-0198

Cochiti Pueblo Court
P.O. Box 70
Cochiti Pueblo, NM 87041
Phone: (505) 465-2244
Fax: (505) 465-2245

Cocopah Court of Indian Offenses
P.O. Box Bin "G"
Somerton, AZ 85364
Phone: (602) 627-8153
Fax: (602) 627-3173

Coeur d'Alene Tribe Court
Tribal Headquarters
Plummer, ID 83851
Phone: (208) 274-3101
Fax: (208) 274-2824
ICWA Youth Shelter
Phone: (208) 274-3101

Colorado River Tribal Court
Box BH
Parker, AZ 85344
Phone: (602) 669-9211
Fax: (602) 669-5675

Colville Tribal Court
P.O. Box 150
Nespelem, WA 99155
Phone: (509) 634-4711 x211
Fax: (509) 634-4116
ICWA Social Services
Phone: (509) 634-4711 x628, 850

Comanche Nation Tribal Court
HC 32 Box 1720
Lawton, OK 73502
Phone: (405) 492-4988
Fax: (405) 492-4981
ICWA Director
Phone: (405) 492-4988 x70

Crow Tribal Court
Box 489
Crow Agency, MT 59022
Phone: (406) 638-2681
Fax: (406) 638-2359
Attention: Director
Phone: (406) 638-2681

Crow Creek Sioux Tribal Court
P.O. Box 247
Fort Thompson, SD 57339
Phone: (605) 245-2325
Fax: (605) 245-2343
ICWA Director
Phone: (605) 245-2213

Delaware Tribe of Western Oklahoma
CFR COURT
P.O. Box 825
Anadarko, OK 73005
Phone: (405) 247-2448
Fax: (405) 247-9393

Devils Lake Tribal Court
P.O. Box 30
Fort Totten, ND 58335
Phone: (701) 766-4244
Fax: (701) 766-4126
ICWA Social Services
Phone: (701) 766-4404

Duckwater Shoshone Tribe
P.O. Box 68
Duckwater, NV 89832
Phone: (702) 863-0227
Fax: (702) 863-0361
ICWA Director
Phone: (702) 863-0227

Eastern Cherokee Court of Indian Offenses
Cherokee Agency
P.O. Box 455
Cherokee, NC 28719
Phone: (704) 497-7720
Fax: (704) 497-5705

Fallon Colony
8955 Mission Road
Fallon, NV 89406
Phone: (702) 423-8883
Fax: (702) 423-5202

Flandreau Santee Sioux Court
P.O. Box 283
Flandreau, SD 57028
Phone: (605) 997-3593
Fax: (605) 997-3878

Flathead Tribal Court
(Salish & Kootenai Tribes)
P.O. Box 278
Pablo, MT 59855
Phone: (406) 675-2700
Fax: (406) 675-2806
ICWA Director
Phone: (406) 676-2500

Fort Sill Apache Tribe CFR COURT
Route 2, Box 121
Apache, OK 73006
Phone: (405) 588-2298
Fax: (405) 588-3133
ICWA Social Services
Phone: (405) 588-2296

Fort Peck Tribal Court
P.O. Box 1027
Poplar, MT 59255
Phone: (406) 768-5557
Fax: (406) 768-5478
ICWA Social Services
Phone: (406) 653-1590

Fort McDermitt Tribal Court
P.O. Box 397
McDermitt, NV 89421
Phone: (702) 532-8402
Fax: (702) 532-8259
ICWA Director
Phone: (702) 532-8263

Fort Mojave Tribal Court
500 Merriman
Needles, CA 92363
Phone: (619) 326-5293
Fax: (619) 326-2468

Fort Berthold Tribal Court
(Three Affiliated Tribes)
P.O. Box 501
Mandaree, ND 58757
Phone: (701) 759-3328
Fax: (701) 759-3506
ICWA Social Services
Phone: (701) 627-4557

Fort Belknap Tribal Court
Route 1, Box 62
Harlem, MT 59855
Phone: (406) 353-2205
Fax: (406) 353-2797
ICWA Director
Phone: (406) 253-2901

Gila River Indian Community
P.O. Box 97
Sacaton, AZ 85247
Phone: (602) 836-8178
Fax: (602) 562-3422
ICWA Social Services
Phone: (602) 836-8178

Grand Portage Tribal Court
Grand Portage Reservation
Grand Portage, MN 55605
Phone: (218) 475-2277
Fax: (218) 475-2284

Hannahville Community Court
Route 1, Community Center
Wilson, MI 49908
Phone: (906) 466-2342
Fax: (906) 466-2418
ICWA
Phone: (906) 466-2881

Havasupai Tribal Court
P.O. Box 10
Supai, AZ 86435
Phone: (602) 448-2710
Fax: None
ICWA Director
Phone: (602) 448-2661

Hoh Tribal Court
(NORTHWEST INTERNATIONAL COURT SYSTEM)
HC 80 Box 917
Forks, WA 98331
Phone: (206) 374-6582
Fax: (206) 374-6549
ICWA Social Services
Phone: (206) 374-6582

Hoopa Valley Tribal Court
P.O. Box 608
Hoopa, CA 95546
Phone: (916) 625-4305
Fax: (916) 625-4234
ICWA Director
Phone: (916) 625-4305

Hopi Tribal Court
P.O. Box 156
Keams Canyon, AZ 86034
Phone: (602) 738-2288, 2289
Fax: (602) 738-5589
ICWA Director
Phone: (602) 738-2283, 2284

Hualapai Tribal Court
P.O. Box 275
Peach Springs, AZ 86434
Phone: (602) 769-2216
Fax: (602) 769-2343
ICWA Attention: Chairman of Tribal Council
Phone: (602) 769-2216

Iowa Tribe of Oklahoma CFR COURT
P.O. Box 190
Perkins, OK 74059
Phone: (405) 547-2402
Fax: (405) 547-5294
ICWA Director
Phone: (405) 547-2402

Iowa Tribe of Kansas & Nebraska
Route 1, Box 58A
White Cloud, KS 66094
Phone: (913) 595-3258
Fax: (913) 595-6610
(In regard to ICWA matters, ask to speak to the Chairman)

Isleta Pueblo Court
P.O. Box 317
Isleta, NM 87022
Phone: (505) 869-6510
Fax: (505) 869-4236

Jamestown Klallam Tribal Court
305 Old Blyn Highway
Sequim, WA 98382
Phone: (206) 683-1109
Fax: (206) 683-4366
ICWA Director

Jemez Pueblo Court
P.O. Box 100
Jemez Pueblo, NM 87024
Phone: (505) 834-7369
Fax: (505) 834-7573
ICWA Social Worker

Jicarilla Apache Tribal Court
P.O. Box 221
Dulce, NM 87528
Phone: (505) 759-3366
Fax: (505) 759-3005
ICWA Clerk of Court

Kaibab-Paiute Tribal Court
HC 65 Box 2
Fredonia, AZ 86022
Phone: (602) 643-7214
Fax: (602) 643-7260
ICWA Intake Worker
Phone: (602) 643-7245

Kalispel Tribal Court
Box 39
Usk, WA 99180
Phone: (509) 445-1762
Fax: None
ICWA Director
Phone: (509) 445-1762

Kaw Tribe CFR COURT
P.O. Box 50
Kaw City, OK 74641
Phone: (405) 269-2552
Fax: (405) 269-2301
ICWA Director
Phone: (405) 269-2552

Keweenaw Bay Tribal Court
Tribal Center Building
Route 1, Box 45
Baraga, MI 49908
Phone: (906) 353-6623
Fax: (906) 353-7540
ICWA Staff
Phone: (906) 353-6623

Kickapoo Tribal Courts
P.O. Box 70
McLoud, OK 74851
Phone: (405) 964-5856
Fax: (405) 964-2745
ICWA Director
Phone: (405) 964-5856

Kickapoo Traditional Tribe of Texas
P.O. Box 972
Eagle Pass, TX 78853
Phone: (512) 773-2105
Fax: None
(In regard to ICWA matters ask to speak to the Tribal Social Service Worker)

Kiowa Tribe CFR COURT
P.O. Box 368
Anadarko, OK 73005
Phone: (405) 247-6673
Fax: (405) 247-9232

Kootenai Tribal Court
P.O. Box 1269
Bonners Ferry, ID 83805
Phone: (208) 267-3519
Fax: (208) 267-2960
ICWA Social Worker
Phone: (208) 267-3519

Lac Courte Oreilles Tribal Court
Route 2, Box 2700
Hayward, WI 54843
Phone: (715) 634-8934
Fax: (715) 634-4797
ICWA Director
Phone: (715) 634-8934

Laguna Pueblo Court
P.O. Box 194
Laguna, NM 87026
Phone: (505) 552-6687
Fax: (505) 552-7186

Las Vegas Paiute Tribal Court
1 Paiute Drive
Las Vegas, NV 98106
Phone: (702) 386-3926
Fax: (702) 383-4019

Leech Lake Tribal Court
RR 3, Box 100
Cass Lake, MN 56633
Phone: (218) 335-8240
Fax: (218) 335-8390

Lovelock Paiute Colony Tribal Court
P.O. Box 1109
Lovelock, NV 89025
Phone: (702) 273-0328
Fax: (702) 273-7030

Lower Elwha Tribal Court
1666 Lower Elwha Road
Port Angeles, WA 98362
Phone: (206) 452-8471
Fax: (206) 452-3428
ICWA Staff
Phone: (206) 452-8471

Lower Brule Sioux Tribal Court
P.O. Box 802
Lower Brule, SD 57548
Phone: (605) 473-5529
Fax: (605) 473-5606

Lummi Tribal Court
2616 Kwina Road
Bellingham, WA 98226
Phone: (206) 734-9231
Fax: (206) 384-4737

Makah Tribal Court
P.O. Box 192
Neah Bay, WA 98357
Phone: (206) 645-2727
Fax: (206) 645-2707

Director
Makah Family Services
P.O. Box 115
Neah Bay, WA 98547
Phone: (206) 645-2201
Fax: (206) 645-2033

Menominee Tribal Court
P.O. Box 429
Keshena, WI 54135
Phone: (715) 799-3348
Fax: (715) 799-4061

Director
Menominee Tribal Social Services
P.O. Box 520
Keshena, WI 54135
Phone: (715) 799-5161
Fax: (715) 799-4525

Mescalero Apache Tribal Court
P.O. Box 176
Mescalero, NM 88340
Phone: (505) 671-4489, 4821
Fax: (505) 671-4863

Metlakatla Magistrate Court
P.O. Box 8
Metlakatla, AK 99626
Phone: (907) 886-4021
Fax: (907) 886-4441

Miccosukee Tribal Court
P.O. Box 440021
Tamiami Station
Miami, FL 87053
Phone: (305) 223-8380
Fax: (305) 223-8383

Minnesota Chippewa Court of Indian Offenses
P.O. Box 608
Nett Lake, MN 55772
Phone: (218) 757-3162
Fax: (218) 757-3166

Moapa Paiute Tribal Court
P.O. Box 187
Moapa, NV 98025
Phone: (702) 865-2845
Fax: (702) 865-2865

Muckleshoot Tribal Court
39015 172nd Avenue, S.E.
Auburn, WA 98002
Phone: (206) 939-3311
Fax: (206) 939-5311

Muscogee (Creek) Nation Supreme Court
P.O. Box 652
Okmulgee, OK 74447
Phone: (918) 758-1412
Fax: (918) 758-1413

ICWA Office
(Muscogee (Creek) Nation)
313 West 8th Street
Okmulgee, OK 74447
Phone: (918) 756-4224
Fax: (918) 756-2882

Nambe Pueblo Court
Route 1, Box 177-B
Santa Fe, NM 87501
Phone: (505) 455-2036
Fax: (505) 455-2038

Navajo Nation Supreme Court
P.O. Box 250
Window Rock, AZ 86515
Phone: (602) 871-6763
Fax: (602) 871-5704
(ICWA contact at extension 608 - who will connect you to the correct District Personnel)

Shiprock District Court
(NAVAJO NATION)
P.O. Box 1148
Shiprock, NM 87420
Phone: (505) 368-4306
Fax: (505) 368-4175

Crownpoint District Court
(NAVAJO NATION)
P.O. Box 6
Crownpoint, NM 87313
Phone: (505) 786-5334, 5391
Fax: (505) 786-7038

Chinle District Court
(NAVAJO NATION)
P.O. Box 547
Chinle, AZ 86503
Phone: (602) 674-5367
Fax: (602) 674-5036

Tuba City District Court
(NAVAJO NATION)
P.O. Box 725
Tuba City, AZ 86045
Phone: (602) 283-6283, 5244
Fax: (602) 283-6857

Kayenta District Court
(NAVAJO NATION)
P.O. Box 1248
Katenta, AZ 86033
Phone: (602) 697-8668, 8669
Fax: (602) 697-3633

Ramah District Court
(NAVAJO NATION)
P.O. Box 291
Ramah, NM 87321
Phone: (505) 775-3218
Fax: (505) 775-3399

Window Rock District Court
(NAVAJO NATION)
P.O. Box 447
Window Rock, AZ 86515
Phone: (602) 871-6476
Fax: (602) 871-7560

Nez Perce Tribal Court
P.O. Box 305
Lapwai, ID 83540
Phone: (208) 843-2253, x328
Fax: (208) 843-2718

Nisqually Tribal Court
4820 She-Nah-Num Drive SE
Olympia, WA 98503
Phone: (206) 456-5221
Fax: (206) 456-5280
ICWA Supervisor
Phone: (206) 456-5221

Nooksack Tribal Court
(NORTHWEST INTERTRIBAL COURT SYSTEM)
P.O. Box 157
Deming, WA 98244
Phone: (206) 592-5176
Fax: (206) 592-5753

Northern Plains Intertribal Court of Appeals
P.O. Box 57
Aberdeen, SD 57402-0057
Phone: (605) 226-3165
Fax: (605) 226-3244

Northern Cheyenne Tribal Court
P.O. Box 128
Lame Deer, MT 59043
Phone: (406) 477-8340
Fax: (406) 477-6210

Oglala Sioux Tribal Court (IRA)
P.O. Box 280
Pine Ridge, SD 57770
Phone: (605) 867-5151
Fax: (605) 867-5659

Omaha Tribe Court of Indian Offenses (IRA)
P.O. Box 508
Macy, NE 68039
Phone: (402) 837-5814
Fax: (402) 837-5308

Otoe-Missouria Tribe CFR COURT
P.O. Box 62
Red Rock, OK 74651
Phone: (405) 723-4426
Fax: (405) 723-4273

Ottawa Tribe
P.O. Box 110
Miami, OK 74355
Phone: (918) 540-1536
Fax: None

Pascua Yaqui Tribal Court
7474 S. Camino De Oeste
Tucson, AZ 85746
Phone: (602) 578-2853, 1219
Fax: (602) 883-7770

Passamaqoddy Tribal Court
P.O. Box 343
Perry, ME 04667
Phone: (207) 853-2551
Fax: (207) 853-6039

Pawnee Tribe CFR COURT
P.O. Box 470
Pawnee, OK 74058
Phone: (918) 762-3624
Fax: (918) 762-2389

Penobscot Nation Judicial System
Community Building
6 River Road - Indian Island
Old Town, ME 04468
Phone: (207) 827-7776
Fax: (207) 827-6042

Peoria Tribe
P.O. Box 1527
Miami, OK 74355
Phone: (918) 540-2535
Fax: (918) 540-2538

Picuris Pueblo Court
P.O. Box 127
Penasco, NM 87553
Phone: (505) 587-2519
Fax: (505) 587-1071
(please send duplicate copies to the Lieutenant Governor)

Ponca Tribe
P.O. Box 2, White Eagle
Ponca City, OK 74601
Phone: (405) 762-8104
Fax: (405) 762-7136
ICWA Office
Phone: (405) 762-8104

Port Gamble S'Kallam Tribe
(NORTHWEST INTERTRIBAL COURT SYSTEM)
P.O. Box 280
Kingston, WA 98346
Phone: (206) 464-7281
Fax: (206) 297-7091

Prairie Band of Potawatomi
Route 2, Box 50A
Mayetta, KS 66504
Phone: (913) 966-2255
Fax: (913) 966-2144
(In regard to ICWA matters ask for the Indian Child Welfare Administrative Court and/or the Tribal Chairperson)

Yavapai-Prescott Tribe
P.O. Box 348
Prescott, AZ 86301
Phone: (602) 445-3500
Fax: None
(Contact President)

Pyramid Lake Tribal Court
P.O. Box 257
Nixon, NV 89424
Phone: (702) 574-0299
Fax: (702) 574-0310

Puyallup Tribal Court
2002 E. 28th Street
Tacoma, WA 98404
Phone: (206) 593-0212
Fax: (206) 272-9614

Quapaw Tribe
P.O. Box 765
Quapaw, OK 74363
Phone: (918) 542-1853
Fax: (918) 542-4694

Social Services Technician
Quechan Tribe
P.O. Box 11352
Yuma, AZ 85366
Phone: (619) 572-0201
Fax: (619) 572-0213
(In regard to ICWA matters ask for Social Services or call (619) 572-0213 and ask for Tribal President)

Quileute Tribal Court
P.O. Box 279
La Push, WA 98350
Phone: (206) 374-6163 x230
Fax: (206) 374-6311
ICWA Case Worker
Phone: (206) 374-6163 x324

Quinault Nation
Tribal Court
P.O. Box 189
Taholah, WA 98587
Phone: (206) 276-8211 x223
Fax: (206) 276-4191
ICWA Director
Phone: (206) 276-8211 x353

Red Cliff Chippewa Tribal Court
P.O. Box 529
Bayfield, WI 54814
Phone: (715) 779-3701
Fax: (715) 779-3151
ICWA Director
Phone: (715) 779-3747

Red Lake Tribal Court
General Delivery
Red Lake, MN 56671
Phone: (218) 679-3303
Fax: (218) 679-2194
ICWA Director
Phone: (218) 679-2122

Reno Sparks Tribal Court
98 Colony Road
Reno, NV 89502
Phone: (702) 329-2936
Fax: (702) 329-8710

Administrator
Family & Support Services
Reno Sparks Tribe
34-A Reservation Road
Reno, NV 89502
Phone: (702) 329-5071
Fax: (702) 329-8710

Rosebud Sioux Tribal Court
P.O. Box 129
Rosebud, SD 57570
Phone: (605) 747-2278
Fax: (605) 747-2243

Indian Child Welfare Advocate
Child & Family Services Program
Rosebud Sioux Tribe
P.O. Box 430
Rosebud, SD 57570
Phone: (605) 747-2258

Sac & Fox Nation CFR COURT
Route 2, Box 246
Stroud, OK 74079
Phone: (918) 968-2031
Fax: (918) 968-3887

Director
Indian Child Welfare Office
2013 S. Gordon Cooper
Shawnee, OK 74801
Phone: (405) 275-2281
Fax: (405) 275-5637
(ICWA contact for Sac & Fox Nation)

Sac & Fox Tribe of Missouri
Route 1, Box 60
Reserve, KS 66434
Phone: (913) 742-7471
Fax: (913) 742-3785
(In regard to ICWA matters, please ask to speak to the Tribal Chairperson)

Saginaw-Chippewa Tribal Court
7070 E. Broadway
Mt. Pleasant, MI 48858
Phone: (517) 772-5700 x210
Fax: (517) 772-3508
ICWA Director
Phone: (517) 772-5700 x233

Salt River Pima Maricopa Court
Route 1, Box 216
Scottsdale, AZ 85256
Phone: (602) 941-7212
Fax: (602) 949-2904
ICWA Director
Phone: (602) 941-7201
Fax: (602) 949-2909

San Juan Pueblo Court
P.O. Box 1099
San Juan Pueblo, NM 87566
Phone: (505) 852-4475
Fax: (505) 852-4820

Director
Department of Social Services
Northern Pueblo's Agency - BIA
4269 Fairview Station
Espanola, NM 87533
Phone: (505) 753-1436
Fax: (505) 753-1404
(ICWA contact for San Juan Pueblo)

Pueblo of San Felipe Court
P.O. Box A
San Felipe Pueblo, NM 87001
Phone: (505) 867-9737
Fax: (505) 867-3383
ICWA Director
Phone: (505) 867-9740

San Ildefonso Pueblo Court
Route 5, Box 315A
Santa Fe, NM 87501
Phone: (505) 455-7500
Fax: (505) 455-7351

Director
Department of Social Services
Northern Pueblo's Agency - BIA
4269 Fairview Station
Espanola, NM 87533
Phone: (505) 753-1436
Fax: (505) 753-1404
(ICWA contact for San Ildefonso Pueblo)

San Carlos Juvenile Court
P.O. Box 0
San Carlos, AZ 85550
Phone: (602) 475-2874
Fax: None
ICWA Director
Phone: (602) 475-2874

Sandia Pueblo Court
P.O. Box 6008
Bernalillo, NM 87004
Phone: (505) 867-3317, 3318
Fax: (505) 867-9235
ICWA Officer
Phone: (505) 867-3317, 3318

Santa Ana Pueblo Court
Star Route Box 37
Bernalillo, NM 87004
Phone: (505) 867-3301
Fax: (505) 867-3395

Social Worker
Southern Pueblo's Agency - BIA
P.O. Box 1667
Albuquerque, NM 87103
Phone: (505) 766-3036
Fax: (505) 766-3023
(ICWA contact in regard to Santa Ana Pueblo)

Santa Clara Pueblo Court
P.O. Box 580
Espanola, NM 87532
Phone: (505) 753-7326
Fax: (505) 753-8988
ICWA Director
Phone: (505) 753-7326

Santee Sioux Tribe of Nebraska
(IRA - No Existing Tribal Courts)
Route 2
Nobrara, NE 68760
Phone: (402) 857-3302
Fax: (402) 857-3307
(Request to speak to Chairman or any of the tribal officers regarding Indian Child Welfare matters)

Santo Domingo Pueblo Court
P.O. Box 99
Santo Domingo Pueblo, NM 87052
Phone: (505) 465-2214 x15
Fax: (505) 465-2688
ICWA Director
Phone: (505) 465-2214 x32

Sault Marie Chippewa Tribal Court
1301 Marquette Avenue
Sault Ste Marie, MI 49783
Phone: (906) 635-6540
Fax: (906) 632-0741
*(ICWA contact **Binogii** (means child) at (906) 632-6537)*

Sauk-Suiattle Tribal Court
(NORTHWEST INTERTRIBAL COURT SYSTEM)
5318 Chief Brown Lane
Darrington, WA 98241
Phone: (206) 435-8366
Fax: (206) 436-1511
Indian Child Welfare Committee
Phone: (206) 435-8366

Seminole Nation Court of Indian Offenses
530 East Arlington
Ada, OK 74820
Phone: (405) 436-0784
Fax: (405) 436-3215

Indian Child Welfare Specialist
Seminole Nation of Oklahoma
P.O. Box 1498
Wewoka, OK 74884
Phone: (405) 257-6287
Fax: (405) 257-5017

Senneca Nation Peacemakers & Surrogate Courts
P.O. Box 231
Salamanca, NY 14779
Phone: (716) 945-1790
Fax: (716) 945-3917
ICWA Director - Rainbow House
Phone: (716) 945-1195

CRF COURT
(Seneca-Cayuga)
P.O. Box 391
Miami, OK 74355
Phone: (918) 542-3396
Fax: (918) 542-7202

Director
Indian Child Welfare Program
Seneca-Cayuga Tribe
P.O. Box 1283
Miami, OK 74355
Phone: (918) 542-6609
Fax: (918) 542-3684

Northwest Intertribal Court System
(Shoalwater Bay Tribe)
121 5th Avenue N., Suite 305
Edmonds, WA 98020
Phone: (206) 774-5808
Fax: (206) 778-7704

Indian Child Welfare Advisory Committee
Shoalwater Bay Tribe
P.O. Box 130
Tokeland, WA 98590
Phone: (206) 267-6766
Fax: (206) 267-6778

Shoshone/Arapahoe Tribal Court
P.O. Box 217
Fort Washaie, WY 82514
Phone: (307) 332-3532
Fax: (307) 332-3055
ICWA Director
Phone: (307) 332-3532

Shoshone Paiute Tribal Court
P.O. Box 219
Owyhee, NV 89832
Phone: (702) 757-2741
Fax: (702) 757-2219
ICWA Social Worker
Phone: (702) 757-3161, 3211

Shoshone-Bannock Tribal Court
P.O. Box 306
Ft. Hall, ID 83203
Phone: (208) 238-3902
Fax: (208) 237-9432
ICWA Coordinator
Phone: (208) 238-3943
Fax: (208) 237-0797

Sitka Tribal Court
456 Katlian
Sitka, AK 99835-7505
Phone: (907) 747-3207
Fax: (907) 747-4915
ICWA Director
Phone: (907) 747-3207

Siletz Tribal Court
P.O. Box 549
Siletz, OR 97380
Phone: (503) 444-2532
Fax: (503) 444-2307
ICWA Case Worker
Phone: (503) 444-1030
Fax: (503) 444-1278

Sisseton Wahpeton Sioux CFR COURT
P.O. Box 568
Agency Village, SD 57262
Phone: (605) 698-7629
Fax: None

Director
Department of Social Services
Sisseton Agency - BIA
P.O. Box 688
Agency Village, SD 57262
Phone: (605) 698-7676
Fax: (605) 698-7784
(for Sisseton Wahpeton Sioux Tribe)

Skokomish Tribal Court
(NORTHWEST INTERTRIBAL COURT SYSTEM)
North 80, Tribal Center Road
Shelton, WA 98584
Phone: (206) 426-4232
Fax: (206) 877-5943
ICWA Case Worker
Phone: (206) 426-4232

Southern Ute Tribal Court
Justice Complex
P.O. Box 737
Ignacio, CO 81137
Phone: (303) 563-4525
Fax: (303) 563-4033
ICWA Director
Phone: (303) 563-4525
Fax: (303) 563-4229

Southwest Intertribal Court of Appeals
P.O. Box 4456 - Station A
Albuquerque, NM 87196
Phone: (505) 277-5462
Fax: (505) 277-0068
ICWA Director
Phone: (505) 277-5462

Spokane Tribal Court
P.O. Box 225
Wellpinit, WA 99040
Phone: (509) 258-4569
Fax: (509) 258-7018
ICWA Director
Phone: (509) 258-7012
Fax: (509) 258-4452

Squaxin Island Tribal Court
(NORTHWEST INTERTRIBAL COURT SYSTEM)
SE 70 Squaxin Lane
Shelton, WA 98584
Phone: (206) 426-9781
Fax: (206) 426-6577
ICWA Coordinator
Phone: (206) 426-9781

St. Croix Tribal Court
P.O. Box 287
Hertel, WI 54845
Phone: (715) 349-2195
Fax: (715) 349-5768
ICWA Director
Phone: (715) 349-2195

St. Regis Mohawk Tribal Court
Route 37 - Community Building
Hogansburg, NY 13655
Phone: (518) 358-2272
Fax: (518) 358-3203
ICWA Director
Phone: (518) 358-3216, 2933

Standing Rock Sioux Tribal Court
P.O. Box 363
Fort Yates, ND 58538
Phone: (701) 854-3807
Fax: (701) 854-7543
ICWA Children's Advocate
Phone: (701) 854-3807

Stillaquamish Tribal Court
3439 Stoluckquamish Lane
Arlington, WA 98223
Phone: (206) 652-7362
Fax: (206) 435-2204
ICWA Director
Phone: (206) 435-9338

Suquamish Tribal Court
P.O. Box 1021
Suquamish, WA 98392
Phone: (206) 598-4334
Fax: (206) 598-4414

ICWA Director
Suquamish Tribe
P.O. Box 498
Suquamish, WA 98392
Phone: (206) 598-3311
Fax: (206) 598-6295

Swinomish Tribal Court
(NORTHWEST INTERTRIBAL COURT SYSTEM)
P.O. Box 817
LaConner, WA 98257
Phone: (206) 466-7217
Fax: (206) 466-3610
ICWA Worker
Phone: (206) 466-7222, 7214

Taos Pueblo Court
P.O. Box 1846
Taos, NM 87566
Phone: (505) 758-8626
Fax: (505) 758-8831

ICWA Director
Taos Pueblo
P.O. Box 1956
Taos, NM 87566
Phone: (505) 758-4224
Fax: (505) 758-1882

Te-Moak Court of Indian Offenses
525 Sunset Street
Elko, NV 89801
Phone: (702) 738-9251
Fax: (702) 738-2345
ICWA Coordinator
Phone: (702) 738-9251

Tesuque Pueblo Court
Route 11, Box 1
Santa Fe, NM 87501
Phone: (505) 983-2667
Fax: (505) 455-3815
(please contact Governor)

Tohono O'odham Judiciary System
P.O. Box 761
Sells, AZ 85634
Phone: (602) 383-3193
Fax: (602) 383-2781

ICWA Director
Tohono O'odham Tribe
P.O. Box 837
Sells, AZ 85634
Phone: (602) 383-3206
Fax: (602) 383-2417

Tonkawa Tribe CFR COURT
P.O. Box 70
Tonkawa, OK 74653
Phone: (405) 628-3763
Fax: (405) 628-3774

Tonto Apache Tribal Court
#30 Tonto Reservation
Payson, AZ 85541
Phone: (602) 474-8625
Fax: (602) 474-9125
ICWA Director
Phone: (602) 474-5000

Tulalip Tribal Court
(NORTHWEST INTERTRIBAL
COURT SYSTEM)
6700 Totem Beach Road
Marysville, WA 98271
Phone: (206) 653-4585
Fax: (206) 653-0278
ICWA Director
Phone: (206) 653-0225, 0226

Turtle Mountain Chippewa Tribal
Court
P.O. Box 900
Belcourt, ND 58316
Phone: (701) 477-6121
Fax: (701) 477-6836
ICWA Director
Phone: (701) 477-5688

Umatilla Tribal Court
Box 1083
Pendleton, OR 97801
Phone: (503) 276-2033
Fax: (503) 278-0554

ICWA Director
Umatilla Tribe
Box 638
Pendleton, OR 97801
Phone: (503) 276-7011
Fax: (503) 278-9060

Upper Skagit Tribal Court
(NORTHWEST INTERTRIBAL
COURT SYSTEM)
2284 Community Plaza
Sedro Woolley, WA 98284
Phone: (206) 856-5501
Fax: (206) 856-3175

Uintah and Ouray Juvenile Court
P.O. Box 190
Ft. Duchesne, UT 84026
Phone: (801) 722-3633
Fax: (801) 722-2374
ICWA Director
Phone: (801) 722-2314

Ute Mountain Ute Tribal Court
BIA - Ute Montain Ute Agency
Towaoc, CO 81334
Phone: (303) 565-8471
Fax: (303) 565-8906

ICWA Director
Ute Mountain Ute Tribe
Tribal Office Building
Towaoc, CO 81334
Phone: (303) 565-3751
Fax: (303) 565-7412

Walker River Paiute Tribal Court
P.O. Box 225
Schurz, NV 89427
Phone: (702) 773-2306
Fax: (702) 773-2585

ICWA Director
Walker River Paiute Tribe
P.O. Box 220
Schurz, NV 89427
Phone: (702) 773-2306
Fax: (702) 773-2585

Warm Springs Tribal Court
P.O. Box 850
Warm Springs, OR 97761
Phone: (503) 553-3278
Fax: (503) 553-3281

Director
Children's Protective Service
Warm Springs Tribe
Box C
Warm Springs, OR 97761
Phohe: (503) 553-3216
Fax: (503) 553-1924

Washoe Court of Indian Offenses
919 Hwy 395 South
Gardenville, NV 98410
Phone: (702) 883-1446
Fax: (702) 265-6240
ICWA Director
Phone: (702) 883-1446

White Earth Tribal Court
Box 418
White Earth, MN 56591
Phone: (218) 983-3285
Fax: (218) 983-3641
ICWA Director
Phone: (218) 983-3285

White Mountain Apache Tribal Court
P.O. Box 598
Whiteriver, AZ 85941
Phone: (602) 338-4720
Fax: (602) 338-4778

ICWA Director
White Mountain Apache Tribe
P.O. Box 1870
Whiteriver, AZ 85941
Phone: (602) 338-4164
Fax: (602) 338-1469

Wichita Tribe CFR COURT
P.O. Box 729
Anadarko, OK 73005
Phone: (405) 247-6673
Fax: (405) 247-2005
ICWA Director
Phone: (405) 247-6673

Winnebago Tribal Children's Court (IRA)
P.O. Box 626
Winnebago, NB 68071
Phone: (402) 878-2570
Fax: (402) 878-2963
ICWA Director
Phone: (402) 878-2570

Winnemucca Colony Council
(contact Chairman Glenn Wasson)
420 Pardee *(Home address & phone)*
Susanville, CA 96130
Phone: (916) 257-7093
Fax: None

Wyandotte Tribe
P.O. Box 250
Wyandotte, OK 74370
Phone: (918) 678-2297
Fax: (918) 678-2944
(Contact Chief)

Yakima Tribal Court
P.O. Box 151
Toppenish, WA 98948
Phone: (509) 865-5121
Fax: (509) 865-5528
ICWA Director
Phone: (509) 865-5121

Yankton Sioux Tribal Court
P.O. Box 577
Wagner, SD 57380
Phone: (605) 384-5578
Fax: (605) 384-5706

ICWA Director
Yankton Sioux Tribe
P.O. Box 248
Wagner, AD 57380
Phone: (605) 384-3614
Fax: (605) 384-5687

Yerington Paiute Tribal Court
171 Campell Lane
Yerington, NV 89447
Phone: (702) 463-3301
Fax: (702) 463-2416
ICWA Worker
Phone: (702) 463-3301

Yomba Court of Indian Offenses
Route 1, Box 24
Austin, NV 89310
Phone: (702) 964-2463
Fax: (702) 964-2443

Zia Pubelo Court
General Delivery
San Ysidro, NM 87053
Phone: (505) 867-2196
Fax: (505) 867-3308
ICWA Director
Phone: (505) 867-3304

Zuni Tribal Court
P.O. Box 339
Zuni, NM 87327
Phone: (505) 782-4501
Fax: (505) 782-2250
ICWA Director
Phone: (505) 782-4481
Fax: (505) 782-2700

APPENDIX • F

Checklist for Adoption Clearance

Voluntary Termination Record

Mom	Dad	
____	____	1. Birth Certificate of Child
____	____	2. Petition
____	____	3. Verification
____	____	4. DSS Consent/Verification
____	____	5. Waiver of Notice
____	____	- Consent to Adopt/PA (Father only, mother must be present at hearing)
____	____	6. Order Terminating Parental Rights
____	____	7. Notice of Entry of Order
____	____	- Waived?
____	____	- Other? ________________

ICWA
Tribe Notice Best Although Not Specifically Required By ICWA
No Notice if Parent Objects

Additional Documents Required by 25 U.S.C. § 1913:

____ ____ Consent must be executed in writing and recorded in court file; and

____ ____ Judge's certificate must be filed indicating that the terms and consequences of the consent were fully explained in detail and fully understood by the parent or Indian custodian to whom the explanation was made in English or interpreted into a language the parent or Indian custodian understood.

Also Note:

1. No consent give prior to, or within 10 days after, birth of an Indian child, is valid.
2. A parent of an Indian child may withdraw consent for any reason at any time prior to the entry of a final decree of termination or adoption, as the case may be, and the child shall be returned to the parent.
3. Up to two years after the entry of the adoption decree in state court, the parent of an Indian child may withdraw consent upon grounds that consent was obtained through fraud or duress and may petition the court to vacate such decree.

Involuntary Termination

Mom	Dad		
____	____	1.	Child's Birth Certificate
____	____	2.	Notice of Temporary Custody 48-Hour Hearing (SDCL 26-7A-15)
____	____	3.	A & N Summons/Petition*
____	____	4.	Proof of Service of Summons/Petition** (If non-noticed, see SDCL 26-7A-13, 14)
____	____	5.	Notice of Adjudicatory Hearing
____	____	6.	Proof of Service of Notice of Adjudicatory Hearing**
____	____	7.	Adjudicatory Findings of Fact and Conclusions of Law (clear and convincing evidence)
____	____	8.	Adjudicatory Order
____	____	9.	Proof of Service of Adjudicatory Order**
____	____	10.	Interim Dispositional Orders (if any) and Proof of Service
____	____	11.	Notice of Review Hearings (if any) and Proof of Service
____	____	12.	Notice of Dispositional Hearing
____	____	13.	Proof of Service of Notice of Dispositional Hearing **
____	____	14.	Dispositional Findings of Fact and Conclusions of Law (clear and convincing evidence but beyond a reasonable doubt in ICWA cases)***
____	____	15.	Dispositional Order
____	____	16.	Notice of Entry of Final Dispositional Order
____	____	17.	Proof of Service of Notice of Entry**

* Summons must contain statements that termination of parental rights is a possible remedy, whether or not ICWA is applicable and give date of advisory hearing (an adjudicatory hearing date if same).

** Proof of service may be filed showing personal service on the parent OR by publication if whereabouts of parent unknown. If proof of service is shown by publication, we must have:

(1) Affidavit of Publication (from newspaper);

(2) Affidavit (or application) of SA to Court for authority to serve absent parent by publication, listing all reasons publication is necessary;
(3) Court Order authorizing service by publication.

NB: If service is made by publication, it is much easier, under the new statutory requirements, for the SA to make one application and get one court order authorizing publication pending all proceedings. If parent's whereabouts are found, or course, simply revert to personal service and file proof of that.

*** ICWA Findings must include a finding that the termination is supported by evidence beyond a reasonable doubt including testimony of qualified expert witness that:

(1) The continued custody of the child by the parent or Indian custodian is likely to result in serious emotional or physical damage to the child, and
(2) Active efforts have been made to provide remedial services and rehabilitative programs designed to prevent the breakup of the Indian family and these efforts have proven unsuccessful.

ICWA

Yes	No	
____	____	Is the child "Indian"?: Under 18 and either

(a) A member of an Indian tribe; or
(b) Eligible for membership in an Indian tribe AND is the biological child of a member of an Indian tribe.

If "yes" MUST SEND NOTICE OF THE PENDING PROCEEDINGS

By: Certified Mail - Return Receipt Requested, Registered by law (ICWA)
To: Indian child's parents/Indian custodians AND child's Tribe AND the Secretary (of Interior) and appropriate BIA Area Director [See updated regulations 23.11(a) and 23.11(e)].

NB: BEST PRACTICE IS TO SEND "NOTICE" OF EACH PROCEEDING TO TRIBE AS WELL AS PARENTS UNLESS TRIBE OPTS OUT IN WRITING.

APPENDIX • G

Form Motions

Notice To Child's Tribe
Instructions

This is the agency's notice to a child's Indian tribe that a petition has been filed in state court. This notice *must be* sent by Registered Mail, Return Receipt Requested. Send the original to the Indian tribe, retain a second for the child's case record, and send the third to the clerk of court.

When mailing this Notice to the tribe, also include:

- A copy of the Petition
- Staffing Recommendations
- Family Tree Chart
- Notice of Intervention and Request for Continuance
- Motion to Transfer Jurisdiction

In The Juvenile Court of the City and County of Denver or Juvenile Division of the District Court of the State of Colorado

In Re The Welfare Of)
)
(Name))
An Indian Child)

Pursuant to the Indian Child Welfare Act of 1978 (25 USC 1912), Department of Social Services, as petitioner in the above matter, gives notice to the (Name or Tribe) of a child custody proceeding now pending in the above-named court. This hearing has been scheduled for (Date) at (Time) a.m./p.m. before the Honorable (Name), Judge. The name, address and phone number of the courthouse are:

The name of the child in question is ___(Child's Name)___, born ___(Date)___ in ___(City, County, State)___. It is believed that ___(Child's Name)___ is a member of or eligible for membership in the ___(Name)___ Tribe of ___(Reservation)___.

Father: ___(Name)___, born ___(Date)___ in ___(City, County, State)___
Address: ______________________ ___(Tribe/Enrollment Number)___

Mother: ___(Name)___, born ___(Date)___ in ___(City, County, State)___
Address: ______________________ ___(Tribe/Enrollment Number)___

Under the Indian Child Welfare Act, 25 USC 1911, the biological parents or Indian custodian of the child, and the child's tribe have the right to intervene at any point in this proceeding. You also have the right to petition the above-named court to transfer this proceeding to the tribe's jurisdiction.

No proceeding involving the above-named child shall take place until at least 10 days after receipt of this notice. Upon request, the parent(s) or Indian custodian(s) of the child and the child's tribe can be granted an additional twenty (20) days to prepare for these proceedings. A form for you to notify us of your desire to intervene, or transfer the proceeding, is enclosed, or you may wish to call the court clerk at the number in paragraph one. The potential outcome of the hearing in this proceeding, if there is no intervention by the child's parents, custodians or tribe, will be (an order from the court awarding temporary custody of ___(Child's Name)___ to the Department of Social Services) OR ______________.

If your tribe is not federally recognized, you may petition to intervene, but it is up to the judge to grant or deny the petition. You may wish to contact another tribe or Indian organization for referral, consultation and/or possible intervention. Since custody proceedings are conducted on a confidential basis, you are requested to keep confidential all information contained in this notice.

If the parents or Indian custodians of the child wish legal counsel but cannot afford attorney fees, court-appointed counsel may be requested. Under the Indian Child Welfare Act, 25 USC 1911(c), each party has the right to examine all reports or other documents filed with the above-named court. The case was (or will be) staffed on ___(Date)___. The recommendations are (enclosed/summarized below):

I have enclosed a Family Tree Chart with further background on the child's ancestors and a copy of the petition. If you need more information, I ask that you call me at ___(Phone Number)___. Your earliest response would be most appreciated.

Respectfully,

______________________ ______________________

(Caseworker Name) (Social Services Attorney's Name/Phone)

______________________ ______________________

(Address) (Date of this Mailing)

In The Juvenile Court of The City and County of Denver or Juvenile Division of the District Court of the State of Colorado

In RE the Welfare of) No.
)
) Notice to Secretary of United States Department
) of the Interior Regarding an Indian Child
______________________________)
An Indian Child)

To: ____

Pursuant to the provisions of 25 U.S.C. 1901, Section 1912, you are hereby notified that the above-named Indian child is the subject of an involuntary child custody proceeding in the above-entitled court. You are further notified that the following information cannot be determined.

[ ] The identity of said child's parents.
[ ] The location of said child's parents.
[ ] The identity of said child's Indian tribe.

The following information regarding said child and his or her family is known to Department of Social Services.

[ ] Child's full name: ______________________________
[ ] Child's birth date: ______________________________
[ ] Child's birthplace: ______________________________
[ ] Names of child's parents or Indian custodian: ______________
[ ] Mother's maiden name: ______________________________
[ ] Birth date of mother: ______________ Birthplace of mother: __________
Birth date of father: ______________ Birthplace of father: __________
[ ] Location of child's parents or Indian custodian:
[ ] Tribal affiliations:
Mother: ______________________ Enrollment number: __________
Father: ______________________ Enrollment number: __________
Child: ______________________ Enrollment number: __________
[ ] Any additional information:

Since the child's legal status in regard to the Indian Child Welfare Act is uncertain, we are unable to properly plan for the child in the absence of the information requested. Please respond within fifteen days of receipt of this Notice.

DATED THIS ______________ DAY OF ______________, 19___.

______________________________ ______________________________
Caseworker Name File Number

______________________________ ______________________________
Address Phone Number

Notice To Bureau of Indian Affairs
Instructions

In some very rare instances, client information is so sketchy that inquires about tribal affiliation must be sent to a Bureau of Indian Affairs (BIA) office. BIA office addresses are listed in the Resource Section of this handbook.

Send one copy of this letter to the appropriate BIA office and retain a copy in the case file.

Notice To Canadian Band

File No.______________

To:______________ Canadian Indian Band.

This letter is to advise you that a court hearing is scheduled for ___(Name of Child)___ ___(Birth date of Child)___ on ___(Date and Time)___ at ___(Place of Hearing)___, ___(Telephone Number)___, Case No. __________. The hearing may result in [ ] foster care, [ ] temporary or permanent loss of parental rights, [ ] other.

There is reason to believe that ___(Name of Child)___ is a member of the _______ Canadian Indian Band. The child's mother is ____________________, her address is ____________________, the child's father is ____________________, his address is ____.

This letter is for purposes of notification only. As a Canadian Indian Band, you do not have the automatic right to intervene in a judicial proceeding of the United States, nor to request that the case be transferred to the jurisdiction of your band.

However, please contact me if you want more information about the situation and /or if you have services that you would like to offer to the child or family. I will look forward to hearing from you.

____
Caseworker's Name

____
Address

____

____
Telephone Number

Notice To Canadian Indian Band
Instructions

Canadian Indian Bands do not come under the Indian Child Welfare Act, but tribes can petition the U.S. courts to intervene. If your client is Canadian Indian, send a copy of this letter to the Canadian Band, if known, and retain a copy for your file.

If you do not have an address, contact and ICWA Consultant or use the address below.

Director of Policy & Research
Assembly of First Nations
Health Commission
55 Murray Street, 5th Floor
Ottawa, ON K1N 5M3
(613) 236-0673

Motion To Transfer Jurisdiction and Dismiss The Case
Instructions

Since tribes are permitted to request a transfer of proceedings to their own courts, you should mail this form to the tribe when you send it the official "Notice to Tribe" letter. If it wishes to request a transfer of the proceeding, having this form may expedite the tribe's request.

If the tribe uses this form, or its own, to request a transfer, keep a copy in your file and make sure the court has received a copy.

In The Juvenile Court

FOR __________ COUNTY, STATE OF __________

In the Matter of ____________	)	No.
________________________	)	
_________, D.O.B. _________	)	MOTION TO TRANSFER JURISDICTION
	)	AND DISMISS THE CASE
A Person Under Eighteen	)	
Years of Age.	)	
________________________	)	

Comes Now the Tribe, by and through its attorney undersigned, and petitions the Court to transfer this action to the ____(Tribe)____ Tribal Court, ____(City)____, ____(State)____, and to dismiss the state court proceeding, pursuant to the Indian Child Welfare Act of 1978, 25 U.S.C. 1911 (b). As grounds therefore, the tribes states:

1. The minor child involved in this proceeding is an "Indian child" as defined by the Indian Child Welfare Act of 1978, 25 U.S.C. § 1903 (4), in that the

child is under eighteen years of age, D.O.B. __________, and the child is a member of the ___(Tribe)___ or eligible for membership in the ___(Tribe)___, Enrollment No. __________.

2. The ___(Tribe)___ is an "Indian tribe" as defined by the Indian Child Welfare Act of 1978, 25 U.S.C. § 1903 (8), and by this fact is entitled to judicial notice by virtue of publication in the Federal Register, 48 Fed. Reg. 56862 (Dec. 23, 1983).

3. The ___(Tribe)___ is the "Indian child's tribe" as defined by the Indian Child Welfare Act of 1978, 25 U.S.C. § 1903 (5), in that the child is a member of or eligible for membership in the ___(Tribe)___.

4. This is a child custody proceeding as defined by the Indian Child Welfare Act of 1978, 25 U.S.C. § 1903 (1), in that it involves foster care placement, termination of parental rights, pre-adoptive placement of adoptive placement.

5. The Indian Child Welfare Act of 1978, 25 U.S.C. § 1911 (b), requires that the state court transfer a child custody proceeding involving an Indian child to the jurisdiction of the tribe when the Indian child's tribe petitions the state court.

6. Good cause does not exist to deny transfer of this proceeding.

7. The ___(Tribe)___ seeks to take jurisdiction of this proceeding, and to provide planning and placement for the above named child.

WHEREFORE Petitioner prays the Court to transfer the above captioned proceeding to the ___(Tribe)___, ___(Tribal Court)___, ___(City)___, ___(State)___, to dismiss the state court proceeding involving the above named Indian child, and to grant such other relief as the Court deems just and proper.

____
Tribe Attorney

____
Address

____
Phone

I hereby certify that copies of this Motion have been mailed to opposing counsel, this ________________ day of ________________, 19___.

By: ______________________________

In The District Juvenile Court

FOR __________ COUNTY, STATE OF ___________

In The Matter of____________,	)	
	)	Consent To (Foster Care Placement or
A Minor Child, D.O.B.: _______,	)	Termination of Parental Rights) And
	)	Certification
And Concerning____________,	)	
Natural Parent. _______	)	

Pursuant to the Indian Child Welfare Act of 1978, 25 U.S.C. § 1913, I do hereby consent to the (foster care placement or termination of parental rights for adoption) to my child, _________________, D.O.B.: ___________, and request his/her placement with _________________ for a foster care placement/adoption.

Before this Court I do State:

1. That I am an enrolled member of the ___________ Tribe of the State of _________________ with an enrollment number of_________________.

2. That my child,_________________, is a member of or eligible for membership with the _________________ Tribe of the state of_________________, with an enrollment number of_________________.

3. That I desire to (place my child in foster care or terminate my rights to said child or consent to adoption) and prefer that he be placed with _________________, (name), my _________________, (relationship if any), pursuant to the placement preferences of the Indian Child Welfare Act of 1978, 25 U.S.C. § 1915 (a) and (c).

4. That I fully understand the consequences of my actions and no threats or promises have been made to me to get me to sign this consent.

5. That I have the right to withdraw my consent to (foster care placement at any time and regain the custody of my child, termination of parental rights before the entry of an order terminating my rights or an order of adoption and regain the custody of my child), at which time _________________ will be returned to my custody.

6. That I wish to be notified if the final decree of adoption is set aside or vacated so that I may exercise my right to petition the court for a return of custody and custody shall be returned if the Court finds that it is in the child's best interest to be returned to me.

7. That I do not intend to waive any of my rights under the Indian Child Welfare Act by signing this consent.
8. That this consent was not signed prior to, or within ten days after the birth

of ________________.

9. That I prefer that this consent be signed in closed court because I wish to remain anonymous. I do not wish that my Tribe be notified of this proceeding, although I acknowledge that should the Tribe become aware of this proceeding it may entitled to participate.

10. I acknowledge that at the time of the execution of this consent I am not domiciled on or residing upon any Indian reservation.

Verification

Executed the __________ day of ________________, 199__, in open (closed) court before a judge of the ________________ District Court for the state of __________.

____

Natural Parent or Indian Custodian

Certification

Pursuant to the Indian Child Welfare Act of 1978, 25 U.S.C. Section 1913 (a), I, the Honorable ________________, Judge of the ________________ District Court for the State of ________________, do certify that this consent was executed in writing and recorded before me in open court (or closed court upon the request of the parent), that the terms and consequences were explained in detail to ________ , and that the parent fully understood the consequences and understood English or that it was interpreted into a language that she understood.

Certified this ________________ day of ________________, 199___.

____

Judge of District Court

Index